CYBER FRAUDS, SCAMS AND THEIR VICTIMS

Crime is undergoing a metamorphosis. The online technological revolution has created new opportunities for a wide variety of crimes which can be perpetrated on an industrial scale, and crimes traditionally committed in an offline environment are increasingly being transitioned to an online environment.

This book takes a case study-based approach to exploring the types, perpetrators and victims of cyber frauds. Topics covered include:

- An in-depth breakdown of the most common types of cyber fraud and scams.
- The victim selection techniques and perpetration strategies of fraudsters.
- An exploration of the impact of fraud upon victims and best practice examples of support systems for victims.
- Current approaches for policing, punishing and preventing cyber frauds and scams.

This book argues for a greater need to understand and respond to cyber fraud and scams in a more effective and victim-centred manner. It explores the victim-blaming discourse, before moving on to examine the structures of support in place to assist victims, noting some of the interesting initiatives from around the world and the emerging strategies to counter this problem. This book is essential reading for students and researchers engaged in cyber crime, victimology and international fraud.

Mark Button is Professor and Director of the Centre for Counter Fraud Studies at the Institute of Criminal Justice Studies, University of Portsmouth, UK.

Cassandra Cross is a Senior Lecturer in Criminology at the School of Justice, Queensland University of Technology, Australia.

'A much needed publication, drawing together a body of evidence that shines the light on the devastating phenomenon of cyber fraud! This book dispels the myths and exposes the truths. Nobody should carry the misconception that they are safe or protected from fraudsters. Who should read it and exhort dialogue – it's everyone's responsibility!'

David Clark, *Detective Chief Superintendent, Head of Economic Crime, City of London Police, UK*

'The authors have performed a valuable academic and practical service by pulling together a large range of studies, a significant proportion by themselves, to illuminate the types, impact and criminal methodologies of online fraud, and to discuss what has been done and could be done to help victims of fraud and to reduce those harms.'

Michael Levi, *Professor of Criminology, Cardiff University, UK*

CYBER FRAUDS, SCAMS AND THEIR VICTIMS

Mark Button and Cassandra Cross

Routledge
Taylor & Francis Group
LONDON AND NEW YORK

First published 2017
by Routledge
4 Park Square, Milton Park, Abingdon, Oxon OX14 4RN
605 Third Avenue, New York, NY 10017

Routledge is an imprint of the Taylor & Francis Group, an informa business

British Library Cataloguing-in-Publication Data
A catalogue record for this book is available from the British Library

Library of Congress Cataloging-in-Publication Data
Names: Button, Mark, author. | Cross, Cassandra, author.
Title: Cyber frauds, scams and their victims / Mark Button and Cassandra Cross.
Description: Abingdon, Oxon; New York, NY: Routledge, 2017. | Includes bibliographical references and index.
Identifiers: LCCN 2016054853 | ISBN 9781138931190 (hardback) | ISBN 9781138931206 (pbk.) | ISBN 9781315679877 (ebook)
Subjects: LCSH: Computer crimes. | Fraud. | Victims of crimes.
Classification: LCC HV6773 .B87 2017 | DDC 364.16/302854678—dc23
LC record available at https://lccn.loc.gov/2016054853

ISBN: 978-1-138-93119-0 (hbk)
ISBN: 978-1-138-93120-6 (pbk)
ISBN: 978-1-315-67987-7 (ebk)

Typeset in Bembo
by codeMantra

Mark

To Emma, Conrad and George for all their support and love.

Cassandra

To Lachlan, for his unfailing love and support of all my endeavours.

CONTENTS

FIGURES

TABLES

CASES

ABOUT THE AUTHORS

Professor Mark Button is Director of the Centre for Counter Fraud Studies at the Institute of Criminal Justice Studies, University of Portsmouth, UK. Mark has written extensively on counter fraud and private policing issues, publishing many articles and chapters and completing eight books. His latest book (co-authored with Martin Tunley, Andrew Whittaker and Jim Gee) is titled *The Accredited Counter Fraud Specialist's Handbook*. Some of the most significant research projects include leading the research on behalf of the National Fraud Authority and ACPO on fraud victims; the Department for International Development on Fraud Measurement; Acromas (AA and Saga) on 'Cash-for-Crash fraudsters'; the Midlands Fraud Forum, Eversheds; and PKF on 'Sanctioning Fraudsters'. Mark has also acted as a consultant for the United Nations Offices on Drugs and Crime on developing international standards for Civilian Private Security Services and the United Nations Development Programme/European Union on enhancing civilian oversight of the Turkish private security industry. Mark also holds the position of Head of Secretariat of the Counter Fraud Professional Accreditation Board. He is also a former Director of the Security Institute. Before joining the University of Portsmouth he was a Research Assistant to the Rt Hon Bruce George MP, specialising in policing, security and home affairs issues. Mark completed his undergraduate studies at the University of Exeter, his Masters at the University of Warwick and his Doctorate at the London School of Economics.

Dr Cassandra Cross is a Senior Lecturer in the School of Justice, Queensland University of Technology, Australia. Previously, she worked as a research/policy officer with the Queensland Police Service, where she commenced research on the topic of online fraud and was awarded a Churchill Fellowship in 2011 to study the prevention and support of online fraud victims. This enabled her to travel to the UK, USA and Canada to learn how international jurisdictions were responding to the issues posed by cyber crime. Since taking up her position at QUT, she has published in this area across several journals and continued her research into online fraud, focusing across the prevention, victim support and policing aspects of this crime. She has received three highly competitive Criminology Research Grants, the first in 2013 to conduct the first Australian study into the reporting experiences and support needs of online fraud victims, the second in 2015 to examine the restoration of identity for identity theft victims, and the third in 2016 to examine the policing of cyber crime in Australia. Cassandra completed all her undergraduate and postgraduate studies at the School of Justice, Queensland University of Technology, where she was awarded her doctorate in 2008.

ACKNOWLEDGEMENTS

The authors would like to acknowledge the many brave victims who have shared their often painful and traumatic victimisation stories as part of our research across the years. While not being able to improve your individual situations, we hope that this book and our ongoing research in this area will enable a societal shift to improve the prevention, policing and victim support aspects of cyber fraud and scams experienced by all too many people across the globe.

The authors would also like to acknowledge the many police and other agencies worldwide who are working tirelessly in this area, faced with enormous challenges to respond to the problems posed by such large numbers of cyber fraud victimisation.

Lastly, the authors would like to acknowledge the support of their respective universities and colleagues, and the relevant funding bodies, without whom the research underpinning this book would not have been possible. They would also like to thank the many colleagues they have worked with on research projects and publications linked to research which has been used in this book.

In particular Mark would like to thank Dean Blackbourn, Chris Lewis, Jacki Tapley, Carol McNaughton Nicholls, Jane Kerr and Rachael Owen.

In particular Cassandra would like to thank Kelly Richards, Michael Kelly, Dom Blackshaw, Russell Smith, and the staff at the Queensland Police Service, West Australia Police, South Australia Police and the Australian Competition and Consumer Commission.

1

'THE DARK SIDE OF CRIME'

Cyber frauds and scams

Introduction[1]

For many industrialised countries over the last 20 years there has been a decline in recorded crime. This has led some criminologists to question this fall and to seek to explain it. Some have pointed to better crime prevention (Farrell et al., 2011), some – more preoccupied with violent crime – have pointed to the liberalisation of abortion (Donohue and Levitt, 2001) or removal of lead from petrol (Nevin, 2007). A small number, however, have suggested crime may be changing, that it is morphing into new online forms (Fitzgerald, 2014). There is a strong argument to be made that crimes committed in a traditional offline environment, are increasingly being transitioned and instead perpetrated in an online environment. As authors, we are firmly of the view that crime has changed and that the online technological revolution has fuelled significantly different ways in which crimes occur. This can be attributed largely to the evolution of the internet, however it is important to acknowledge the development of technology in a much broader sense and its impact on offending behaviour as well as victimisation.

However, it is also important to acknowledge the longevity of fraud and deception offences. Fraud and scams are not a new phenomenon that has emerged out of the technological revolution, which has been taking place over recent decades. Rather there is evidence that frauds and scams have been a much bigger problem for some time, preceding the expansion of the internet and related technologies. The central issue is that fraud offences have largely been ignored and excluded from mainstream crime reporting. There is strong evidence to suggest that fraud has not been a priority of policing agencies for a long time (Button et al., 2015) and this has translated into inaccurate understandings and measures relating to the prevalence and impact of these offences, as well as a lack of resources allocated to investigating and prosecuting alleged offenders. Sadly, this same trend has also been observed with fraud perpetrated in an online environment. Cyber frauds and scams have been largely excluded from the main measures of crime, and there is a momentous task ahead to better record and accurately depict the extent and prevalence of these offences worldwide. The challenge also stems from the criminal justice community – and by this we mean politicians, law enforcement, and criminologists to name a few – and the importance that is placed with crime statistics largely of offences outside the cyber realm. Their preoccupation with these measures and other types of crime has meant that cyber frauds and scams have been neglected. They therefore represent the dark side of crime, subject to much less interest from the criminal justice system as well as criminologists, compared to traditional volume crimes, although this is beginning to change. Cyber fraud and scams are certainly not the only type of crime to suffer the consequences of under-reporting and other challenges associated with reporting, but nevertheless, there is still a critical need to improve understandings and practices associated with this particular type of crime.

This book attempts to address the lack of scholarly literature that specifically examines the issue of fraud perpetrated in an online context. While there has been an emerging field of studies around cyber crime more broadly (Clough, 2015; Yar, 2013), which point to some of the issues raised by cyber fraud and scams, this book is dedicated to an examination and analysis of the many facets of cyber fraud and scams which currently pose significant challenges to society. By focusing exclusively on the issues associated with cyber fraud and scams in a global context, it is our hope as authors to be able to instigate further interest and scholarly debate on this topic as well as provide a solid foundation for further research in the area.

Globally, there have been recent events that have marked a significant shift in recognising the true extent of cyber fraud and scams and their impact across society. For example, in 2016 in England and Wales, the Office of National Statistics (ONS) included fraud and computer misuse offences in its official statistics for the first time. This was a significant step for government and police, as the inclusion of these additional crime categories added 5.8 million new offences to the existing 6.3 million, almost doubling the overall crime figures. While this may seem extraordinary, it is an important step to acknowledging the common nature and prevalence of cyber crime offences and the impact they can have on individuals, businesses and government.

It is clear that there are some positive signs that point to an increased recognition of cyber fraud and scams and its associated harms and impacts. However, in order to effect positive change, we would argue that there needs to be cultural change across society, which recognises the severity of these offences and promotes a response from the fraud justice network (which includes the criminal justice system), commensurate with the harm caused.

The following chapters each seek to provide an in-depth examination of the many facets of cyber fraud and scams within a global context. This book draws heavily on the individual research of the authors, which examines cyber fraud and scams across victim experiences, policing responses, prevention efforts and the need for support services, across the United Kingdom, Australia and Canada. What can be taken from this collective research is a realisation that the victim experience and police response for cyber frauds and scams appears to be consistent across each of these jurisdictions. Unlike other types of crimes whereby the geographical and cultural context can be an important factor to consider, in the case of fraud perpetrated in a virtual environment it can be understood as one global jurisdiction. As will become evident throughout the book, the experiences of victims in the UK mirror those in Australia as well as Canada. Unfortunately, this book will also highlight the overwhelmingly negative experiences suffered by victims both as a result of the fraud itself, and then as a result of seeking to report or gain a response through the fraud justice network. The following chapters will demonstrate many areas where much needed positive change is clearly evident.

This first chapter introduces the premise of the book. It provides a context to the problem of cyber frauds and scams globally. It illustrates some of the measures currently used to show the significant scale of the problem of cyber fraud and scams and the impact on victims. However, before this is undertaken, it is important to define some of the key concepts which underpin the book, including the terms 'cyber fraud' and 'scams'. In doing this, the chapter will provide a typology of frauds which will be considered throughout this book. The chapter examines some of the changes in society that are taking place, changes which are fuelling the growth in cyber fraud and scams and are focused around the evolution of technology, though it is important to note that fraud has existed for centuries and cannot solely be attributed to the development of current technologies. Rather, these add a new dimension to the ways in which fraud can be perpetrated and understood. The chapter ends with a brief consideration of those who become engaged in such criminal activities.

Chapter 2 begins an in-depth examination of the large variety of cyber frauds and scams that exist. It uses the framework established in the opening chapter to further explore the most common fraudulent approaches and also provides some of the known statistics which illustrate the extent of known victimisation in this area (noting that this is one of the most under-reported crime types that exist). Lastly, the chapter explores victim profiles, and the current state of knowledge on who becomes a victim of fraud, highlighting the vulnerabilities of certain individuals and populations to certain fraud types. This culminates in the presentation of a segmentation approach, which breaks down the entire population according to their vulnerability and likelihood of experiencing certain types of fraud. An acknowledgement of the pervasiveness of fraud underpins several arguments across the book.

Chapter 3 focuses on victims through an analysis of how people become victims of cyber fraud and scams. It does this through an illustration of the large number of techniques and methods that offenders use to target potential victims.

This encompasses a combination of both traditional offline approaches with evolving online methods. However, the role of technology and the role it has played in opening up channels of communication to target potential victims is highlighted as a dominant enabler of cyber fraud. This chapter reaffirms the notion that there is a fraud for everyone, and that everyone could be a victim of fraud, if approached in the right way at the right time, by a highly skilled offender. This chapter also begins to challenge the common misconceptions of who becomes a victim of cyber fraud and sheds light on the stereotype that exists.

Chapter 4 looks at the impact that cyber frauds and scams can have on the individual. It asserts that, while there is a common belief that fraud is a 'victimless' crime, this is far from the truth. It presents the small but growing body of research that argues that the effects of fraud on its victims can be as severe as on those who experience violent crime. In doing this, the chapter details the, often devastating, impact that fraud can have across many facets of an individual victim's life. This includes both financial and non-financial harms. To demonstrate the reality of cyber fraud victimisation, this chapter uses a large number of case studies taken from current research to highlight the diverse effects of this crime.

Chapter 5 focuses on the discourses surrounding cyber fraud victimisation. In particular, it examines the negative stereotype that is commonly associated with cyber fraud and scams, asserting victims to be greedy, gullible, uneducated and somewhat deserving of their victimisation. This discourse places a large degree of blame and responsibility on the individual victim for not being able to discern the fraudulent approach in the first place. This chapter seeks to challenge this stereotype and the misconceptions associated with victimisation. Of interest, it does this through the identification of how humour plays an active role in reinforcing these perceived norms and beliefs. Again, this chapter draws upon the narratives of several victims to highlight the reality of their victimisation and seeks to present the reality of victimisation. It also establishes these discourses and negative stereotypes as barriers that inhibit the disclosures of these crimes to family and friends, discourage their reporting of these crimes to authorities, and prevent victims from seeking support (either informal or formal) to assist in their recovery.

Chapter 6 shifts the focus to the current lack of support services to assist victims of cyber fraud and scams. Despite the severity of its impact, as illustrated in Chapter 4, this chapter argues that there are very few services that are available to support this category of victims. This can be seen to result from a number of factors, including the victim blaming discourse outlined in Chapter 5, which does not acknowledge cyber fraud victims as genuine victims who require assistance to aid in their recovery. In spite of this, the needs of cyber fraud victims are outlined and the few examples of victim support available worldwide are explored. While small in number, these programmes offer some best practice examples that can be expanded upon and implemented in a greater number of countries.

Chapter 7 turns to an examination of current policing practices and responses to cyber fraud and scams, as well as a brief consideration of current sentencing and punishment practices for those convicted of cyber fraud. This chapter provides an in-depth analysis of the many challenges that face police and other agencies in seeking to implement traditional responses to cyber frauds and scams. The complexity of the policing landscape is presented, which comprises general state police bodies and bodies from hybrid, private, voluntary and finally international policing. The chapter examines many of the challenges such mixed provision creates, before exploring a case study of good practice in policing in this area. Policing cyber frauds and scams presents many unique challenges through the characteristics of these incidents, and while traditional policing methods are important, there needs to be an adaptation and development of new strategies to specifically respond to this crime type.

Chapter 8 uses the challenges posed by cyber frauds and scams as a platform for arguing the importance of prevention efforts to reduce the harm incurred by these events. It asserts that preventing victims from sending money or personal information in the first place, is a more effective and appropriate approach to cyber fraud and scams in general, compared to a reactive approach after the fact. Subsequent to a discussion on the similarities and differences which exist between crimes committed across offline and online environments, the chapter focuses on the adaptation of situational crime prevention techniques to target cyber frauds and scams. It then uses the example of Project Sunbird (an Australian programme which uses financial intelligence to target cyber fraud victims) to demonstrate the importance and impact that prevention efforts can achieve. Lastly, the chapter analyses the current prevention messages that surround cyber frauds and scams, and argues for a simplification of these to focus purely on the transfer of money or personal information.

Chapter 9 brings the book to an end, through a summary of the main arguments found within the book, arguing that this book has brought together a body of evidence that clearly agitates for the need to improve current practices, across the prevention, policing, and victim support aspects of cyber frauds and scams. It outlines the main challenges that lay ahead, and how these will impact on the field into the future. Despite the inadequacies that currently exist in the area, this chapter is optimistic and advocates positive change into the future, with the hope that this book is a starting point for the much needed dialogue to commence.

Overall this book argues the need to better understand and respond to cyber fraud and scams in a more effective and victim-centred manner. Across our individual research projects, we have seen the reality of cyber fraud victimisation and the impact it can have on individuals and businesses. We have also seen firsthand, the challenges faced by police and other relevant organisations in attempting to respond to these incidents and address victim complaints and concerns. However, as the book will highlight, there are several barriers that exist in the current conceptualisation of cyber fraud and scams and what can be done. The ultimate goal of the current analysis is to provide a catalyst for greater public and academic discussion on this particular crime type, with a view to improving policing, prevention and support services for victims into the future. Cyber frauds and scams are unlikely to abate any time in the near future, therefore it is imperative that these offences are afforded the appropriate degree of priority and acknowledgement across society, the criminal justice system, the fraud justice network more broadly, and academia.

However, before attempting to examine these issues in detail, it is important to lay down the conceptual foundations and definitions that underpin the analysis in this book. It is towards these that this chapter now turns.

Defining fraud and scams

Fraud covers a broad range of activities united by some form of misrepresentation by a party to secure an advantage for that party or cause a disadvantage to others. It covers criminal, civil and regulatory acts of deviance. While current conceptualisations of fraud are strongly linked to new technologies (such as the internet), it is important to note that older technologies provided the means for deception in previous centuries. Frauds have occurred since people have been able to speak and own assets.

As means of communication and trade have advanced, so have the opportunity and nature of fraud. The introduction of mail facilitated frauds to be conducted by postage, the telephone led to tele-marketing frauds and now the internet and related technologies have fuelled 'cyber fraudsters'. The evolution of technology has not changed the desire or willingness of offenders to engage in fraud, rather it has simply altered the means through which these offences are executed.

Fraud is an unusual crime, because unlike crimes like burglary or theft, where the crime is usually very visible, such as signs of a break-in or the disappearance of a bicycle, with frauds there is not always unambiguous evidence that a crime has occurred. Worthless share certificates sold by boiler room fraudsters might not be discovered until the victim attempts to cash them in or a counterfeit designer handbag purchased on the internet might not be detected until a friend questions its authenticity. Many frauds – which are clear – initially are not always; such as the U2 fan who thinks they have purchased tickets to one of their concerts, who only discovers when they try and enter that they are counterfeit.

Unlike many other volume crimes such as burglary or theft, it is not always clear with frauds whether they actually are 'criminal' frauds or whether they are civil or regulatory issues or just plain 'unethical'. Before exploring Figure 1.1, which illustrates this issue, it is important at this point to briefly examine what is meant by 'scams' as this is a term often used interchangeably with frauds. 'Scam' is defined in dictionaries as, 'A dishonest scheme; a fraud' (Oxford English Dictionary); 'an illegal plan for making money, especially one that involves tricking people' (Cambridge Dictionary); and 'a dishonest way to make money by deceiving people' (Miriam Webster Dictionary). The latter does not denote criminality and it is this broader definition that we wish to use to distinguish

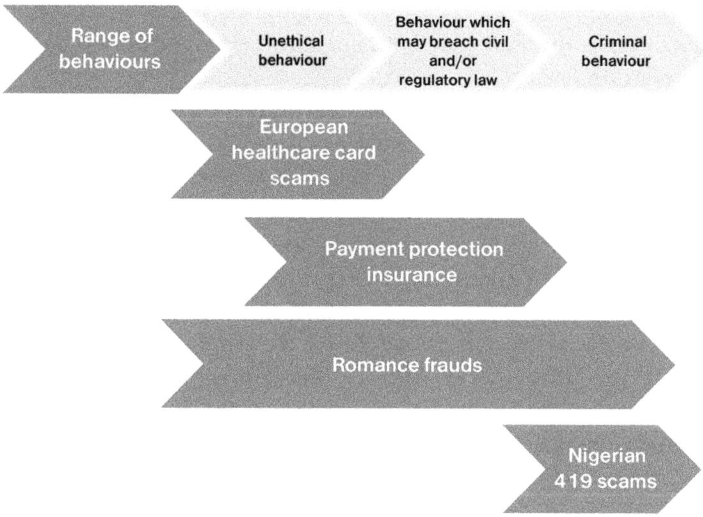

FIGURE 1.1 The legal spectrum of 'frauds' and 'scams'.

scams from fraud. In this book we use scams to distinguish 'a deceptive scheme that seeks to trick a person (s) out of money and/or personal information which is unethical and may also be a civil, regulatory or criminal issue too'. The term 'scams' therefore covers the wide range of behaviours listed in Figure 1.1, from criminal to unethical – it is the universal term, whereas frauds are more clearly located at the criminal/civil end of the spectrum. Figure 1.1 illustrates this issue when it comes to fraud and scams.

Figure 1.1 shows the continuum of behaviours from unethical, civil/regulatory breaches to outright criminal behaviours. Some 'scams' are framed such that they are not illegal. A good example of this is European healthcare card scams. These are free cards available to citizens of the European Union, which enable them to access healthcare services. Several websites have been set up which will source these cards for the applicant for a fee, usually in the region of £20. It has been suggested almost a million have used such websites to secure these cards. So long as the websites note in the small print that they can be secured free of charge from the official website, they are not breaking any law (Massey, 2011). From a consumer perspective if you are paying for something, which is in reality free, this is a financial loss and would be regarded as a scam, not a fraud. This is therefore classified in the figure above as unethical behaviour.

Second in the figure is payment protection insurance. In the UK there has been a major problem with financial institutions selling payment protection insurance to those taking out loans, or credit cards for example, who either do not need it or would not be covered by it if they ever needed to make a claim. As a result of this scandal the regulators for financial services have intervened resulting in the institutions having to repay the monies to their customers. As of October

2016 around £25 billion had been paid to customers (FCA, 2016). The breaches by the financial institutions were both unethical and breaches of the regulations, but were not criminal.

Third in the figure is romance fraud. This covers the full range of behaviours because, depending upon the nature of the scam, the type of breach varies. For instance, if a person goes onto a romance website and lies about their relationship status with the purpose to secure additional liaisons this would be, to most, unethical, but would not be breaching any laws in most countries. At the other extreme, if they used a false identity to secure multiple partners and fabricated scenarios to secure funds from their victims, this would be deemed unlawful; dozens of individuals have been convicted in the criminal courts for such behaviours. There are, however, behaviours in-between which might be more difficult to prove as criminal, might be civil torts and certainly unethical, such as a person using a real identity to seduce victims and encourage them to send gifts. Romance fraud therefore covers a variety of behaviours, which, depending upon the case, would fit different levels of behaviour in the figure above.

Finally, there are some frauds that are clearly criminal alone. The classic Nigerian 419 scam where a 'corrupt official' contacts a person on the basis of an offer to transfer illegally gained monies, for which in return the victim would receive a fee – but to secure confidence a monetary transfer is required to be made to the official – if true, would be an act of money laundering. The scheme is built upon a false representation and identity, which is clearly criminal.

It is important to identify these differences in this book and to also note that the focus of it will be more towards the criminal end of the spectrum in terms of frauds and scams. In this context it is important to note what constitutes criminal acts. In many countries, the criminal acts of fraud are often covered by a complex mix of legislation. England and Wales are two of the few countries to have codified the criminal act of fraud with the *Fraud Act 2006* (although many criminal acts of fraud are still dealt with by other legislation, such as tax frauds, social security frauds and the like). Under the 2006 Act there are a number of ways in which fraud can be committed:

- Fraud by False Representation (providing false information to secure a gain or cause a loss)
- Fraud by Failing to Disclose Information (failing to disclose information which leads to a gain or a loss to the victim)
- Fraud by Abuse of Position (this is where a person in a position of trust abuses their position, such as an accountant diverting funds to their own personal account).

The legislation also set out a series of other offences such as:

- Possession of articles for use in frauds and making or supplying articles for use in frauds (this is very wide ranging and could include catching someone at home with a paper or electronic copy of a false invoice which could be submitted to a company).

- Participating in a fraudulent business (this could be a car dealership founded on enhancing the value of cars by turning back the mileage clocks).
- Obtaining services dishonestly (this could be securing an insurance policy by providing false or inaccurate information).

(Farrell et al., 2007)

It is important not to become too preoccupied with the legal definitions, because they often mask the diversity and breadth of fraud. This book is concerned with cyber frauds and scams directed at the general public. These account for a significant proportion of frauds in society, but there are many more, such as the frauds against organisations by their own employees, by outsiders, and of course, the frauds perpetrated by organisations (Smith et al., 2010). This book has used the title 'cyber frauds and scams'. 'Scam' is a term widely used and this could have been utilised to cover cyber frauds too. However, such is the increase in the use of cyber-related technology it was felt important to clearly distinguish that this book is concerned with such frauds. To use this term alone, however, would negate the many frauds and scams that are still perpetrated by traditional means. Therefore scams, which can be defined as a 'dishonest scheme', has also been used.

There are a number of definitions and typologies which are important to this subject, which will now be explored. In the UK, the growing technological element to crime has led the police to divide such crimes between cyber-enabled and cyber-dependent. McGuire and Dowling (2013) define these as:

> Cyber-dependent crimes (or 'pure' cyber crimes) are offences that can only be committed using a computer, computer networks or other form of information communications technology (ICT).
>
> Cyber-enabled crimes are traditional crimes, which can be increased in their scale or reach by use of computers, computer networks or other forms of information communications technology (ICT). Unlike cyber dependent crimes, they can be committed without the use of ICT. Two of the most widely published instances of cyber enabled crime relate to fraud and theft.

Cyber crime is much broader than fraud, covering illegal pornography, online harassment to hacking, to name some. It would therefore be useful to illustrate the two types of cyber crime vis-à-vis fraud in Table 1.1 below.

Table 1.1 shows the wide diversity of cyber-related frauds. There is much interest and focus upon cyber-dependent crimes and frauds. These clearly are a major problem, but the vast majority of cyber-related frauds arise from the cyber-enabled frauds. Indeed at a conference in 2015, Commander Head of the City of London Police (drawing upon Action Fraud data) estimated 70 per cent of frauds reported to Action Fraud were cyber-enabled (Head, 2015) (the other 30 per cent also includes non-cyber-related fraud). Clearly the skills necessary to

TABLE 1.1 Selected examples of cyber-enabled and cyber-dependent frauds*

Cyber-dependent frauds	*Cyber-enabled frauds*
Hacking The computer systems of organisations and individuals are hacked to secure personal information to perpetrate frauds or to actually divert monies.	Card Not Present Fraud Fraudsters secure the relevant numbers from plastic cards and then use them to purchase goods and services online.
Monitoring Aids such as key-sniffers/spyware placed on computers to enable passwords and personal details to be identified to perpetrate frauds. This also includes computer viruses targeting machines in order to gain passwords and personal information, or to enable control to facilitate other actions (such as Dedicated denial of service (DDoS) attacks.	Fraudulent Sales Goods and services which are non-existent or not as described sold online.
	Phishing Scams Emails sent purporting to be from an official body which persuade the respondent into supplying personal information which can then be used for a fraud.
	Mass Marketing Frauds (also known as Advanced Fee Fraud) A wide variety of frauds which seek to secure a payment from the victim, ranging from fake lottery prizes, to inheritance notifications to business investment opportunities.
	Romance Frauds The method in which offenders use dating websites and other social media sites under the guise of legitimate relationships to trick 'lovers' into sending (often recurring amounts of) money.

Source: Adapted from McGuire and Dowling (2013).

* Identity frauds where a person's personal information is used to commit a fraud such as apply for a loan in their name or use their credit card details to purchase goods and services may be either the result of cyber-dependent or cyber-enabled means and often the victim will not know how their personal details were gained.

perpetrate cyber-enabled fraud are much less than for cyber-dependent. Setting up websites, sending emails and the like do not require significant information technology skills, whereas most cyber-dependent frauds do.

Central to this book is also the term 'mass marketing fraud' which can be used to encapsulate much of the cyber frauds and scams that will be considered in this book. The Office of Fair Trading (2006: 12) has attempted to produce a definition of mass marketing scams as 'a misleading or deceptive business practice where you receive an unsolicited or uninvited contact (for example by email, letter, phone, or ad) and false promises are made to con you out of money'. This is reiterated by Whitty (2015: 84) who defines a mass market scam as that which 'exploits mass communication techniques (e.g., email, instant messenger, bulk mailing, social networking sites) to con people out of money' (Whitty, 2015: 84). Both of these definitions focus on the use of technology to target a large number of victims at the one time. In this respect, the development of the internet has facilitated the ability for offenders to target a greater number of potential victims, in a much more cost-effective manner. The sending of bulk emails is a cost-effective means of distributing fraudulent pitches to a large number of victims, compared to the costs (both financial and time) involved in telephoning individual persons or sending out physical letters through the mail. While each of these methods is still in existence, the evolution of the internet has seen the proliferation of mass marketing fraud approaches, specifically those around phishing (attempts to gain a potential victims username, password or other personal details).

As is evident, central to mass marketing fraud is the attempt to con money out of the potential victim. Therefore it is important to note that mass marketing fraud would not cover many identity frauds, where the aim is to deceive a victim into providing personal information that they would otherwise not share, to enable offenders to perpetrate fraud against that victim or for the information to be sold to those who wish to perpetrate frauds. This is an important distinction that Beals et al. (2015) make in the most comprehensive attempt to date to develop a taxonomy of fraud. Influenced by the *UN Principles and Framework for International Classification of Crime for Statistical Purposes*, and drawing on an impressive panel of experts and scholars, Beals et al. (2015) identify a very comprehensive taxonomy.

The taxonomy begins at Level 1 and distinguishes between fraud against the individual and the organisation. The taxonomy then, in Level 2, identifies seven sub-categories, which are built upon the 'expected benefit or expected consequence of the transaction' (Beals et al., 2015: 11). These seven categories include:

Consumer Investment Fraud: the expected benefit is investment returns and includes fake shares, Ponzi schemes, film frauds.

Consumer Products and Services Fraud: the expected benefit is the product or service and this includes fake tickets, bogus holidays, dietary pills that don't work, products that don't arrive.

Employment Fraud: the expected benefit is employment and these include fake opportunities for jobs such as work at home scams, model agency work.

Prize and Grant Fraud: the expected benefit is winning a prize or other windfall and this includes fake lotteries, 419 scams.

Phantom Debt Collection Fraud: the expected benefit is avoiding the consequences of failing to pay debts the victim did not know were previously owed and this includes bogus demands for payment for debts, taxes.

Charity Fraud: the expected benefit is contributing to a charity, but the reality is that the victim is contributing to the fraudsters, not a legitimate cause.

Relationship and Trust Fraud: the expected benefit is a relationship, but the reality is usually a fake identity aimed at securing monies from the victim.

(Beals et al., 2015: 11–12)

The taxonomy is further developed through Levels 3, 4 and 5; which further divide the 7 categories above. Thus, for the first category, Consumer Investment Fraud, at Level 3 this can be divided between securities and commodities. These sub-categories can then be further divided, such as commodities between precious metals and films. The taxonomy, depending upon the complexity, therefore creates a tree-like structure from most of the seven base frauds. All these frauds vary to the extent to which they are perpetrated using cyber-dependent or enabled techniques or more traditional means.

Beals et al. (2015) excluded identity frauds from their classification, because the aim in these frauds is to secure information, rather than monies (although they do include phishing under consumer products and services fraud) and that information can be secured by many means, often not involving the victim's actions. Many identity frauds do meet this condition. However, the use of deceptive methods to secure information from victims that can then be used to perpetrate frauds is a significant problem. Identity fraud in all its forms is also a significant problem as Table 1.3 later in this chapter will show, as with further evidence in Chapter 2. Identity fraud involves the use of another person's (or organisation's) details unlawfully for gain or to avoid an obligation (Pascoe et al., 2006). Identity fraud is to be distinguished from 'identity theft', which is where the victim's identity is permanently appropriated (Semmens, 2005). There are a wide variety of tactics used by fraudsters to secure sensitive important information. Here the cyber-dependent and enabled basis of the crime are important because both can yield such information. As mentioned, phishing scams can appear in two distinct formats, the first uses fake emails from legitimate organisations (such as banks, telephone/internet service providers) to deceive customers into yielding personal information (cyber-enabled) while the second uses emails to distribute malware onto a victims computer to enable offenders to gain access to personal details held on that computer or network. This again is different to straightforward hacking of computers by skilled computer savvy experts (cyber-dependent) to gain personal information. It is also important to note than many identity fraud victims play no part in their victimisation, because the offenders secure the sensitive information from their banks or other organisations holding their financial information through what is known as a 'third party data breach'. It is therefore important to add identity fraud, where the purpose of the fraud is to secure personal information which could be used to conduct identity fraud, to Beal et al.'s seven base categories. Table 1.2, below, therefore captures the broad categories of fraud, which will be the focus of this book. These eight frauds can target both individuals and organisations. This book will largely focus upon individual victims, but it is important to note that some target both. In the next chapter a more detailed overview of the eight broad categories will be undertaken to unpick the diversity of frauds that fall beneath them.

The extent of cyber fraud and scams

Cyber fraud and scams are a major problem in many countries, but often official statistics, particularly crime statistics, do not show this. This section will

TABLE 1.2 Eight broad categories of fraud considered in this book

Individuals or organisations
Consumer Investment Fraud
Consumer Products and Services Fraud
Employment Fraud
Prize and Grant Fraud
Phantom Debt Collection Fraud
Charity Fraud
Relationship and Trust Fraud
Identity Fraud

examine the evidence for the extent of the problem in a number of countries, using the different measures that are utilised.

Crime statistics

The reliability of crime statistics for measuring the extent of crime is a well-debated issue amongst criminologists (Fitzgerald, 2014; Maguire, 2012). The lack of reporting for some crimes and the way that official bodies filter out some crimes through recording practices have been well documented (Maguire, 2012). For fraud, however, the problems are even greater in many countries. First of all, many victims do not know they are victims. A person who has bought fake shares will not know they are so until they come to cash them in or the fraudster gets caught and the police inform the victims. Second, fraud victims might be reluctant to report their fraud. This might be because the sum lost is low or they are simply too embarrassed to report it. Third, in many countries fraud is a crime that often can be reported to multiple bodies. This results in some victims finding it difficult to report their crime to the correct body and sometimes victims might be sent on a 'merry-go-round' of agencies, leading some to give up. Fourth, where the police are responsible for receiving reports in some countries, they view fraud as low priority and may even blame the victim, further inhibiting reporting. These all combine to create substantial attrition in the volume of fraud (Button et al., 2014).

Even when frauds are then reported they are combined with a wide variety of frauds, such as occupational fraud, insurance fraud, social security fraud, tax fraud, which makes it difficult to ascertain accurate levels of fraud against individuals, which is the main focus of this book.

Victimisation surveys

For most criminologists, victimisation surveys are the gold standard of crime measurement. Interviews with thousands of individuals, selected in a way that allows statistical methods to be applied to determine actual levels of victimisation within a statistical range and level of confidence, are used. These types of surveys are used in a number of countries to accurately measure levels of crime victimisation in the general population (Maguire, 2012). It is these surveys that, in many industrialised countries, have been falling over the last 15 years, leading many criminologists to debate the 'crime fall'. The fact they exclude organisations is well documented. However, the central problem in relation to fraud is that many of these surveys simply do not ask questions about fraud victimisation. As cited earlier, the English and Wales Crime Survey had previously not captured the extent to which individuals were victims of cyber crime. Until the publication of a pilot in 2015, it had only asked interviewees about their victimisation relating to plastic card fraud. The pilot study (which was not added to the main survey findings), suggested there were 2.6 million fraud victims with a loss and a further 2.4 million fraud victims with no loss. Added to this, just over 2 million had experienced a virus and 0.4 million unauthorised access to their computer (hacking) (ONS, 2015). If these had been added to the 6.6 million crime incidents in the main survey, crime would have more than doubled (ONS, 2016). This doubling of crime statistics was a reality in 2016, when these cyber crime statistics were officially incorporated for the first time. This saw the survey report 6.3 million offences in the preceding year, and with the addition of two questions targeting fraud and cyber offences, a further 3.8 million fraud offences and 2 million computer misuse offences (ONS, 2016). While traditional crime statistics continue to fall (with the 6.3 million offences down 6 per cent from a previously recorded 6.8 million offences) (ONS, 2016), our earlier assertion that crime is not necessarily falling, but changing its form, is supported by these statistics. This survey recorded an additional 5.8 million offences, which were previously not officially recognised, almost reaching parity between offline and online offences.

While the inclusion of cyber crime statistics within the England and Wales crime survey is an important and positive step forward to gaining a more informed picture of the extent of this type of victimisation, there are still many factors associated with the under-reporting of cyber fraud and scams. This is still unlikely to capture the true extent of fraud, because of the factors cited earlier, namely the unknowing victims and the embarrassed victims. The former are unlikely ever to be accurately measured, and form part of the well-established 'dark figure' of crime. It is impossible for a victim to report a crime against them that they are unaware of. The latter, however, because of the use of face-to-face interviews to secure data, may mean some victims will be unwilling to reveal an embarrassing fraud to an interviewer. For these types of victims – as is used to secure data on domestic violence – the opportunity to complete an anonymous questionnaire online, on a laptop or other device, would be more likely to yield more accurate results from this type of victim. A more detailed examination of the shame and embarrassment associated with cyber fraud is covered in Chapter 5. Nevertheless it is welcome that at last one of the gold standard measures of crime victimisation is covering fraud across both online and offline contexts.

In the USA the main national crime survey is the National Crime Victimisation Survey (NCVS) and in 2004 questions on the prevalence of identity theft were added. The USA therefore can provide more detailed statistics on the trends in identify theft. Research published in 2011 showed that the percentage of households with an identity theft victim had risen from 5.5 per cent of households in 2005 to 7 per cent in 2010 (Langton, 2011).

Within Australia, the Australian Bureau of Statistics (ABS) undertakes regular prevalence surveys focused on fraud victimisation, with the latest released in 2016. The overall report found that 'in the 12 months prior to interview in 2014–15, an estimated 1.6 million Australians experienced personal fraud, or 8.5 per cent of the population aged 15 and over. This is an increase from the proportion of persons who experienced personal fraud in 2010–11 (6.7%)' (ABS, 2016). Within this report, personal fraud encompasses card fraud, identity theft and scam fraud. Main findings indicate that an estimated 126,300 Australians experienced identity theft (or 0.7 per cent of the population aged 15 years and over) (ABS, 2016). Of significance, over half (56%) of the Australian population were exposed to at least one scam (10.4 million persons), and of those who were exposed, 4 per cent responded through the sending of money or personal information (449,100 persons or 2.4 per cent of the population aged 15 years and over) (ABS, 2016). The financial losses to fraud are significant, with the total estimated financial loss at AU$3 billion (ABS, 2016).

The Australian Competition and Consumer Commission (ACCC) is another source of data related to cyber frauds and scams and provides an annual report based on victim complaints to their Scamwatch portal. This is a web-based mechanism whereby victims can self-report across a wide range of frauds and scams experienced. In their annual report for 2015, the ACCC highlighted financial losses of AU$84.9 million from Australians who reported frauds or scams. The top two schemes were investment and dating and romance fraud, which made up less than 3.7 per cent of overall reports but accounted for 56 per cent of financial losses (ACCC, 2016). Of interest in these findings, telephone approaches dominated with 40.9 per cent of overall approaches, with email second at 27.7 per cent. However, given the dominance of investment fraud and romance fraud approaches, it is likely that there is a strong use of the internet and a cyber element to facilitate these types of frauds. Again, it is important to recognise that these figures represent a group of Australians who have self-identified as victims and made the decision to report themselves. It does not necessarily provide an accurate representation of victimisation across the country.

Despite the lack of general crime victimisation surveys covering fraud, some countries have commissioned bespoke victimisation surveys, using the same principles as the general crime surveys, to try and gauge the size of the problem. Table 1.3 below illustrates some of these surveys from different countries, some of which have been previously discussed above.

Table 1.3 illustrates data from three industrialised countries to illustrate the large numbers of people who fall victim to frauds. It would be fair, based upon these findings, to say that a conservative figure of between 5 and 10 per cent of the adult population falling victims to fraud would be appropriate. The lack of

TABLE 1.3 The prevalence of fraud: evidence from selected countries

Country	*Type of research*	*Findings*
Australia	Prevalence Survey (ABS)	2014–15 8.5% of population aged at least 15 and victim of one personal fraud in previous 12 months (1.6 million people. Above includes 5.9% victim of credit card fraud 0.7% victims of identity theft 2.4% victims of scam
England and Wales	ONS Crime Survey England and Wales Pilot	2015 5.8% of adults victim of fraud with loss (2.6 million) 5.4% of adults victim of fraud no loss (2.4 million) 0.9% of adults victim of unauthorised access to personal information (0.4 million) 4.5% of adults victim of computer virus (2 million)
	National Fraud Authority commissioned survey	2012 8.8% victims of identity fraud in previous 12 months
	Specific Office of Fair Trading Report (UK Wide)	2006 48% targeted 8% a victim
USA	Federal Trade Commission Consumer Fraud Survey 2011	2011 10.8% of US adults (25.6 million) victim of consumer fraud during 2011
	National Crime Victimisation Survey	2015 7% of US residents aged 16 and over victim of identity theft in 2014 (17.6 million)

Sources: Australian Bureau of Statistics (2016); Federal Trade Commission (2013); Harrell (2015); National Fraud Authority (2013).

longitudinal comparative data makes trends difficult to determine accurately. The data from the USA discussed above clearly showed an increase in identity theft victimisation in the USA. As some of the other surveys begin to be undertaken more regularly, data on trends will become more available. Some of the research on the types of fraud, the losses and how victims discovered they had become so, will be teased out in subsequent chapters.

Central reporting agencies

Several countries have established central agencies for reporting fraud and cyber crime. This includes Action Fraud in the UK, the Internet Crime Complaint Centre (IC3) in the USA, the Australian Cybercrime Online Reporting Network (ACORN) in Australia and the Canadian AntiFraud Centre (CAFC) in Canada. The creation of these single agencies for reporting is an attempt to consolidate data for these specific types of crimes as well as improve the ability of the public to lodge complaints regarding their victimisation and provides an alternative source of self-reported victimisation figures.

Internet Crime Complaint Centre (IC3)

The IC3 was established in 2000 and is based within the Federal Bureau of Investigation (FBI). It is an online self-report mechanism that receives complaints from victims across the world who have experienced a variety of cyber crimes with an American link or association. The types of crimes encompassed can include 'intellectual property rights (IPR) matters, computer intrusions (hacking), economic espionage (theft of trade secrets), online extortion, international money laundering, identity theft, and a growing list of internet facilitated crimes' (IC3, n.d.). Originally named the 'Internet Fraud Complaint Centre', this was revised in 2003 with the realisation that many fraud incidents overlapped with other types of criminal offences also perpetrated in an online environment. The latest annual report indicated that in 2015, 288,012 complaints were received with 44 per cent of these reporting a financial loss (IC3, 2016: 12). In total, combined losses were estimated at $1,070,711,522 (IC3, 2016: 12).

Australian Cybercrime Online Reporting Network (ACORN)

In late 2014, the ACORN was established as the central reporting agency for cyber crime within Australia. Cyber crime is defined for this purpose as crimes 'directed at computers or other devices (for example, hacking), and where computers or other devices are integral to the offence (for example, online fraud, identity theft and the distribution of child exploitation material)' (ACORN, 2014). This is similar to the cyber-dependent and cyber-enabled definitions cited earlier. Within the Australian context, cyber frauds and scams and identity theft are now required to be reported through this portal, rather than through local police at state and territory level. ACORN is a web-based mechanism and some police agencies in Australia will no longer accept a complaint at a police station, but will instead direct a victim to self-report through the ACORN website. ACORN publishes quarterly reports, and the latest one available (1 October to 31 December 2015) indicates that ACORN received 9,291 reports, of which 46 per cent related to scams or fraud (ACORN, 2016). Across the year 2015, ACORN reports indicate that 39,492 reports were made online (ACORN, 2016). It is unlikely that these statistics by themselves represent the true extent of cyber crime that is occurring within Australia, and instead reflect the early stages of this new reporting platform being made available as a means to report cyber frauds and scams in Australia.

Canadian Anti-Fraud Centre (CAFC)

The CAFC was first established in 1993, under the name 'Project PhoneBusers' as a local initiative through the work of police in the Ontario Provincial Police (OPP) and the Royal Canadian Mounted Police (RCMP) in targeting telemarketing fraud (CAFC, 2015a). After undergoing several expansions across the years, in 2010, the CAFC came into being as it is known today, and is a joint partnership approach with the OPP, RCMP and the Competition Bureau Canada, with a mandate to target many forms of mass marketing fraud across Canada. The CAFC is the central reporting agency for mass marketing schemes for victims across Canada, but also those from outside where there is a Canadian link. There are two means of contacting the CAFC to lodge a complaint, the first is through a call centre, which is based out of North Bay, Ontario, and the second is through a web-based form. In 2014, the CAFC recorded losses of over $74 million to mass marketing fraud (CAFC, 2015b). Of this total reported dollar loss, the solicitation method for Canadian complainants was predominantly via email and the internet, at 66 per cent (CAFC, 2015b).

The existence of central reporting agencies for cyber frauds and scams is a positive step towards improving the experience of victims by seeking to determine the most appropriate authority with which to lodge a complaint. The establishment of these central bodies can also assist police with providing a more accurate picture of offending and victimisation patterns across their jurisdictions. However against these positives, there remain challenges and areas for improvement in operating central reporting agencies. As will be discussed in later chapters, despite the establishment of these central reporting agencies, there are still many challenges experienced by victims in their ability to navigate the fraud justice network, lodge a complaint, and receive a response which is satisfactory to them.

Special fraud statistics

The other source of data on levels of fraud can be found in some of the specialist bodies that receive and publish statistics that exist in many countries throughout the world. In the USA, for example, the Federal Trade Commission through the Consumer Sentinel Network (CSN) publishes annual statistics on reported frauds. This contains reports of frauds recorded by a variety of American enforcement bodies at the Federal and state levels. Figure 1.2 reflects the total complaints for fraud and identity theft received by the CSN from 2001 to 2015, illustrating the substantial increase. The rising graph may not be totally linked to a rise in the problem as, like any detected statistics, better mechanisms to encourage reporting may also explain some of the changes. However, such is the rise and the other evidence from above it is highly likely to reflect the prevailing increase in this type of fraud.

Overall, this section has demonstrated the challenges involved in recording accurate statistics for cyber fraud and scams globally. It has also illustrated the variety of bodies in the fraud justice network who collect and publish statistics on this topic. The variety of figures that is produced demonstrates the lack of consistency there is in defining cyber fraud and scams across multiple jurisdictions and the additional challenges of being able to track trends within a country and between countries. The global nature of these offences also provides challenges, and documenting cyber fraud within a singular jurisdiction may not encapsulate the true extent of victimisation of the criminal networks globally, who perpetrate these types of offences. This is a topic which will be further explored in the later chapter on policing efforts.

Having established the definitions underpinning the categories of cyber fraud and scams covered in this book, and the challenges associated with determining an accurate depiction of victimisation in this area, the remainder of this chapter turns to a specific examination of technology, and how this has significantly impacted our understanding of fraud and how it operates today. In particular, this

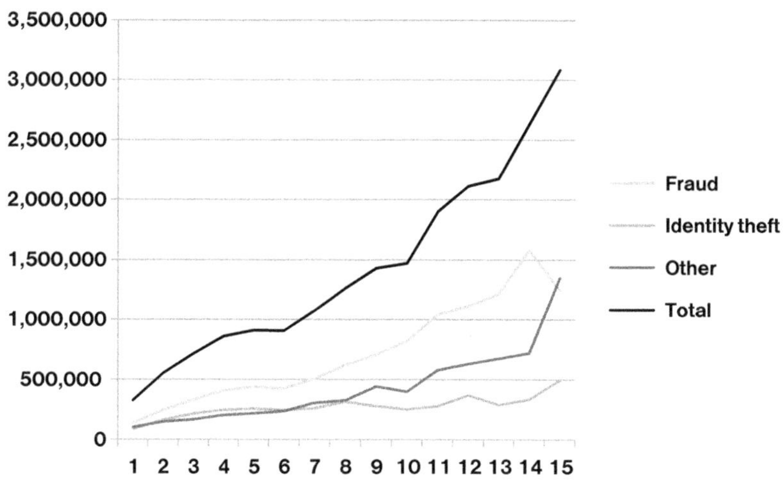

FIGURE 1.2 2001–2015 Reports to Consumer Sentinel Network.

emphasises the historical nature of fraud offences, but points to technology as a disruptive mechanism that has changed the way fraud operates, particularly in an online environment.

Technology, change and the fraudogenic consequences

> A scam artist is committing malpractice if he's [sic] not using the Internet.
> *(Danner, 2000 cited in Langenderfer and Shimp, 2001: 764)*

The above quote by Danner sums up the importance of the technological changes which have occurred over the last two decades. Technology, particularly the internet, has opened up new ways to perpetrate frauds and to industrialise old ones. It is worth illustrating some of the technological changes that have occurred to give a context to the substantial changes occurring around the world, before we look more specifically at its impact upon fraud.

The expansion of the internet

In a relatively short period of time access to the internet has risen from a few million in the industrialised world to the majority of the world population. In December 1995, across the globe there were estimated to be 16 million users of the internet (Jewkes and Yar, 2010). By 2000, there were around 361 million users of the internet worldwide (Internet World Stats, 2012). This had grown to almost 2.5 billion in 2011, amounting to 35 per cent of the world's population and by October 2016 it was estimated there were over 3.4 billion users (Internet Live Stats, 2016). The advancement of mobile computing devices has also increased access across many countries. Access to the internet has expanded from desk-based computers, to laptops, to tablets, to televisions, to mobile phones to now the 'internet of things', with connectivity of televisions, heating systems, buildings and vehicles, to name some. In 2015, mobile-cellular telephone subscriptions were 120.6 (per 100) in the developed world compared to 91.8 (per 100) in developing countries. Smart phones, which have advanced computing and internet access facilities, have also been growing substantially. Research has estimated over 1.8 billion worldwide with access to smart phones in 2015 (Statista, 2016b). A significant portion of these, are users in the developing world, which illustrates the huge potential for connectivity to engage in a wide range of behaviours across the world, both legitimate and illegitimate.

The growth of social networking

Completely new forms of social interaction have emerged through social networking sites such as Facebook, Tinder and LinkedIn. Indeed Facebook, which was only launched in 2004 in the USA, has grown to over a billion users, with 1.13 billion daily active users recorded on average in June 2016 (Facebook, 2016).

Social networking sites dedicated to people seeking love, sex and friendship have also emerged. Research by YouGov in the UK found that 1 in 5 relationships now begin online (Nolan, 2012).

The growth of online shopping and banking

The way people buy goods and services and manage their finances has also substantially changed. Increasingly, people purchase goods online via their home computers or mobile phones and manage their finances through online banking services in the same way. Symbolic of this is eBay, formed in 1995, and now has a global customer base of 233 million enabling millions to trade globally with one another on a daily basis (eBay, n.d.). Another icon of this change is Amazon, which went online in 1995 selling books and now sells virtually every consumer item and had global revenues of over US$100 billion in 2015 (Statista, 2016a). The internet has also changed the way that financial transactions and business are conducted. In the USA it is estimated that just over half of adults bank online (Pew Research Centre, 2013), but more significantly a survey of the American population in 2014 found that 87 per cent of the US population in 2014 possessed a mobile phone, that 71 per cent of these phones were smart and that 52 per cent of smart phone owners with a bank account had used it for online banking in the previous 12 months (Board of Governors of the Federal Reserve System, 2015). Such rises in the prevalence of the use of such technology are typical across the globe. In 2014 in Great Britain, for instance, 76 per cent of the population accessed the internet everyday, 74 per cent bought goods and services online and 53 per cent used online banking services (ONS, 2014).

Technology and commerce

Further to this, the use of technology (such as computers, the internet, mobile phones) has also fuelled completely new ways of doing business and providing services. Take the application for jobs. Many organisations advertise opportunities online and provide websites where applications are completed online. Many payments by both organisations and individuals are done so through online banking or through automated telephone systems, rather than paper cheques. Loans, social security benefits, grants, tax returns, and passports are also increasingly secured via online and automated telephone technology. Methods of communication, between companies, their staff and customers have also shifted from traditional face-to-face interactions to that of email and other modern forms of communication. There is no doubt that the internet has revolutionised and somewhat disrupted traditional methods of business, communication and knowledge production. This in and of itself is not a negative thing, as they can provide new and more efficient means to provide services. However, they can also create new threats and more opportunities for fraud to occur, as the following section will demonstrate.

The impact of technology on fraud

These changes in technology and the way things are done have had a significant impact on fraud. This chapter will note these changes under the following key themes, most of which are underpinned by the proliferation of opportunities for fraud to occur. Second, the transformation of technology has fuelled the globalisation of fraud, where frauds increasingly take place at a global cross-border level. Third, these changes have fuelled an increased exposure and likelihood of becoming a victim of fraud for both individuals and organisations, through the course of conducting legitimate business or other activities. Traditional understandings of crime risk and exposure are no longer adequate to explain the potential targeting and victimisation of an individual in the virtual environment. Indeed there are now persons who, 20 years ago, were designated at a very low risk of crime victimisation, that are now regularly exposed to the risk of crime in the form of cyber-enabled fraud.

Opportunities for fraud

There is extensive research illustrating the links between crime and opportunity (Cohen and Felson, 1979; Clarke, 1980; Mayhew et al., 1976). The importance of opportunity has also been noted in fraud (Cressey, 1973; Newman and Clarke, 2003). The technological changes that have occurred have increased the potential opportunities for fraud exponentially. First and foremost, completely new opportunities for frauds have occurred. The cyber-dependent frauds for the technologically skilled provide new opportunities to secure sensitive information, which can be used to perpetrate a fraud or sold to someone else to do so.

i) New types of fraud

Advances in technology have created opportunities for new types of fraud, which either did not exist before or were much more difficult to successfully pursue. The internet needs to be viewed as a set of 'social practices' and it is through these legitimate social practices that some people will create distinct opportunities for offending (Yar, 2013: 6). Therefore, illegitimate online activities must be viewed in conjunction with their legitimate counterparts. For instance the expansion of online dating and social networking sites has created new opportunities to develop friendships and romances, but they have also created opportunities to use these situations to perpetrate frauds. One of the recurring themes of many cyber-enabled frauds is the 'at-a-distance' aspect, which makes the frauds easier to perpetrate (Duffield and Grabosky, 2001) and makes the use of false and stolen identities a more attractive option for offenders, which in turn, is harder to detect by victims. This issue will be developed further in its own right shortly.

This is also evident in phishing emails, whereby potential victims receive an authoritative-looking email from a legitimate organisation (such as a bank or other service provider). This email generally claims there has been a security breach and requests potential victims to confirm their identity or 'reset' their passwords. Again such scams were possible before email, but would have required much more effort and resources to perpetrate. These two examples illustrate how the emerging technologies have fuelled new opportunities for fraud from legitimate activities, which are now dominant within a virtual environment. Indeed it is estimated globally there are 29 billion spam emails daily and that the email virus rate is 1 in 196 and phishing emails are 1 in 392 (Symantec 2014).

ii) Adapting to new technology

A second strand is the ease and convenience through which technology has created opportunities to undertake frauds via new methods. For example, the advent of online sales platforms such as eBay and Gumtree has made it simpler for fraudsters to sell non-existent and fake goods. Indeed Treadwell (2011) has noted how traditional criminals have moved from car boot sales to eBay to sell counterfeit goods. The proliferation of technology that is relatively easy to use has also enabled many ordinary people (and criminals) to use computer software such as 'Photoshop' and related technologies to create documents which can be used to perpetrate fraud.

iii) Industrialisation of 'old frauds'

Perhaps the biggest increase in opportunities has come from the ability for fraudsters to 'industrialise' old frauds. Just as the advent of modern technology has increased opportunities for businesses to reach larger markets to sell goods and services, this is also evident with fraudsters. At one level there are a number of frauds, which were already perpetrated on a mass scale through traditional communications such as mail and telephone that have become even easier to perpetrate using the internet, email and also to be done so more cheaply. Advanced fee fraud schemes (also known as Nigerian 419 scams, named after the section of the Nigerian Criminal Code relevant to fraud offences), where a potential victim is presented with a scenario where they are asked to pay a small amount of money up-front in return for a promised larger amount down the track, have moved from paper letters to email (Smith et al., 1999). Such scenarios can include inheritance notifications, business/investment opportunities and corrupt officials seeking assistance. The fraudsters can send out millions of emails at little cost hoping to hook a tiny few. The same applies to the very common fake lottery scams, where emails can replace paper notifications of a win in a foreign lottery which requires a 'fee' to release the substantial prize (although paper versions of this fraud are still common, particularly for targeting pensioners).

iv) 'Normalising' fraud

The technological changes have also created new opportunities for fraud, which could almost be described as the 'normalisation' of fraud. By this we mean the 'dark web', which now contains websites where individuals can purchase credit card details to undertake fraud. In the same way that eBay and Gumtree engage in legitimate trade, there are websites on the dark web which are dedicated to the sale and trade of stolen credentials (such as credit card numbers/passwords/personal information) which facilitates further criminal activity. Indeed some of the websites even 'ape' legitimate website sales techniques such that there are 'free tests for regular customers' and 'discounts for regular clients' (RSA, 2015). Other illegitimate services are also offered such as the bespoke writing of malware and denial of services attacks, for example. Thus anyone with access of the internet and knowledge of where to find such websites can purchase the tools to conduct fraud, just as easily as they can buy any other goods and services.

v) Fraud entrepreneurs

The substantial number of opportunities that have arisen has given rise to the growth of fraud entrepreneurs or scampreneurs (Button et al., 2009). These are persons who have realised the potential of the technological changes and used these to invent scams to target victims and make large sums of money. Many are 'traditional' criminals who have adapted to the new opportunities, but some are a new breed of persons lured into criminality who see the easy money to be made and the low risks. Indeed in 2011, a teenager who had attended an exclusive British Public School (an elite fee-paying school) was convicted of running an £18 million internet scam, which involved a social networking site for crooks and the selling of stolen credit card details amongst others (Mailonline, 2011). In addition, in many countries worldwide there has been a sharp decline in the number of armed robberies of banks and other financial institutions across the past decade. While increased security and crime prevention measures are undoubtedly a strong contributing factor (Brown, 2015; Weatherburn and Holmes, 2013), many also assert the notion that offenders have turned their efforts to online crime, as it is seen to be lower risk and reap higher rewards compared to its offline counterpart (Nicas, 2013). More consideration to those who engage in such frauds will be considered later in this chapter.

vi) The neutralisation of fraud

The changes in the way many activities take place have also facilitated much greater opportunities for fraudsters to neutralise what they are doing. Many frauds can take place with the perpetrator having no personal contact with the victim. Emails can be sent and websites created where interactions are driven by the exchange of information electronically. This 'at a distance' approach is much easier for many to perpetrate (Duffield and Grabosky, 2001); traditional frauds where face-to-face contact or even speaking to the victim are not always necessary. For many potential fraudsters conducting frauds by having to speak direct or over the telephone is unpalatable. New forms of communication make it easier for some to engage in such activities and the process of neutralisation, which is so important to fraud-related crimes, becomes much easier (Sykes and Matza, 1957).

vii) Costs of technology

The evolution in technology has seen a large reduction in the costs associated with targeting potential fraud victims, and offenders have sought to exploit this as far as possible. Historically, offenders were required to send physical letters or make direct phone calls to potential victims in order to sell their particular fraudulent approach. However, the internet enables offenders to send out an infinite number of emails with the hope of soliciting a few successful pitches. This is reiterated in the concept of mass marketing fraud, as detailed earlier. Costs associated with targeting victims (such as postage) are no longer relevant, instead the offender only needs an internet connection. The ever increasing speed of the internet is also facilitating an increased ability for offenders to send out mass marketing emails and phishing attempts. The return on benefit works in the favour of the offender, who has to make little effort with the likelihood of gaining a few replies from unsuspecting victims.

This is not to say that fraud is no longer perpetrated through older technologies such as physical mail and the telephone. These methods are still in existence, as demonstrated through the work of Think Jessica in campaigning to reduce the number of fraudulent letters received particularly by older persons. The cost of telephones has also reduced, and there is an availability of mobile phones and pre-paid sim cards, which can be used by offenders without having to link specifically to their own identity. These phones and sim cards are easily disposable and therefore make attractive tools for criminals as part of their overall fraud efforts.

Globalisation of fraud

As previously stated, one of the unique characteristics of cyber crime more broadly is its transnational nature, whereby offenders will seek to exploit geographic jurisdictional boundaries to avoid police detection and prosecution. Technological changes have enabled those inclined to fraud to broaden their horizons and target victims across the world. There are a number of dimensions to this globalisation. First there are those from the poorer parts of the world who now have the capacity and opportunity to target those in the richer parts. Second, there are fraudsters based in industrialised countries who can reach a global audience with their scams. Third, there are more organised fraudsters who move their operations to a third country to target other countries in order to avoid detection. Each of these dimensions to globalisation will now be explored.

Technological changes have opened up opportunities for poor but skilled persons in developing nations to target citizens in richer countries. In 2014, a report by investment bank Credit Suisse found that 1 per cent of the world's population owned 48 per cent of global wealth (Credit Suisse, 2014). The same report found the bottom 50 per cent of the world's population owned less than 1 per cent of global wealth. This demonstrates a huge inequality in the distribution of wealth in the world. For individuals in the poorer parts of the world equipped with appropriate technological skills and the increasing ease and lower costs of connecting with the richer parts of the world, this has provided the opportunity to target them with frauds. Indeed a report on advanced fee frauds estimated there were over 800,000 active perpetrators of such frauds globally with 'too many to count' in Nigeria, but also substantial numbers operating in countries such as Ghana, India, South Africa, Cameroon, to name some (Ultrascan Global Investigations, 2014). Many attribute cyber fraud to predominantly West African nations such as Nigeria and Ghana, and while historically this may have been accurate (evidenced by terms such as 'Nigerian fraud' and '419 fraud', being the section of the Nigerian Criminal Code which refers to these criminal acts), it is now a worldwide phenomenon (Australian Crime Commission, 2012; see also Schoenmakers et al., 2009).

Globalisation has also enabled some scammers to establish a scam that lures victims from around the globe. The sale of bogus goods and services has been particularly open to this. For example in 2009, a group in the UK were convicted of selling counterfeit premium brand golf clubs on eBay, which had made them 'millions'. The counterfeit clubs were manufactured in China and marketed on eBay. Victims were drawn from the UK, China, Thailand, Australia, Germany, USA, Singapore and Hong Kong (This is Money, 2009).

The other aspect to globalisation is that is has enabled some organised fraudsters to locate in one country and target another. This can be done at much lower costs using telephones, the internet and related technologies. Location in other countries is often associated with local law enforcement who are unlikely to be interested due to their own citizens not being targeted. For example, in Europe many boiler rooms selling bogus investments have been based in Spain, around Marbella and have targeted the UK. In North America there have been groups that have located in Canada to target the USA (Button, 2012). In Australia, victims have been targeted from countries all over the world, and continue to send money to West African countries (Cross and Blackshaw, 2015) as well as Europe, North America and Asia.

Risk of fraud

The impact of technology has ultimately led to the increased risk of an individual being targeted and becoming a victim of fraud. As was illustrated earlier in this chapter, millions of people fall victim to frauds and even more are targeted. On an individual level most people who use modern technology run the daily gauntlet of fraud attempts upon them. Most people regularly receive phishing emails, notifications of lottery wins, offerings of bogus products, to name some. When we scan the internet for bargains there is the risk of stumbling across bogus websites and legitimate sites too, selling counterfeit and non-existent products and services. Seeking love and friendship online runs the risk of internet fraudsters with fake identities befriending you. Downloading a potential job opportunity or 'amusing video' sent to us could also mean putting malware on our computers and smartphones, which could be used to steal our identity. Our computers and smartphones have become the windows through which a potentially global community of fraudsters can target and defraud us. Many segments of society, which traditionally have been at very low risk of crime victimisation, have in a short period of time, become much more high risk. For example many crime surveys show young men as the most likely to be victims of crime (theft and violence) and older people to be the least likely victims of crime (ONS, 2013). However, the technological changes that have emerged have opened up many older people to be at a high risk of being victimised by a variety of frauds (OFT, 2006). Thus the pensioner, safe in their home and at very low risk of suffering a property-related crime, as soon as they switch on their computer or smartphone, check their email, surf the web or answer the phone is suddenly connecting to a much higher-risk world. There are many who readily accept that older people are attractive targets for potential fraud offenders (Reiboldt and Vogel, 2001), arguably through factors such as access to life savings, superannuation, ability to access additional lines of credit and their likely ownership of property. Many offenders will seek to target older people specifically based on these circumstances and use the internet to perpetrate this.

To develop this point further the impact of technology has created a completely new habitus in which we live, work and play; but, unlike the traditional world, many have not yet learnt to appreciate the risks. For example, many people would know the risks and how to manage them of purchasing goods from a 'carboot' sale, of visiting certain locations at night and of talking to strangers. The internet, however, has created a completely new habitus in which we operate and many are still learning how to gauge and manage the risks of this new technology. The application of traditional crime prevention measures (such as locking the front door, keeping valuables out of sight in a vehicle, and shredding personal documents) are not always as readily applicable to the virtual environment and, therefore, need to be modified to ensure safety. Digital networks, including the internet, also pose new threats to our safety that we are yet to comprehend or effectively combat and this remains a challenge into the future.

Perpetrators of fraud

This chapter will now end with a consideration of the perpetrators of the frauds. The wide range of potential behaviours means that the range of persons and bodies engaged in these types of frauds is very broad. As was noted earlier in this chapter many scams and frauds are not criminal breaches and at worst might be regulatory/civil breaches or merely unethical behaviour. As such there is a spectrum of those who commit such acts. There are, for example, legitimate organisations, such as banks and other companies who have been found to have used deceptive practices. Earlier, the problems of payment protection insurance mis-selling and European health insurance cards were illustrated. The financial collapse in 2008 also exposed huge negligence, if not fraud, by financial institutions in packaging up and hiding worthless debts known as 'sub-prime mortgages' with other better products. Many corporate investors and ultimately individuals lost large sums of money as a result of these acts (National Commission on the Causes of the Financial and Economic Crisis in the United States, 2011). Indeed, the cost of the Global Financial Crisis of 2008–09 has been estimated at $12.8 trillion to the US economy alone (Weise, 2012). These acts were not perpetrated by loan conmen, organised criminals or fraudsters, but by well-known and up until this point, respected financial institutions. The mis-selling of endowment mortgages in the UK by legitimate financial institutions has also left an estimated 4.4 million product holders substantially short in the value of their funds to repay mortgages (Fooks, 2003). Again, this was largely undertaken by financial institutions.

Frauds are also perpetrated by organised criminal groups as well as individuals (Garner et al., 2016). The individuals who commit such frauds may start with honourable intentions and slip into fraud (Levi's slippery slope fraudsters, which will shortly be explained) or may have started out with clear criminal intentions. The focus of this section will be to consider more the individual fraudsters, with clear criminal intentions and what is known about them. It is nevertheless important to recognise the 'criminal' corporations and many individuals operating in the legal hinterland who have also become involved, but which are not the main focus of this book.

It is also important to note, before this discussion commences, that the 'newness' of many of these frauds means there is limited academic research. Indeed fraud in general has been the subject of much less research than other areas of criminology (Levi, 2008a). The interest in fraud in general and the 'newness' of the crimes combined, makes for a very limited research base.

Origin

The diversity of the frauds, however, makes such generalisation very difficult. This becomes apparent when considering fraudsters and where they originate from. For instance Nigeria has become associated with a variety of frauds, leading to serious concerns amongst many in their country over the image for their country. Nigerians and other West Africans have become associated with the 419 scams, but Smith et al. (1999) have also suggested involvement of Nigerians in credit card fraud, identity card fraud, forgery and immigration fraud as well. Many internet-based frauds – often involving phishing – have been linked to Eastern European criminal groups in Russia, Romania, Lithuania, to name some (Levi, 2008a).

Nigeria and Eastern Europe have been, and continue to be, the source of many frauds. However, as this section will reveal, the origin of fraudsters is much more diverse than this; it depends upon the type of fraud and many countries should look much more closely to home for many of their fraudsters.

One of the best sources of information in this limited area is the United States Federal Trade Commission (FTC), which, through the Consumer Sentinel Network, provides a variety of statistics relating to frauds against Americans. The report for 2014 identified over 98,000 cross-border frauds reported in the USA. However, of these types of frauds (largely the mass marketing and identity fraud that are the subject of this book) they accounted for only 6 per cent of all the frauds reported. This compares to 9 per cent in 2013 and 10 per cent in 2010 illustrating a downward trend in the proportion of fraud emanating across borders (Consumer Sentinel Network, 2015). Thus, the first significant finding this illustrates is that the USA is the largest source of fraud attacks against the USA. Further the largest source of attacks after the USA was Canada, accounting for just over 16,500, then followed by Nigeria at 9,858, then the UK at 7,371, China at 6,847 and Jamaica at 6,159, representing the top five. Thus, although Nigeria features in the top five it accounted for a tiny proportion of the frauds affecting the USA.

The origin of fraudsters is further illustrated by some of the data that is released by the private companies that offer services to organisations to detect and prevent frauds. ThreatMetrix is one such company and in the report for the last quarter of 2015, which largely related to attacks against organisations, rather than individuals, the top five countries for origin of attack were the USA, UK, France, India and Bangladesh, and Nigeria didn't even make it into the top 10 (ThreatMetrix, 2015). Further, when hacking is considered (which is used for purposes much wider than fraud) one of the leading perpetrators is Indonesia, which took over from China as the number one source of attack globally, with 38 per cent of hacking-related traffic on their servers, followed by China at 33 per cent, and the USA at 6.9 per cent (Milian, 2013).

These brief snapshots of origin of attack serve to illustrate the first key theme. Cross-border frauds are clearly a problem and account for a large number of frauds. There are clearly some of the more technical frauds, which are associated with specific countries, and these tend to be in the Far East and former communist countries. From wherever the origin of the attack occurs, many fraudsters will be keen to 'launder' their money in safe havens overseas, so even when some fraudsters are based in their own country they might still seek to divert their gains to a perceived safer third country.

Academic studies

Research studies based upon interviews with offenders are surprisingly rare, for white-collar criminals they are even rarer and for the fraudsters that are the focus of this book, rarer still (Shover and Hunter, 2010). Levi (2008b) has conducted research on 'long firm fraudsters', which involved interviews with them. Long firm fraudsters set up businesses and build up credit gradually, ordering more goods, and then eventually disappearing and not paying the debts. The scam is oriented more at organisations than individuals, although it could affect the latter. In conducting this research Levi distinguished three useful categories of fraudsters, which probably has relevance to some mass marketing fraudsters (Levi, 2008a). These are:

> *Slippery slope*: generally have no prior convictions and fall into frauds through pressures combined with identification of opportunities.
>
> *Intermediate long firm fraudsters*: some with prior convictions who started out with legitimate intentions, but eventually turn to fraud.
>
> *Pre-planned long firm fraudsters*: the perpetrators start with the purpose of fraud and generally have past criminal convictions although may use 'front' people without convictions. Some may be involved in organised crime in the 'traditional' sense: i.e. drugs, racketeering, or links to them, or may focus solely on certain types of frauds.

There have also been a handful of studies on the types of fraudsters who commit some of the frauds considered in this book. The findings from these studies relating to the backgrounds and profiles of these types of fraudsters will be considered here. Some of the insights on their rationale for engaging in fraud and how they went about it, amongst others, will be developed in later chapters.

i) Telemarketing fraudsters

Some of the frauds considered in this book are perpetrated via the telephone. The victim is ensnared into the fraud by an individual calling them on the telephone. There are a variety of scams perpetrated using this method, but one of the most common is the selling of worthless or fake investments. Others include securing donations to non-existent charities, selling tickets to fake lotteries or non-existent or bogus products. Shover et al. (2003, 2004) have conducted the largest study of these types of fraudsters to date, interviewing 47, largely in prison with some on probation, convicted for engagement in this type of fraud in the USA. They found the offenders had been involved in criminal telemarketing for 8.25 years on average, with an age range of 26 to 69 and mean of 42.4 years old. Forty-one were male, with six female and all bar three, who were black, were white. They found these fraudsters differed significantly from street criminals, largely coming from conventional hard-working family backgrounds. Some 68 per cent of the interviewees had fathers who were business owners or managers and, as Shover et al. (2004: 65) note, 'a substantial proportion of the men and women interviewed for this research were exposed to entrepreneurial perspectives and understandings while young'. In terms of education, five claimed a degree, 21 had attended college, and eight had dropped out of high school. The picture of these types of fraudsters is therefore very different from traditional street criminals, but there exists some similarities to studies of occupational fraudsters, where there has been a dominance of middle-aged men, and those from typical working family backgrounds (Shover et al., 2004).

ii) Identity fraudsters

Another group of fraudsters, which has been the subject of in-depth academic research involving interviews with them, are identity fraudsters (Copes and Vieraitis, 2007). This study covered those offenders who use the personal information of a person (such as social security number or banking details) to commit frauds, such as taking out loans in the person's name. In this study, 59 individuals convicted of identity theft-related crimes in the USA incarcerated in federal prisons were interviewed. As with the Shover et al. (2003, 2004) research on fraudulent telemarketers, this group were significantly different from street criminals, coming predominantly from the middle-classes. Their sample included 61 per cent male to 39 per cent female, 44 per cent white, 52 per cent black and three per cent Asian. The age ranged from 23 to 60 with a mean age of 38. Forty-two per cent of the interviewees came from middle-class or upper-middle-class backgrounds, but 37 per cent were from working-class backgrounds and 10 per cent from the underclass. In terms of education, 20 per cent had a degree, 32 per cent had attended some college and almost 80 per cent had held down jobs at some point in their lives. This study also noted 63 per cent had been arrested for crimes other than what they had been incarcerated for, with the biggest crime group being other identity theft and fraud, followed by property crimes. The nature of sampling for interviews led Copes and Vieraitis (2007) to suggest that the sampling strategy led to certain biases, particularly in terms of the bias towards women. However, they found, 'identity theft to be quite democratic with participants from all walks of life. In fact they were just as likely to resemble persistent street offenders as they were middle-class offenders' (Copes and Vieraitis, 2007: 17).

iii) eBay fraudsters

A significant numbers of frauds are perpetrated by the use of an existing website to sell fake, faulty or non-existent goods. eBay is one of the biggest online means to sell goods and Treadwell (2011) has conducted a small study based upon interviews with ten persons selling stolen and counterfeit goods online. In this small study he found evidence of traditional working-class criminals moving to this type of criminal venture. Albeit a small sample and not generalisable, it does offer at least one snapshot on this type of fraud.

A central debate emerging in recent years with the growing interest in cyber fraud has been to what extent those engaging in such crimes are the 'usual suspects' moving from traditional street crimes to more lucrative opportunities with less law enforcement interest in the cyber world. Alongside this debate is also the question of the extent to which fraudsters are from other countries, using the benefits of the technological changes to target other countries. The research discussed above only provides a few snapshots of different types of fraud, largely in the USA. As more research is conducted in this area we will be confident of the types of persons who become involved in such frauds. However, the limited research so far does offer evidence of not only traditional street criminals turning to fraud, but also other groups not normally strongly associated with crimes engaged in fraud. The overseas risk, at least in terms of the USA, would also seem to be small but significant, but clearly not the majority threat. It is important therefore to cast our gaze much wider than traditional street criminals and West Africans when considering who might be the fraudsters.

Conclusion

This chapter has introduced the types of fraud that will be considered in this book, along with a typology of them. It has set out some of the main terms and definitions. The huge scale of the problem of cyber fraud and scams was then detailed. The chapter also provided some context to the changes that are taking place globally, particularly technologically, which are fuelling the growth in cyber fraud and scams. Some of these key themes include the expansion of access to the internet, the changing ways in which relationships are formed, as well as the ways goods and services are bought, to name some. The chapter ended with some of the small but limited insights from research on who these fraudsters are and where they come from. It showed that the small research published so far suggests we should be much more focused upon home grown 'talent' from ordinary working families. The next chapter will now move to consider the victims and, amongst a number of issues, explore their characteristics.

Note

1 Part of this chapter first appeared as Button, M. and Cross, C. (2017) Technology and fraud: The 'fraudogenic' consequences of the internet revolution. In: McGuire, M. and Holt, T. (eds) *The Routledge Handbook of Technology, Crime and Justice*. London: Routledge, pp. 78–95.

References

Australian Bureau of Statistics (2016) *4528.0 Personal Fraud 2014–15*. Available at: http://www.abs.gov.au/AUSSTATS/abs@.nsf/0/1FF970676E24FDFECA2574740015CA71?Opendocument (accessed 21 October 2016).

Australian Competition and Consumer Commission (2015) *Targeting Scams: Report of the ACCC on Scams Activity 2014*. Canberra: Australian Competition and Consumer Commission. Available at: http://www.accc.gov.au/publications/targeting-scams-report-on-scam-activity/targeting-scams-report-of-the-accc-on-scam-activity-2014 (accessed 21 October 2016).

Australian Competition and Consumer Commission (2016) *Targeting Scams: Report of the ACCC on Scams Activity 2015.* Canberra: Australian Competition and Consumer Commission. Available at: http://www.accc.gov.au/publications/targeting-scams-report-on-scam-activity/targeting-scams-report-of-the-accc-on-scam-activity-2015 (accessed 21 October 2016).

Australian Crime Commission (ACC) and Australian Institute of Criminology (AIC) (2012) *Serious and Organised Investment Fraud in Australia.* Canberra, Australia: Australian Crime Commission and Australian Institute of Criminology.

Australian Cybercrime Online Reporting Network (2014) *Learn about Cybercrime.* Available at: https://www.acorn.gov.au/learn-about-cybercrime (accessed 21 October 2016).

Australian Cybercrime Online Reporting Network (2016) *ACORN Statistics Reports.* Available at: https://www.acorn.gov.au/resources (accessed October 2016).

Beals, M., DeLiema, M. and Deevy, M. (2015) *Framework for a Taxonomy of Fraud.* Stanford: Stanford Center on Longevity. Available at: http://fraudresearchcenter.org/wp-content/uploads/2015/07/FFRC_Taxonomy_FullReport_7-22-15.pdf (accessed 21 October 2016).

Board of Governors of the Federal Reserve System (2015) *Consumer and Mobile Services 2015.* Washington DC: Federal Reserve Publications.

Brown, R. (2015) Explaining the property crime drop: The offender perspective. *Trends and Issues in Crime and Criminal Justice*, no. 495. Available at: http://www.aic.gov.au/publications/current%20series/tandi/481-500/tandi495.html (accessed 21 October 2016).

Button, M. (2012) Cross-border fraud and the case for an 'interfraud'. *Policing: An International Journal of Police Strategies & Management* 35(2): 285–303. Doi: 10.1108/13639511211230057.

Button, M., Blackbourn, D. and Tunley, M. (2015) 'The not so thin blue line after all?' Investigative resources dedicated to fighting fraud/economic crime in the United Kingdom. *Policing: A Journal of Policy and Practice* 9(2): 129–142. Doi: 10.1093/police/pau037.

Button, M., Lewis, C. and Tapley, J. (2009) *Fraud Typologies and the Victims of Fraud Literature Review*, London: National Fraud Authority.

Button, M., Lewis, C. and Tapley, J. (2014) Not a victimless crime: The impact of fraud on individual victims and their families. *Security Journal* 27(1) 36–54. Doi: 10.1057/sj.2012.11.

Canadian Anti-Fraud Centre (2015a) *About the CAFC.* Available at: http://www.antifraudcentre-centreantifraude.ca/about-ausujet/index-eng.htm (accessed 21 October 2016).

Canadian Anti-Fraud Centre (2015b) *Annual Statistics Report 2014.* Available at: http://www.antifraudcentre-centreantifraude.ca/reports-rapports/2014/ann-ann-eng.htm (accessed 21 October 2016).

Clarke, R. V. G. (1980) Situational crime prevention: Theory and practice. *British Journal of Criminology* 20(2): 136–147.

Clough, J. (2015) *Principles of Cybercrime*, 2nd edition, Cambridge: Cambridge University Press. Doi: 10.1017/CBO9781139540803.

Cohen, L. E. and Felson, M. (1979) Social changes and crime rates: A routine activities approach. *American Sociological Review* 44(4): 588–608.

Consumer Sentinel (2015) *International Consumer Complaints Jan–Dec 2014.* Available at https://www.ftc.gov/enforcement/consumer-sentinel-network/reports (accessed 3 November 2016).

Copes, H. and Vieraitis, L. (2007) *Identity Theft: Assessing Offenders' Strategies and Perceptions of Risk.* Available at: https://www.ncjrs.gov/pdffiles1/nij/grants/219122.pdf (accessed 21 October 2016).

Credit Suisse (2014) *Global Wealth Report*. Available at: https://publications.credit-suisse.com/tasks/render/file/?fileID=60931FDE-A2D2-F568-B041B58C5EA591A4 (accessed 21 October 2016).

Cressey, D. (1973) *Other People's Money*, Montclair, NJ: Patterson Smith.

Cross, C. and Blackshaw, D. (2015) Improving the police response to online fraud. *Policing: A Journal of Policy and Practice* 9(2): 119–128. Doi: 10.1093/police/pau044.

Donohue, J. J. and Levitt, S. D. (2001) The impact of legalized abortion on crime. *Quarterly Journal of Economics* 116(2): 379–420. Doi: 10.1162/00335530151144050.

Duffield, G. and Grabosky, P. (2001) The psychology of fraud. *Trends and Issues in Crime and Criminal Justice*, no. 199, Canberra: Australian Institute of Criminology. Available at: http://www.aic.gov.au/media_library/publications/tandi_pdf/tandi199.pdf (accessed 21 October 2016).

eBay (n.d.) *The Company*. Available at: http://pages.ebay.co.uk/aboutebay/thecompany/companyoverview.html (accessed 21 October 2016).

Facebook (2016) *Stats*. Available at: http://newsroom.fb.com/company-info/ (accessed 21 October 2016).

Farrell, G., Tseloni, A., Mailley, J. and Tilley, N. (2011) The crime drop and the security hypothesis. *Journal of Research in Crime and Delinquency* 48(2): 147–175. Doi: 10.1177/0022427810391539.

Farrell, S., Yeo, N, and Ladenburg, G. (2007) *Blackstone's Guide to the Fraud Act 2006*, Oxford: Oxford University Press.

Federal Trade Commission (2013) *Consumer Fraud in the United States: The Third FTC Survey*. Available at: https://www.ftc.gov/sites/default/files/documents/reports/consumer-fraud-united-states-2011-third-ftc-survey/130419fraudsurvey_0.pdf (accessed 21 October 2016).

Financial Conduct Authority (2016) *Monthly PPI Refunds and Compensation*. Available at: https://www.fca.org.uk/consumers/payment-protection-insurance/monthly-ppi-refunds-and-compensation (accessed 21 October 2016).

Fitzgerald, M. (2014) *Falling Crime or Flawed Statistics?* Presentation at British Society of Criminology Mannheim seminar, London School of Economics, 15 January 2014.

Fooks, G. (2003) In the valley of the blind the one-eyed man is King: Corporate crime and the myopia of financial regulation. In: Tombs, S. and Whyte, D. (eds) *Unmasking the Crimes of the Powerful: Scrutinizing States and Corporations*, New York: Peter Lang.

Garner, S., Crocker, R., Skidmore, M., Webb, S., Graham, J. and Gill, M. (2016) *Organised Fraud in Local Communities*, London: Police Foundation.

Harrell, E. (2015) *Victims of Identity Theft, 2014*, Bureau of Justice Statistics, US Department of Justice. Available at: https://www.bjs.gov/content/pub/pdf/vit14.pdf (accessed 24 October 2016).

Head, S. (2015) *Presentation to the 2015 Annual Counter Fraud and Forensic Accounting Conference*, University of Portsmouth, 2nd June, 2015. Available at: https://vimeo.com/130322766 (accessed 21 October 2016).

Internet Crime Complaint Center (n.d.) *About Us*. Available at: https://www.ic3.gov/about/default.aspx (accessed 21 October 2016).

Internet Crime Complaint Center (2016) *2015 Internet Crime Report*. Available at: https://pdf.ic3.gov/2015_IC3Report.pdf (accessed 21 October 2016).

Internet Live Stats (2016) *Internet Live Stats*. Available at: http://www.internetlivestats.com/ (accessed 21 October 2016).

Internet World Stats (2012) *Internet Usage Statistics*. Available at: http://www.internetworldstats.com/stats.htm (accessed 21 October 2016).

Jewkes, Y. and Yar, M. (2010) Introduction: The Internet, cybercrime, and the challenges of the 21st Century. In: Jewkes, Y. and Yar, M. (eds) *Handbook of Internet Crime*, Cullompton: Wiley, pp. 1–8.

Langenderfer, J., and Shimp, T. A. (2001) Consumer vulnerability to scams, swindles, and fraud: A new theory of visceral influences on persuasion. *Psychology & Marketing* 18(7): 763–783. Doi: 10.1002/mar.1029.

Langton, L. (2011) *Identity Theft Reported by Households, 2005–2010*. Bureau of Justice Statistics: US Department of Justice. Available at: https://www.bjs.gov/index.cfm?ty=pbdetail&iid=2207 (accessed 21 October 2016).

Levi, M. (2008a) Organized frauds and organising frauds: Unpacking the research on networks and organisation. *Criminology and Criminal Justice* 8(4): 389–419. Doi: 10.1177/1748895808096470/.

Levi, M. (2008b) *The Phantom Capitalists*, revised edition. Aldershot: Ashgate.

Maguire, M. (2012) Criminal statistics and the construction of crime. In: Maguire, M., Morgan, R. and Reiner, R. (eds) *The Oxford Handbook of Criminology*. Oxford: Oxford University Press.

Mailonline (2011) *Pictured with Piles of Cash: The Public Schoolboy Jailed for Five Years for Masterminding £18 Million Internet Scam*. Available at: http://www.dailymail.co.uk/news/article-1362207/Public-school-boy-masterminded-18million-Internet-scam-jailed-years.html (accessed 21 October 2016).

Massey, R. (2011) *Millions of Britons Duped Over the Internet into Paying for Free EU Health Cards*. Available at: http://www.dailymail.co.uk/news/article-2010441/Millions-duped-paying-free-EU-health-cards.html (accessed 21 October 2016).

Mayhew, P., Clarke, R. V. G., Sturman, A. and Hough, J. M. (1976) *Crime as Opportunity*, London: HMSO.

McGuire, M. and Dowling, S. (2013) *Cybercrime a Review of the Evidence*. Home Office Research Study 75. Available at: https://www.gov.uk/government/publications/cyber-crime-a-review-of-the-evidence (accessed 14 July 2015).

Milian, M. (2013) *Indonesia Passes China to Become Top Source of Cyber-Attack Traffic*. Available at: http://www.bloomberg.com/news/2013-10-15/indonesia-passes-china-to-become-top-source-of-cyber-attack-traffic.html (accessed 21 October 2016).

National Commission on the Causes of the Financial and Economic Crisis in the United States (2011) *The Financial Crisis Inquiry Report*. USA: Pacific Publishing Studio.

National Fraud Authority (2013) *Annual Fraud Indicator*, London: National Fraud Authority.

Nevin, R. (2007) Understanding international crime trends: The legacy of preschool lead exposure. *Environmental Research* 104(3): 315–336. Doi: 10.1016/j.envres.2007.02.008.

Newman, G. R. and Clarke, R. V. (2003) *Superhighway Robbery*, Cullompton: Willan.

Nicas, J. (2013) Crime that no longer pays? *Wall Street Journal*. Available at: http://www.wsj.com/articles/SB10001424127887323926104578274541161239474 (accessed 21 October 2016).

Nolan, S. (2012) *Huge Spike in Online Dating After Christmas as Holiday Spirit Encourages Thousands to Cure Their Loneliness*. Available at: http://www.dailymail.co.uk/news/article-2254968/Online-dating-statistics-Huge-spike-Christmas-holiday-spirit-encourages-thousands-cure-loneliness.html#axzz2K7uODPCt (accessed 21 October 2016).

Office of Fair Trading (2006) *Research on Impact of Mass Marketed Scams*, London: Office of Fair Trading.

Office for National Statistics (2013) *The Likelihood of Becoming a Victim of Crime*. Available at: http://www.ons.gov.uk/ons/rel/crime-stats/crime-statistics/period-ending-march-2012/sty-a-victim-of-crime.html (accessed 21 October 2016).

Office for National Statistics (2014) *Internet Access – Households and Individuals: 2014*. London: Office for National Statistics.

Office for National Statistics (2015) *Fraud and Cyber-crime Development Trial: Field Trial*, London: Office for National Statistics.

Office for National Statistics (2016) *Crime in England and Wales: Year Ending March 2016*. Available at: https://www.ons.gov.uk/peoplepopulationandcommunity/crimeandjustice/bulletins/crimeinenglandandwales/yearendingmar2016 (accessed 21 October 2016).

Pascoe, T., Owen, K., Keats, G. and Gill, M. (2006) *Identity Fraud: What About the Victim*, Leicester: Perpetuity Research and Consultancy International.

Pew Research Centre (2013) *51% of U.S. adults bank online*. Available at: http://www.pewinternet.org/2013/08/07/51-of-u-s-adults-bank-online/ (accessed 18 January 2017).

Reiboldt, W. and Vogel, R. (2001) A critical analysis of telemarketing fraud in a gated senior community. *Journal of Elder Abuse and Neglect* 13(4): 21–38. Doi: 10.1300/J084v13n04_02.

RSA (2015) *Cybercrime 2015 An Insider Look at the Changing Threat Landscape*, London: RSA. Available at: https://www.emc.com/collateral/white-paper/rsa-white-paper-cybercrime-trends-2015.pdf (accessed 21 October 2016).

Schoenmakers, Y., de Vries, R. and van Wijk, A. (2009) *Mountains of Gold: An Exploratory Research in Nigerian 419 Fraud*, Netherlands: SWP.

Semmens, N. (2005) When the world knows your name: Identity theft and fraud in the UK. *Scottish Journal of Criminal Justice Studies* 11: 80–91.

Shover, N. and Hunter, B. W. (2010) Blue-collar, white-collar: Crimes and mistakes. In: Bernasco, W. (ed.) *Offenders on Offending*. Cullompton: Wilan.

Shover, N., Coffey, G. S. and Hobbs, D. (2003) Crime on the line: Telemarketing and the changing nature of professional crime. *British Journal of Criminology* 43(3): 489–505. Doi: 10.1093/bjc/43.3.489.

Shover, N., Coffey, G. S. and Sanders, C. R. (2004) Dialling for dollars: Opportunities, justifications and telemarketing fraud. *Qualitative Sociology* 27(1): 59–75. Doi: 10.1023/B:QUAS.0000015544.69646.f1.

Smith, G., Button, M., Johnston, L. and Frimpong, F. (2010) *Studying Fraud as White Collar Crime*, Basingstoke: Palgrave.

Smith, R. G., Holmes, M. N. and Kaufmann, R. G. (1999) Nigerian advanced fee fraud. *Trends and Issues in Crime and Criminal Justice*, no. 121, Canberra: Australian Institute of Criminology. Available at: http://www.aic.gov.au/media_library/publications/tandi_pdf/tandi121.pdf (accessed 21 October 2016).

Statista (2016a) *Net sales revenue of Amazon from 2004 to 2015 (in billion U.S. dollars)*. https://www.statista.com/statistics/266282/annual-net-revenue-of-amazoncom/.

Statista (2016b) *Number of Smartphone Users Worldwide From 2014 to 2019 (in millions)* http://www.statista.com/statistics/330695/number-of-smartphone-users-worldwide/.

Sykes, G. and Matza, D. (1957) Techniques of neutralization: A theory of delinquency. *American Sociological Review* 22(6): 665–670.

Symantec (2014) *Internet Security Threat Report 2014*. Available at: http://www.symantec.com/content/en/us/enterprise/other_resources/b-istr_main_report_v19_21291018.en-us.pdf (accessed 21 October 2016).

This is Money (2009) *eBay fraudster made millions from fake clubs*. Available at: http://www.thisismoney.co.uk/money/bills/article-1685712/Ebay-fraudster-made-millions-from-fake-golf-clubs.html (accessed 21 October 2016).

ThreatMetrix (2015) *2015 Q4 Cybercrime Report*. San José (USA): ThreatMetrix.

Treadwell, J. (2011) From the car boot to booting it up? eBay, online counterfeit crime and the transformation of the criminal marketplace. *Criminology and Criminal Justice* 12(2): 175–191. Doi: 10.1177/1748895811428173.

Ultrascan Global Investigations (2014) 419 *Advanced Fee Fraud Statistics 2013*. Available at: http://www.ultrascan-agi.com/public_html/html/pdf_files/Pre-Release-419_Advance_Fee_Fraud_Statistics_2013-July-10-2014-NOT-FINAL-1.pdf (accessed 31 October 2016).

Weatherburn, D. and Holmes, J. (2013) The decline in robbery and theft: Inter-state comparisons. *Crime and Justice Statistics: Bureau Brief*, no. 89. Available at: http://www.bocsar.nsw.gov.au/Documents/BB/bb89.pdf (accessed 21 October 2016).

Weise, K. (2012) *Tallying the Full Cost of the Financial Crisis*. Available at: http://www.bloomberg.com/news/articles/2012-09-14/tallying-the-full-cost-of-the-financial-crisis (accessed 21 October 2016).

Whitty, M. (2015) Mass-marketing fraud: A growing concern. *IEEE Security and Privacy* 13(4), 84–87. Doi: 10.1109/MSP.2015.85.

Yar, M. (2013) *Cybercrime and Society*, 2nd edition, London: Sage.

2

'IT COULD BE YOU'

Victims and the diversity of fraud

Introduction

In this chapter the diversity of frauds and victims is considered. The chapter will show there is a very wide range of frauds, which provides the basis for almost everyone in society to become a potential victim. The chapter starts by picking up on the amended Beals et al. (2015) classification from Chapter 1, offering more depth to the different types of fraud that fall under these broad categories. The chapter then considers some of the limited data that exists which shows the more common types of frauds in volume. In the final part of the chapter, it turns to a consideration of fraud victim profiles and what the research currently asserts, highlighting the vulnerability of some segments of society who are more likely to fall victim to certain frauds.

The diversity and dynamism of frauds

In Chapter 1 this book adapted the typology of Beals et al. (2015) to identify eight broad categories of fraud. The original typology developed consists of seven categories which unfold to further sub-categories. It is not the intention to go into great depth, breaking down each of the frauds and creating a large 'tree like' structure of frauds. Rather, this section will look at some of the most significant and common types of frauds from around the world, which fit under each of these categories. There are literally thousands of frauds and it would not be possible, and would be very boring, to examine them all. This book will, however, throughout its chapters illustrate a large number of different types of fraud. The diversity of frauds is important to note because most frauds are targeted at a particular group. All of these different frauds combined mean that almost everyone in society is at risk from a certain type of fraud. A non-gambler might be highly unlikely to fall for a lottery scam, but that same person who may be lonely and looking for love might be susceptible to a romance fraud. It is also important to note the dynamism of frauds as they change and adapt to keep ahead of law enforcement and victims and identify new niches to maximise the returns for the fraudster. However, there are also frauds which stand the test of time, and require very little adaptation on the part of the offender.

Consumer investment fraud

There are a wide variety of frauds and scams which centre on investments. The attraction of above average returns on monies invested is a lure for many people with the cash to invest. Investment scams and frauds, however, often occupy the grey area of fraudulent activity noted in the previous chapter, which may not always be criminal, but civil/regulatory or just unethical. Those who instigate such acts are also drawn from the clear criminal fraternity through to household names. For instance the global financial crisis of 2008, which started in the USA and spread throughout the world, was largely caused by sub-prime mortgages which have been extensively linked to unethical and fraudulent behaviours (although with virtually no successful criminal prosecutions) (National Commission on the Causes of the Financial and Economic Crisis in the United States, 2011). Many ordinary investors have lost monies as a result of this crisis. The focus of this section, however, will be on those investment frauds that are very clearly at the criminal end of the spectrum.

The essence of most investment frauds is a victim being sold something such as a share, asset or property, which is promoted as likely to increase substantially in value or to provide very good returns; but in reality is worthless, overvalued or fictitious. Some of the most commonly traded fraudulent investments include: shares, bonds, property, wine, movie production, carbon trading credits, oil and gas prospects, though this is not an exhaustive list. These types of frauds have secured particularly high-profile attention through scandals such as the Madoff Ponzi Scam, which was an investment scheme targeted at the rich and famous. There have also been a number of films portraying such scams, such as 'Wolf of Wall Street' (2013), which centred upon the sale of worthless penny stocks and 'Boiler Room' (2000), which focused on illegal trading operations. These frauds vary in their delivery. Some are targeted at small but exclusive groups who are well off, through face-to-face contact, such as the Madoff scheme. Others are promoted through so-called 'boiler rooms' (high pressure telephone sales), online, by email or traditional mail (Shover et al., 2003).

Consumer products and services fraud

The second category of fraud identified by Beals et al. (2015) is consumer products and services frauds. The internet has opened up opportunities for shopping and sales and many consumers are attracted to the potential of securing a bargain, searching the internet for the best priced item or service. Alongside a legitimate online trade, has grown a substantial number of fraudulent transactions. These scams are rooted in the sale of non-existent products and services or they are significantly different from how they were advertised. This covers a very large area,

CONSUMER INVESTMENT FRAUDS

Investments which are non-existent or significantly over-valued.

These include:

Equities investment frauds: penny stock frauds, property trusts, oil and gas exploration scams, alternative energy.

Debt investment frauds: investments linked to corporate/government debts, which include: promissory note fraud, bond fraud.

Commodities trading frauds: frauds linked to trading transactions such as foreign exchange trading, precious metals.

Other investment frauds: film productions, property, rare objects.

Adapted from (Beals et al., 2015).

as any product or service could be advertised and/or sold fraudulently. However, there tends to be some products and services which are particularly prone to this type of scam, such as memorabilia, slimming products, anti-impotence 'cures', holidays and any high-value product that is in demand (such as iPhones). The growth of the internet and the establishment of sales platforms such as eBay and Gumtree have particularly facilitated the opportunities for growth in these types of frauds and, in terms of volume, they are one of the most popular consumer frauds (Personal communication to one of the authors on visit to Action Fraud).

CONSUMER PRODUCTS AND SERVICES FRAUD

Products and services which do not exist or vary significantly from how advertised.

These include:

Worthless or non-existent products: there is a variety of products sold, done so through misleading or blatantly false advertising. Common products include slimming products which do not work, medical products such as anti-impotence drugs, cemetery plots which don't exist, fake memorabilia such as autographs, or fake gemstones. This also includes any product advertised and paid for, but never delivered.

Worthless, unnecessary or non-existent services: there is a wide range of services advertised which fit this category, such as bogus insurance, immigration consultant scams (individuals who charge to secure visas/passports), fraud loss recovery scams (fraudsters who, for a fee, will recover monies lost to a fraud), debt relief scams (individuals who offer to negotiate with creditors for a fee to reduce debts), fake loans/credit cards, fortune-telling frauds, tech support scams (tricking persons to buy worthless support), timeshare frauds, adoption scams (offering non-existent babies for adoption), unnecessary or overpriced repairs and bogus holiday/travel scams.

Unauthorised billing for products and services: consumers are charged for products and services they never agreed to. Some consumers purchase products or services and there is a small box which, if they do not untick it or tick it, results in them being charged for another service. Telephone and internet services are also prone to this type of scam.

Adapted from (Beals et al., 2015).

Employment fraud

In some ways this category could be seen as a sub-category of the previous as the essence is the offer of a fake or inadequate service to secure employment or training which is likely to lead to employment. Nevertheless, Beals et al. (2015) note this as a separate category and that the extent of this type of fraud and the variety linked to it does warrant it as such. These frauds are all linked in that they offer services that will either lead to employment or the acquisition of skills and services which will make employment more likely. These can include training courses through to business opportunity scams. Some of the most common areas where this occurs include modelling, where the victim is offered a package likely to lead to a modelling contract; and currency trading, where an unlikely lucrative career in currency trading is offered for fees in training and set-up costs. Another common variation is where victims are tricked into paying for home assembly kits, for which they will be paid, but are never able to meet all the requirements to secure a fee.

EMPLOYMENT FRAUD

Non-existent or worthless services offered to secure employment or increase the chances of employment.

These include:

Business opportunities fraud: individuals are offered the necessary training, equipment and the like, for them to develop a profitable business. These are often either implausible or very difficult to achieve. Some of the common areas include pyramid schemes, vending equipment/ATM leasing schemes and business coaching scams.

Work-at-home scams: in this variation the victim is offered specific work at home for which they make a payment to become involved, but the work they actually do is not possible to secure payment from. Commonly this includes: home assembly (kit is sold which is assembled by the victim but which they cannot then sell), envelope stuffing, mystery shopper scams where the victim pays to become a mystery shopper which is not likely.

Job placement scams: fraudsters secure payments from victims for placement in jobs that are non-existent. A variation on this is scams where individuals are tricked into paying for a job, or training or other services that will lead to a job. Common areas include highly desirable jobs such as modelling and potentially embarrassing roles such as escorts.

Adapted from (Beals et al., 2015).

Prize and grant fraud

Another very common variety of frauds is linked to prizes and grants. These centre on the victim being informed they have won a prize or payment, but invariably through a variety of means they have to pay a fee to secure access to the financial benefit. The other variation is where the lottery or prize draw is bogus and the victims are tricked into entering it. These have been common for some time and are pursued in significant volume via email and traditional mail.

PRIZE AND GRANT FRAUD

Bogus prize draws or false promises of financial benefits in return for the payment of a fee of some kind.

These include:

Prize promotion/sweepstake/reward scams: fraudsters inform victims they have won a prize or are entitled to a financial reward of some kind in return for a 'release' fee or phoning premium rate telephone lines. Lottery scams where the victim is told they have won the lottery are a common version of this type of scam. Other common variations include tax refund scams, inheritance scams and government grants. This category also includes the famous Nigerian 419 scams where the victim is offered the chance to share the illicitly gained fortune of a corrupt official.

Bogus lotteries/prize draws: scams where prizes are used to entice the entering of draws that are non-existent or not as advertised.

Adapted from (Beals et al., 2015).

Phantom debt collection fraud

These scams centre on individuals being tricked and sometimes pressured into paying debts they do not owe. The collectors may impersonate government bodies, financial institutions or businesses. A very common variation is to impersonate the tax collectors of a country and for a victim to be issued with a letter stating they owe taxes. These can be undertaken online, through email, letters, telephone and even in person. This type of scam may often involve threats of court action, poor credit rating or escalating costs to pressure the victim into complying.

Charity fraud

Charity frauds are straightforward in that they involve a fraudster posing as a legitimate charity (which could be impersonating a real charity or fake charity) in order to secure donations from victims. This could be fairly simple with the fraudster going door-to-door with a money box and fake identity card collecting small change, through to a bogus website or marketing campaign using all the latest technologies.

Relationship and trust fraud

This category includes romance frauds of which there are a variety of forms. The most common variation is the use of a false profile to secure a relationship which is then used to encourage the victim to send gifts, or events occur where the victim is pressured into 'lending' monies to help them. In some cases the victim might even be tricked to engage in sexual acts on line, which are recorded and which might be used at a later date to blackmail the victim (Whitty, 2013). A variation on this is the 'friends or relatives scam', who ask for money for an 'emergency', which often follows the hacking of the email list of an individual. A further variation to this is the 'grandparent scam' where victims receive a phone call/email from their supposed 'grandchild' who is in trouble and requires immediate payment to get them out of their difficulty. The grandchild begs the grandparent not to tell their parent/s what has happened, in an effort to maintain secrecy. Usually the grandparent will transfer the requested amount of money, and by the time they make contact with other family members and realise it is a scam, it is too late and the money has gone (Foxworth, 2012).

Identity fraud

The Beals et al. (2015) taxonomy did not directly include identity fraud for the following reason:

> In our conceptualization of fraud in the taxonomy, the victim must be deceived or persuaded into participating in the fraudulent transaction. As such, we have intentionally excluded identity theft from the framework

> because victims are not persuaded to disclose personal information based on the belief that they will get something in return. Rather, identity theft – and related crimes like credit card fraud – is akin to other forms of personal theft. The difference is that the valuable 'good/property' stolen is the victim's identity and/or financial account information. This theft of information typically occurs beyond the victim's consent, knowledge, and control.
>
> *(2015: 8)*

Identity fraud is perpetrated by a variety of means, some of which do not involve information being sought directly from the intended victim. There are, however, many variations which do involve tricking the victim to disclose important personal information alone (no money is sought directly from the victim). One of the most common attempts to get personal information arises from phishing scams where communications impersonating an official body (such as a bank, government agency, telephone/internet service provider) seek personal information such as name, date of birth, national insurance number, account details, and pin numbers/passwords. This is commonly achieved using email (phishing) but can also be perpetrated through the telephone (vishing), text messages (smishing), redirection to illegitimate websites (pharming) and the creation of bogus websites. It is important to note that there is a difference between compromise and misuse of one's personal details, with there being no guarantee that any personal information supplied (compromise) will lead to an actual fraud loss (misuse). However, the individual has clearly been deceived into supplying the information, which could be used for fraudulent purposes and ultimately lead to the gaining of money from the victim (for example, through the establishment of new lines of credit or personal loans). This type of fraud therefore, in our view, deserves a category in its own right as identity fraud.

Another common means by which this type of fraud occurs is when the victim has been tricked into downloading some form of malware/spyware on their computer or other device, which enables the offender to access key personal information, which can then be used to perpetrate frauds or embarrass or blackmail the victim. A common appearance of this scam occurs when a victim is sent an email with an attachment that the victim is encouraged to download (which could be a photo, invoice, or other document). However, when they open the document, they inadvertently execute the malware onto their device. In many cases, the victim will be unaware of this, and depending on the type of malware downloaded, depends on the type of access that offenders have to their system. This can also be pursued through smishing and pharming.

There is also a version of this fraud where the fraudsters seek to not only secure sensitive information such as passwords and pin numbers, but also the cards as well. In the UK there has been a particular problem with what is termed as 'courier fraud'. There are numerous variations on this approach but the central tenet includes a victim being contacted by an 'official body' (for example, the police or a bank) and told their bank account has been compromised in some way. Often they will be tricked at a 'verification' stage into revealing their pin number and the scam will end with a courier being despatched to pick up the compromised card, which can then be used to empty the victim's account. The above examples of this type of fraud all involve the victim taking some form of action which enables their information to be stolen. It is also important to note many leaks of personal information are not the fault of the victim, but occur through third party breaches such as loss of data, a corrupt employee or a hacking attack.

> **IDENTITY FRAUD**
>
> Disclosure of personal information which could be used to perpetrate fraud
>
> These include:
>
> **Phishing, vishing, smishing, pharming and bogus website scams**: impersonation of official bodies and using storylines to trick the victim into supplying sensitive personal information.
>
> **Downloading scams**: scams that trick victims into downloading malware/spyware which can be used to harvest sensitive personal information, which are often delivered through attachments to an email.
>
> **Personal information and banking card scams**: the victim is tricked to supply personal information in addition to handing over their banking card or other important information such as passwords, and/or pins which enable the fraudster to withdraw/transfer money.
>
> **Loss of personal information due to third party breaches**: victim had no role in loss or compromise of information.

Other classification factors

The Beals et al. (2015: 9–10) classification also lists a number of other factors relevant to the classification of frauds, which are not built into their taxonomy, but which can also be applied. These include:

- *Seriousness*: value of loss and length of time of fraud.
- *Victim and perpetrator characteristics*: gender, age, occupation.
- *Method of advertising fraud*: the means for promoting the fraud, for instance, by advertising, telephone, mail, email.
- *Initial response method/setting*: the place where the fraud took place, whether in person, over the telephone, by email.
- *Method of money transfer*: the means of transfer from victim to fraudster: cash, cheque, electronic transfer, PayPal.

These are a useful starting point in exploring the characteristics of fraud. Later in this chapter we will take some of these factors and develop them further to illustrate the 'mechanics of fraud', that is, the general methods used to perpetrate fraud. Also in Chapter 3, greater depth on the techniques of fraudsters will be considered. However, before this is done it would be useful to explore some of the statistics of the most common frauds and it is this to which the chapter now turns.

The most common frauds

In Chapter 1, some of the evidence on the extent of victimisation was noted as well as the challenges encountered with the accuracy of much of this data. Statistics reporting different types of frauds in terms of numbers – particularly when they are reported statistics – should be viewed with similar caution. However, they may at least provide the relative balance and popularity of different types of scams in terms of the number of victims, although clearly some frauds, which are embarrassing, may be less likely to be reported. They do not, however, offer much in terms of the harm caused in terms of monetary value, as they are largely reports of discrete incidents. Another challenge is that the terminology used to describe frauds and scams is often not consistent and rarely maps over to the typology outlined by Beals et al. (2015) and adapted for this book. Frauds are also very dynamic in nature, and the popularity of different approaches can vary significantly from year to year. Many of the statistics that are reported are often therefore several years behind and are unable to provide an accurate up-to-date picture of offending. Further to this, some reporting bodies do not breakdown fraud statistics by type or have different definitions for similar categories (this is explored later in Chapter 8 on the prevention aspect of fraud). The following tables therefore present a snapshot of the popular frauds and scams perpetrated in a few countries, from where some data has been offered to illustrate the prevalence of different types of fraud.

The first table is from the US Federal Trade Commission Consumer Sentinel Network and shows the top 30 types of complaints received for 2015. While the areas it encompasses go beyond fraud-related behaviours to include other criminal behaviours as well as regulatory and civil breaches (or other categories, as they call them), it is still relevant to the current discussion and provides some insights into a variety of fraud activities. The number one complaint area of debt collection includes a variety of behaviours beyond the scope of this book (such as collectors of legitimate debts calling repeatedly, using threatening behaviours, and failing to identify themselves as a debt collector) (Consumer Sentinel Network, 2016: 77). However, the second overall complaint and the top fraud-related complaint was identity theft, where a person's information had been stolen to perpetrate a fraud. Impostor scams was next on the list and includes persons pretending to be someone in distress seeking money to help them as well as pretending to be an official person to solicit personal information. The fourth on the list (the third fraud category) includes a variety of behaviours some of which relate to misleading advertising for mobile phone contracts, through to unwanted calls and charges for calls not made or to free-phone numbers, and is followed by the fifth-listed prizes, sweepstakes and lotteries frauds. The next category is 'shop-at-home and catalogue sales' which includes purchases which do not arrive. The category of internet services includes a variety of complaints from the downloading of malware and spyware to problems with internet service providers. Healthcare includes misleading claims for health products and services advertised, as well as defective products for weight loss and impotency, to name

TABLE 2.1 Top 30 complaints listed by Consumer Sentinel Network in USA (fraud categories in **bold**)

Type of complaint and position	*Number of complaints*	*Percentage*
1 Debt Collection	897,655	29%
2 **Identity Theft**	**490,220**	**16%**
3 **Impostor Scams**	**353,770**	**11%**
4 **Telephone and Mobile Services**	**275,754**	**9%**
5 **Prizes, Sweepstakes and Lotteries**	**140,136**	**5%**
6 Banks and Lenders	131,875	4%
7 **Shop-at-Home and Catalogue Sales**	**96,363**	**3%**
8 Auto-Related Complaints	93,917	3%
9 Television and Electronic Media	47,728	2%
10 Credit Bureaus, Information Furnishers and Report Users	43,939	1%
11 **Internet Services**	**40,106**	**1%**
12 Credit Cards	37,750	1%
13 **Health Care**	**34,669**	**1%**
14 **Investment-Related Complaints**	**26,453**	**1%**
15 **Foreign Money Offers and Counterfeit Check Scams**	**25,324**	**1%**
16 **Advance Payments for Credit Services**	**24,433**	**1%**
17 **Travel, Vacations and Timeshare Plans**	**24,171**	**1%**
18 **Business and Job Opportunities**	**17,314**	**1%**
19 Office **Supplies and Services**	**10,287**	**<1%**
20 **Mortgage Foreclosure Relief and Debt Management**	**10,210**	**<1%**
21 **Magazines and Books**	**8,866**	**<1%**
22 Home Repair, Improvement and Products	8,364	<1%
23 Computer Equipment and Software	8,119	<1%
24 Education	6,973	<1%
25 **Grants**	**4,077**	**<1%**
26 **Tax Preparers**	**2,991**	**<1%**
27 **Charitable Solicitations**	**2,747**	**<1%**
28 **Internet Auction**	**2,430**	**<1%**
29 **Buyers' Clubs**	**1,168**	**<1%**
30 Funeral Services	1,123	<1%

Source: Adapted from Consumer Sentinel Network (2016: 6).

some. Investment-related companies offering bogus investments and foreign money offers is related to the prize and grant fraud discussed above. The tenth most popular fraud-related scam of advanced payment for credit services covers scams where a fee is paid to secure a credit card or a loan that never transpires.

The second table presented is from the Internet Crime Complaint Centre (IC3) (USA). They publish an annual report each year which lists the most common types of complaints they receive. As the name of IC3 suggests, their focus is on crimes which involve the internet. Table 2.2 has been adapted from their statistics to illustrate the top 10 distinct complaints. Top of the list is non-payment delivery where goods are ordered and paid for, but never arrive. Second are 419/overpayment scams where a promise of a reward is offered in return for the victim offering an upfront payment. Third is identity theft, which is the use of a person's identity to conduct a fraud; followed in fourth place by auction fraud, which is a fraudulent transaction related to online auctions. In fifth place is personal data breach where personal information is lost which could be used for criminal purposes. Sixth are employment-related crimes, which involve employment opportunity scams and money laundering scams. Seventh is extortion where money is extracted from the victim under threat of intimidation or exposure. Eighth are credit card frauds, followed in ninth place by phishing, vishing, smishing and pharming attacks. Finally tenth is advanced fee, which covers the payment of fees for something in return. This category could be merged with the 419/overpayment and some of the other categories could also be merged.

The next table is drawn from the preparatory work for the changes to the England and Wales Crime Survey to include fraud offences. In cyber terms it is a bit dated, but it does offer a snapshot of a valid sample of the population in England and Wales of the most popular consumer frauds which target them. Unfortunately there was no data by fraud type of actual victimisation, therefore this table demonstrates the prevalence of fraud *approaches* used by offenders in targeting potential victims. The table shows that the most popular fraud attempts

TABLE 2.2 Top 10 types of crime reported to the Internet Crime Center (2015*)

Type of crime	*Number of reports*
Non-Payment/Non-Delivery	67,375
419/Overpayment	30,855
Identity Theft	21,949
Auction	21,510
Personal Data Breach	19,632
Employment	18,758
Extortion	17,804
Credit Card Fraud	17,172
Phishing/Vishing/Smishing/Pharming	16,594
Advanced Fee	16,445

Source: Adapted from Internet Crime Complaint Center (2016: 15).

* Reports are from victims and third parties linked to complaint.

were lottery, prize draw, followed by investment fraud, followed by attractive loans and then romance-type relationship frauds.

The following table is taken from data produced by the Australian Competition and Consumer Commission (ACCC) and presents the top 10 fraud categories reported in 2015, according to the number of contacts received.

TABLE 2.3 Percentage of adults experiencing unsolicited mass marketing communications in England and Wales during 2011–15

Type	*Percentage*
A big win in a lottery, prize draw, sweepstakes or competition you haven't entered	40
The chance to make an investment with a guaranteed high return	16
A loan on very attractive terms	15
Someone who invites you to get to know them with a view to a possible friendship or relationship	13
Help in moving large sums of money from abroad	12
A job offer, a franchise offer or other business opportunity	10
Help in releasing an inheritance	9
An urgent request to help someone get out of some sort of financial trouble	8
Adopting or buying a pet	3
Some other type of similar request	7
No communication received	44

Source: Office for National Statistics (2013: 4).

TABLE 2.4 Top 10 categories of fraud reported by the ACCC in 2015 based on total complaint numbers

Fraud category	*Amount reported lost (AU$)*	*Contacts reporting no loss*	*Contacts reporting loss*	*Overall number of contacts*	*Conversion rate*
Phishing	$363,270	15,249	181	15,430	1.2%
Reclaim scams	$1,331,063	12,402	187	12,589	1.5%
Other upfront payment and advanced fee frauds	$3,899,312	10,609	893	11,502	7.8%
ID theft involving spam or phishing	$1,816,361	9,010	318	9,328	3.4%
Other buying and selling scams	$3,959,363	5,703	2,064	7,767	26.6%
Remote access scams	$729,165	5,476	379	5,855	6.5%
Ransomware and malware	$388,167	4,285	154	4,439	3.5%
False billing scams	$616,239	3,721	382	4,103	9.3%
Inheritance scams	$4,391,630	3,697	78	3,775	2.1%
Unexpected prizes and lottery scams	$1,337,296	3,425	258	3,683	7.0%

Source: ACCC (2016: 25).

The above table shows the ten fraud types which had the highest number of complaints from Australians in 2015. It is important to recognise that this table differentiated between those who reported a fraudulent attempt and suffered financial loss and those who did not suffer financial loss. It also demonstrates the overall level of financial losses reported by those individuals who were victims. The conversion rate, listed in the final column of this table is a statistic that is calculated by the ACCC based on the number of complaints received and the difference between those reporting a loss (victims) and those reporting no loss (i.e. were able to successfully identify it was a scam). The conversion rate is seen to be the success rate of these approaches (ACCC, 2016: 14), though it may be difficult to assume that all persons who receive a fraudulent approach will report this if it was unsuccessful. Therefore, the accuracy of this statistic is questionable in a broader context, but provides some interesting observations of the different types of frauds that are reported, and the rates of loss to no loss by those who submit a complaint. The types of frauds evident on this table are similar to those seen across previous tables relating to the USA and UK contexts. When focused on the monetary losses compared to the number of complaints, the following table illustrates a very different picture of the top 10 fraud types.

This table indicates that the top 10 list of frauds based on total complaints is a vastly different picture to the top 10 list of frauds based on reported financial losses. However it is unsurprising to see that investment fraud and dating and romance fraud incur the highest financial losses across all fraud categories.

TABLE 2.5 Top 10 fraud complaints received by the ACCC in 2015 according to reported financial loss

Fraud category	*Amount reported lost (AU$)*	*Contacts reporting no loss*	*Contacts reporting loss*	*Overall number of contacts*	*Conversion rate*
Investment schemes	$24,447,716	886	376	1,262	29.8%
Dating and romance schemes	$22,737,257	1,759	861	2,620	32.9%
Computer prediction software and sports investment schemes	$5,534,878	156	270	426	63.4%
Nigerian scams	$4,549,807	839	141	980	14.4%
Inheritance scams	$4,391,630	3,697	78	3,775	2.1%
Other buying and selling scams	$3,959,363	5,703	2,064	7,767	26.6%
Other upfront payment and advanced fee frauds	$3,899,312	10,609	893	11,502	7.8%
Other business, employment and investment scams	$2,261,762	3,042	324	3,366	9.6%
ID theft involving spam or phishing	$1,816,361	9,010	318	9,328	3.4%
Fake trader websites	$1,458,858	1,148	1,587	2,735	58.0%

Source: ACCC (2016: 26).

Drawing from this data and other better-established data on identity/plastic card-type frauds presented in Table 1.1 in Chapter 1 and returning to the classification of frauds advocated within this book, the three most common fraud categories – in no particular order would seem to be:

- Consumer products and services fraud;
- Identity fraud; and
- Prize and grant fraud.

However, this will clearly vary between countries and if actual losses were added the picture might be very different (as demonstrated by the two Australian tables presented). Perhaps most importantly what this discussion illustrates is the need for greater cooperation worldwide on the classification of different types of frauds and an improvement in the collection of data, which is linked to these. This would enable more accurate data to be compared across countries and for trends to be spotted more effectively. The challenges associated with the different categorisation of fraud types are further covered in Chapter 8, when examining these in terms of prevention messaging.

The 'mechanics' of fraud

Having established the variety of frauds that occur and an indication as to the prevalence of various schemes, this section will briefly characterise the mechanics of how some of these particular frauds are perpetrated. Some of these issues will be developed in further detail in Chapter 3 where the techniques of offenders will be considered in more depth. However, it is important to illustrate the diversity of the methods of contacting victims and then executing the fraud. The starting point for this is the mechanics of contacting victims, as shown in Table 2.6 below.

TABLE 2.6 The mechanics of contacting victims

Method	*Common frauds where technique used (not exhaustive)*
No contact with victim	Identity frauds (some)
Face to face	Investment frauds
Mail	Prize and grant fraud; charity fraud
Advertisement	Consumer product and services fraud; Employment frauds
Telephone	Consumer investment frauds; phantom debt collection frauds
Text message	Identity frauds; prize and grant fraud
Email	Identity frauds; prize and grant fraud
Social networking website	Relationship and trust frauds; Identity frauds
Website	Consumer product and services fraud; employment frauds

The starting point of any fraud is the offender contacting the potential victim. In some cases of identity fraud the offender has no direct contact with the victim (for example in the majority of third party breaches). In most other frauds, there is some form of contact. As technological advances in communication have emerged, so have the techniques of the offenders. The oldest and simplest method of committing fraud involves those that are perpetrated face to face. The offender might meet the victim in a door-to-door situation or in a social setting identified as ripe for potential victims (such as a club or church congregation). Consumer investment frauds are commonly pursued in this way, although they can also be pursued by telephone and email. Traditional mail is also used to contact victims on a variety of scams. Prize and grant frauds, as well as charity frauds, are commonly targeted using traditional mail. Advertising in mediums such as newspapers, magazines, and online is used by some offenders to target potential victims. Consumer product and services frauds and employment frauds are commonly advertised to lure victims. The telephone is also used to perpetrate frauds through so-called 'boiler rooms' (places where high-pressure sales occur). A variety of frauds are marketed in this way, but they are particularly dominant with consumer investment frauds. Text messages can also be used to target victims for identity frauds and prize and grant frauds, as are emails. Social networking sites have become central to the recruitment of victims in relationship and trust frauds, but can also be a source of targeting individuals for identity frauds. Finally, websites are central to many consumer product and services frauds as well as employment frauds, and can assist in creating and/or maintaining the ruse across a variety of different approaches.

Once the victim has been targeted and shows some interest, the offender may then move to other methods of communication to successfully target the victim. For instance relationship and trust frauds may begin on social networking sites, but once the relationship has been established, it is common for offenders to communicate via telephone, messaging services, email, and in some circumstances, face-to-face contact. In contrast, other frauds may stay in the same mode throughout, such as some consumer investment frauds conducted via telephone, which may not move away from that form of communication. In some cases, offenders will use a combination of all the methods listed above in order to gain the trust of the victim and ensure compliance with their requests. This section has provided a brief snapshot of the 'mechanics' of fraud and will be explored in greater depth in Chapter 3.

Existing knowledge of victim profiles

In this section we consider what is known about the profile of fraud victims. As this book has already shown, fraud is very diverse and that, in itself, makes generalisation of fraud victimisation very difficult. There is, however, existing research which highlights vulnerabilities of particular groups to certain frauds. In fact, some frauds are specifically targeted at certain groups because they have the resources and inclination to potentially fall for that type of fraudulent approach. For example, consumer investment frauds require the victim to have spare funds that they are willing to invest. Students who are unlikely to have much cash or a desire to invest any cash they do have would not be a worthwhile group for offenders to target. Rather, well-off pensioners and employed persons with a record of investing would be more likely to invest and therefore be more susceptible to tailored investment approaches. This section will therefore start with some data on what the general victims of fraud look like, and consider some research which has highlighted particular vulnerabilities and weaknesses of individuals and groups to determine the most likely successful approach for each member of the population.

The recent publication of some of the findings from the Office of National Statistics (ONS) England and Wales Crime Survey on the extended questions on fraud victimisation, has offered some new and stronger evidence on the general profile of fraud victims and how fraud has a different profile of victims in comparison to traditional property and violent crimes. The first is that, where most property and violent crimes tend be dominated by younger victims, for frauds it found the 45–54 years age group had higher rates of victimisation than the 16–24 years and 75+ years age groups at 7.9 per cent, compared to 5 per cent and 4 per cent respectively (ONS, 2016).

Given that fraudsters ultimately want to target those with money, it was also no surprise to find that victimisation was greater in households with income of £50,000 plus at 9.1 per cent, compared to 5.6 per cent in households with income less than £10,000. Similarly those from managerial and professional occupations had a victimisation rate of 8 per cent, compared to 5.3 per cent in manual occupations, 4.4 per cent amongst full-time students and 3.8 per cent amongst the long-term unemployed. This again contrasts to violent and burglary offences where students and young people are more at risk (ONS, 2016). The ONS research also highlighted some further differences, such as slightly higher rates of victimisation in Southern England, compared to the North and Wales. It also identified differences between urban and rural areas, noting:

> In some cases the groups typically less likely to be victims of other crime types indicated higher prevalence of victimisation from fraud (although results were not found to be significantly different). For example, individuals living in rural areas were shown to be more likely to be a victim of fraud than those living in urban areas, as were those living in the least deprived areas compared to the most deprived areas.
>
> *(ONS, 2016)*

The ONS data should be treated as very important and relatively up-to-date and accurate data on the profile of fraud victims in England and Wales, given the strong methods used for this research. It is undertaken on an annual basis and based upon interviews with a representative sample of 35,000 adults aged over 16 years who are asked about a variety of issues related to crime victimisation.

The research is undertaken in such a way as to allow very high levels of statistical confidence about the data. There is, however, some data on other countries and insights on the profiles of victims of particular types of fraud which has also been published. Some of this research will now be considered.

It is well established that older people experience lower levels of crime victimisation than their younger counterparts (Carcach et al., 2001). This is consistent across all categories of crime (Graycar and James, 2001). Of the crimes that older people do experience, research consistently suggests that fraud is the largest category (Muscat et al., 2002; Temple, 2007). For example, Australian research has suggested that consumer fraud 'is still the most common personal crime affecting older Australians and … remains an issue of concern' (Smith and Budd, 2009: 4).

While there is consensus on the dominance of fraud in older people's victimisation experiences, there is less agreement as to whether older people are more likely to be victims of fraud than younger people. Kerley and Copes (2002: 22) assert that 'many individuals operate under the misconception that personal frauds occur mostly to older and less educated people'. Similarly, Ross et al. (2014: 427) observe that 'according to psychological and popular opinion, older persons are particularly likely to experience consumer fraud'. While there are studies, which indicate older people are more likely to be victims than their younger counterparts (AARP, 1996; Cohen, 2006; Pak and Shadel, 2011), there are also contradictory findings (FTC in Smith and Budd, 2009; Holtfreter et al., 2006; Kerley and Copes, 2002). There is also a body of research that disputes the overrepresentation of older persons, instead arguing that there is 'no typical victim profile' (Holtfreter et al., 2006; Reiboldt and Vogel, 2003; Titus et al., 1995). In a meta-analysis of 14 studies, which explored the hypothesis that older persons are more vulnerable and therefore more likely to be victims of fraud, Ross et al. (2014) criticise previous research on what they perceive to be methodological flaws and a reliance on anecdotal evidence. They conclude that 'our review fails to support the conventional wisdom that older persons are particularly likely to experience consumer fraud' (Ross et al., 2014: 437). This is furthered by Schiebe et al. (2014: 273) who state that 'no conclusive evidence shows older adults are in fact more susceptible [to fraud]'.

However, many readily accept that older people are attractive *targets* (Reiboldt and Vogel, 2003; Smith, 2003; Sylvester, 2004). Holtfreter et al. (2006: 767) discern that this is the result of three types of vulnerability: physical, financial and social. Regarding their perceived physical vulnerability, Smith (1999: 1) notes that

> a stereotype surrounding older people is that they are easy targets for acts of fraud and deception [which] stems from a perception that they have declining mental abilities and dependence on others due to their physical fragility or mental deterioration.

Wolf (2000: 25) concurs in that 'elders are thought to be particularly susceptible because they seem to be more trusting … and perhaps more easily confused by the fast talking con artist'. The focus on mental deterioration is dominant with authors such as Schiebe et al. (2014: 273), who argue that 'although no conclusive evidence shows older adults are in fact more susceptible, cognitive and motivational changes associated with normal aging may increase older adults' vulnerability because those changes alter the way individuals make decisions'.

The second vulnerability stems from their financial position, in that older persons are more likely to have a variety of assets (such as owning their own property, having access to life savings and/or superannuation funds) which therefore make them attractive targets through potential 'lucrative profits' (Reiboldt and Vogel, 2003: 23). The emergence of self-managed superannuation funds has also contributed to the financial attractiveness of seniors, who are actively looking for opportunities to invest substantial amounts of money and may be open to fraudulent pitches from offenders. In many circumstances, older people also have good credit histories and are less likely to notice any additional lines of credit being taken out in their name, which makes them appealing for potential offenders (Sylvester, 2004). Finally, regarding social vulnerability, Rieboldt and Vogel (2003: 26) observe that 'virtually every study that has examined senior victimisation mentions, on some level, loneliness and isolation'.

In countering the idea that older persons are more likely to be victims of fraud, there are a number of studies where results have demonstrated otherwise. For example, Titus et al. (1995) in a national survey of fraud victims in the USA found older people were three times less likely to be victims of fraud. Another smaller-scale study in the USA, on the other hand, found that the younger were more likely to become victims of fraud (Van Wyk and Benson, 1997). In Australia, Muscat et al. (2002), drawing upon data from the Australian Crime Victims survey, found younger people to be at greater risk of fraud, with 9.3 per 100 persons of 16–64 years compared to 3.9 per 100 persons of 65 years and over, victims of consumer fraud. They found lifestyle factors such as an active social life and working to be more important, as they exposed persons to greater risk of fraudulent transactions. However, compared to other crimes, consumer fraud is a much higher risk than other crimes for the elderly: 2.2 times more frequent than assault, 2.4 more times than theft and thirteen times more than robbery (Caracach et al., 2001). In more recent data from a personal fraud survey conducted in 2014/15 (which included card fraud, identity theft and a variety of scams) it was found that the likelihood of experiencing card fraud was slightly lower for those aged 55 years and over compared to those aged under 55 years (4% and 7% respectively); those aged 55 years and over experienced half the rate of identity theft (0.4% compared to 0.8%); and there was a similar rate of victimisation for scams across both age groups (4% for those aged 55 years and over compared to 5% for those aged under 55 years) (Australian Bureau of Statistics, 2016).

As will be demonstrated in later chapters, there is also a pervasive stereotype that fraud victims are uneducated and are consequently understood to be financially illiterate. However, the existing research highlights the opposite, in that those with greater levels of financial literacy are more likely to become victims of fraud (particularly relevant to investment fraud) compared to those with less (Drew and Cross, 2013). The reasons advocated for this counter-intuitive funding include the 'knowing-doing gap', where it is thought that even though victims know the warning signs to look out for, they fail to apply their knowledge to their specific situation (NASD, 2006). A further explanation is termed the 'expert snare', where those who are more financially literate have an overconfidence in their investment knowledge and ability to determine beneficial opportunities (Gamble et al., 2012). A third explanation offered is the concept of 'low persuasion literacy', whereby victims have strong knowledge of financial literacy but do not have adequate learning on the range of social engineering techniques and methods of persuasion used by offenders to defraud an individual (NASD, 2006). On that basis, Drew and Cross (2013) put forward the PREY model to better explain the relationship between financial literacy and investment fraud, in that victims are able to be *Profiled* by potential offenders, who use the *Relational* aspect of the interaction with victims to build trust and rapport, who see victims as continuously *Exploitable*, in that they will seek to obtain as much money as possible from the victim, and as a result, will do whatever necessary to coerce the victim into *Yielding* to their requests. A better understanding of the social engineering techniques used by offenders is argued to have more effective impacts on investment fraud compared to financial literacy alone (Drew and Cross, 2013).

Other research has shown that those who have a positive attitude to financial risk-taking are more likely to be targeted as victims of fraud (Van Wyk and Benson, 1997). There is also evidence that persons with low self-control – who are often prepared to engage in a range of risky behaviours to seek instant gratification – are also more prone to victimisation (Holtfreter et al., 2008). Overall, it is clear that there are still many gaps in examining the reasons behind fraud victimisation and this should provide an impetus for further research in the area.

Research by OFT (2006) assessed a variety of frauds and scams and identified those more likely to fall victim to them. Given the research is over ten years old and the world of frauds and scams has changed significantly – not least the growth of the internet – it offers an historical snapshot. However, some of these frauds are still common and therefore the profile of the victims may well still be similar and relevant.

1. Scams which men tend to fall for: African advanced fee frauds, internet dialler scams, high risk investments, property investment.
2. Scams which women tend to fall for: Internet matrix, miracle health and slimming cure scams, clairvoyant and psychic scams, career opportunity scams.
3. Scams which seniors tend to fall for: High-risk investments, doorstep service providers.
4. Scams the young tend to fall for: Work-at-home and business opportunities, clairvoyant and psychic scams, internet dialler scams.

Segment #	*% of UK adult population*	*Category description*	*Characteristics*	*Likely type of fraud victimisation*
Segment 1	16%	Avoiding risk but lacking awareness	Moderate to wealthy females, high-worth targets for fraudsters	Identity fraud Bank card fraud Property investment scams
Segment 2	19%	Avoiding risk, exemplary behaviours	Low income, older females	Premium rate telephone scams Charitable donations Foreign lotteries/competitions Clairvoyant/Psychic fraud
Segment 2b	4%	Avoiding risk, but vulnerable to offers	Very low income, pensionable age females	Premium rate telephone scams Foreign lotteries/competitions Clairvoyant/Psychic fraud Miracle health cures
Segment 3	10%	Avoiding risk, but still a victim	Less affluent, older males	Premium rate telephone scams Foreign lotteries/competitions Online dating Pyramid selling
Segment 4	21%	Risk-takers seeking financial gain	Affluent, opportunity-seeking professional males	Identity fraud Phishing emails Bank card fraud Property investment scams Foreign money making investments
Segment 5	10%	Risk-takers, demonstrating naivety	Less affluent, younger females, lacking knowledge	Premium rate telephone scams Bank card fraud Pyramid selling
Segment 6	10%	Risk-taker and sure of themselves	Over-confident men in denial	Online banking scams Bank card fraud Phishing emails
Segment 7	14%	Risk-takers and poor behaviours	Young males and females, complacent and careless	Online banking scams Bank card fraud Online shopping fraud

Source: data used in this table was compiled from NFA, 2011.

There has also been research published by credit reference agencies such as Experian on the profile of identity fraud victims in the past. This also supports the middle-aged, higher-income, professional Southerner profile found by the ONS. This research found males accounted for 60 per cent, of which 50 per cent were 35–54 years old, with a further 36 per cent who were 25–34 years old.

Experian also profiled the victims against their consumer segments classifications and it found two groups stood out at significantly high risk of victimisation: 'Up and Coming Elite' and 'Looking to the Future Groups' and these represent young singles and high-flying graduates who are likely to rent. It also noted, however, the most at risk were the 'Corporate Top Dogs' who are wealth directors and owners of businesses. The research also highlighted London as the highest risk area with the boroughs of Kensington, Chelsea, Victoria, Liverpool St and the West End as some of the areas with the most victims (Experian, 2010).

In 2011, the (former) National Fraud Authority (UK) released a report which broke down the entire population into different segments, based on their risk profiles and likely fraud victimisation. This ascertained that, within society, there are seven core segments and one sub-segment (NFA, 2011: 2). The seven segments and sub-segment along with their key characteristics are summarised in the preceding table.

This table illustrates the various risk profiles that exist for men and women, depending on their age, income, personality and attitudes. It also demonstrates the variety of schemes that are more effectively targeted to their identified vulnerabilities and which are more likely to be successful in terms of victimisation. This segmentation research is an important step to gaining a better understanding of the different ways in which groups within the population can be targeted for fraud, and how to best respond to individual weaknesses and vulnerabilities. While the categories are largely generalisations and would not always hold true, they provide an important step towards better understanding of how offenders think and tailor their fraudulent pitches to solicit potential victims.

Conclusion

This chapter has started to examine the large variety of frauds which exist and in doing this, has also started to unpack the various victim profiles based on existing research. What is clear from the information presented in this chapter is the complexity and enormous variety of frauds that exist and are targeted at victims as a whole. Given the range of techniques, communication platforms and risk profiles available, it is not unreasonable to assert that anyone could be the victim of fraud. Everyone has a weakness or vulnerability, which if targeted in the right way at the right time, could lead to a person becoming a victim of fraud. This chapter has also sought to engage with some of the stereotypes surrounding victims of fraud, in that they are generally older and that they are uneducated. Challenging assumptions such as these is a theme that is continued in later chapters, particularly as it relates to the negative stereotypes of fraud victims. Having established this diversity of fraud and the reality of potential victimisation across all demographics, the following chapter builds on the section which started to examine the techniques used by fraudsters and turns to a more in-depth analysis of the techniques used by these offenders to commit the range of frauds evident in this chapter.

References

AARP (1996) *Telemarketing Fraud Victimization of Older Americans: An AARP Survey.* Washington, DC: AARP.

Australian Bureau of Statistics (2016) *4528.0 Personal Fraud 2014–15.* Available at: http://www.abs.gov.au/AUSSTATS/abs@.nsf/0/1FF970676E24FDFECA2574740015CA71?Opendocument (accessed 21 October 2016).

Australian Competition and Consumer Commission (2016) *Targeting Scams: Report of the ACCC on Scams Activity 2015.* Canberra: Australian Competition and Consumer Commission. Available at: http://www.accc.gov.au/publications/targeting-scams-report-on-scam-activity/targeting-scams-report-of-the-accc-on-scam-activity-2015 (accessed 21 October 2016).

Beals, M., DeLiema, M. and Deevy, M. (2015) *Framework for a Taxonomy of Fraud.* Stanford: Stanford Center on Longevity. Available at: http://fraudresearchcenter.org/wp-content/uploads/2015/07/FFRC_Taxonomy_FullReport_7-22-15.pdf (accessed 21 October 2016).

Carcach, C., Graycar, A. and Muscat, G. (2001) The victimisation of older Australians. *Trends and Issues in Crime and Criminal Justice*, no. 212. Canberra: Australian Institute of Criminology. Available at: http://www.aic.gov.au/media_library/publications/tandi_pdf/tandi212.pdf (accessed 24 October 2016).

Cohen, C. (2006) Consumer fraud and the elderly: A review of Canadian challenges and initiatives. In: Mellor, M. and Brownell, P. (eds) *Elder Abuse and Mistreatment: Policy, Practice and Research*, New York: Haworth Press, pp. 137–144.

Consumer Sentinel Network (2016) *Databook for January to December 2015.* Available at: https://www.ftc.gov/system/files/documents/reports/consumer-sentinel-network-data-book-january-december-2015/160229csn-2015databook.pdf (accessed 21 October 2016).

Drew, J. and Cross, C. (2013) Fraud and its PREY: Conceptualising social engineering tactics and its impact on financial literacy outcomes. *Journal of Financial Services Marketing* 18: 188–198. Doi: 10.1057/fsm.2013.14.

Experian (2010) *The Insight Report. Victims of Fraud Survey – March 2010.* London: Experian. Available at: http://www.experian.co.uk/assets/insight-reports/brochures/The-Insight-Report-Victims-of-fraud-survey-March-2010.pdf (accessed 24 October 2016).

Foxworth, D. (2012) *Beware of the Grandparent scam: Don't let it happen to you.* San Diego, California: Federal Bureau of Investigation. Available at: https://archives.fbi.gov/archives/sandiego/press-releases/2012/beware-of-the-grandparent-scam (accessed 14 September 2016).

Gamble, K., Boyle, P., Yu, L. and Bennett, D. (2012) Aging, financial literacy and fraud. *Social Science Research Network.* Available at: https://papers.ssrn.com/sol3/papers.cfm?abstract_id=2361151 (accessed 17 January 2017).

Graycar, A. and James, M. (2001) Older people and consumer law. Paper presented at 4th National Outlook Symposium on Crime in Australia: New Crimes or New Responses, 22 June. Canberra: Australian Institute of Criminology. Available at: http://www.aic.gov.au/media_library/conferences/outlook4/graycar2.pdf (accessed 24 October 2016).

Holtfreter, K., Reisig, M. and Blomberg, T. (2006) Consumer fraud victimisation in Florida: An empirical study. *St Thomas Law Review* 18(3): 761–789.

Holtfreter, K., Reisig, M. and Pratt, T. (2008) Low self-control, routine activities, and fraud victimization. *Criminology* 46(1): 189–220. Doi: 10.1111/j.1745-9125.2008.00101.x.

Internet Crime Complaint Center (2016) *2015 Internet Crime Report*. Available at: https://pdf.ic3.gov/2015_IC3Report.pdf (accessed 21 October 2016).

Kerley, K. and Copes, H. (2002) Personal fraud victims and their official responses to victimisation. *Journal of Police and Criminal Psychology* 17(1): 19–35. Doi: 10.1007/BF02802859.

Muscat, G., James, M. and Graycar, A. (2002) *Older people and consumer fraud*. Trends & Issues in Crime and Criminal Justice, no. 220. Canberra: Australian Institute of Criminology. Available at: http://aic.gov.au/media_library/publications/tandi_pdf/tandi220.pdf (accessed 24 October 2016).

NASD Investor Education Foundation. (2006) *Investor Fraud Study: Final Report*. Available at: http://www.sec.gov/news/press/extra/seniors/nasdfraudstudy051206.pdf (accessed 24 October 2016).

National Commission on the Causes of the Financial and Economic Crisis in the United States (2011) *The Financial Crisis Inquiry Report*. USA: Pacific Publishing Studio.

National Fraud Authority (2011) *A Quantitative Segmentation of the UK Population: Helping to Determine How, Why and When Citizens Become Victims of Fraud*. Available at: https://www.gov.uk/government/publications/national-fraud-segmentation (accessed 21 October 2016).

Office for National Statistics (2013) *Chapter 4: Mass Marketing Fraud*. Available at: http://www.ons.gov.uk/ons/dcp171776_309772.pdf (accessed 24 October, 2016).

Office for National Statistics (2016) *Overview of Fraud Statistics: Year Ending March 2016*. Available at: https://www.ons.gov.uk/peoplepopulationandcommunity/crimeandjustice/articles/overviewoffraudstatistics/yearendingmarch2016 (accessed 24 October 2016).

Office of Fair Trading (2006) *Research on Impact of Mass Marketed Scams*, London: Office of Fair Trading.

Pak, K. and Shadel, D. (2011) *AARP Foundation National Fraud Victim Study*. Washington, DC: AARP. Available at http://assets.aarp.org/rgcenter/econ/fraud-victims-11.pdf (accessed 24 October 2016).

Reiboldt, W. and Vogel, R. (2003) A critical analysis of telemarketing fraud in a gated senior community. *Journal of Elder Abuse and Neglect* 13(4): 21–38. Doi: 10.1300/J084v13n04_02.

Ross, M., Grossman, I. and Schryer, E. (2014) Contrary to psychological and popular opinion, there is no compelling evidence that older adults are disproportionately victimised by consumer fraud. *Perspectives of Psychological Science* 9(4): 427–442. Doi: 10.1177/1745691614535935.

Schiebe, S., Notthoff, N., Menkin, J., Ross, L., Shadel, D., Deevy, M. and Cartensen, L. (2014) Forewarning reduces fraud susceptibility in vulnerable consumers. *Basic and Applied Social Psychology* 36(3): 272–279. Doi: 10.1080/01973533.2014.903844.

Shover, N., Coffey, G. S. and Hobbs, D. (2003) Crime on the line: Telemarketing and the changing nature of professional crime. *British Journal of Criminology* 43(3): 489–505. Doi: 10.1093/bjc/43.3.489.

Smith, R. G. (1999) Fraud and financial abuse of older persons. *Trends and Issues in Crime and Criminal Justice*, no. 132, Canberra: Australian Institute of Criminology. Available at: http://www.aic.gov.au/media_library/publications/tandi_pdf/tandi132.pdf (accessed 24 October 2016).

Smith, R. G. (2003) Misuse of older persons assets by professionals. Paper presented at *Steps forward for Families: Research, Practice and Policy Conference*, Melbourne, 12 February: Australian Institute of Family Studies.

Smith, R. G. and Budd, C. (2009) Consumer fraud in Australia: Costs, rates and awareness of the risks. *Trends and Issues in Crime and Criminal Justice*, no. 382, Canberra: Australian Institute of Criminology. Available at: http://www.aic.gov.au/publications/current%20series/tandi/381-400/tandi382.html (accessed 24 October 2016).

Sylvester, E. (2004) Identity theft: Are the elderly targeted? *Connecticut Public Interest Law Journal* 3(2): 371–402. Available at http://lsr.nellco.org/cgi/viewcontent.cgi?article=1013&context=uconn_cpilj (accessed 24 October 2016).

Temple, J. (2007) Older people and credit card fraud. *Trends and Issues in Crime and Criminal Justice*, no. 343, Canberra: Australian Institute of Criminology. Available at: http://www.aic.gov.au/publications/current%20series/tandi/341-360/tandi343.html (accessed 24 October 2016).

Titus, R., Heinzelmann, F. and Boyle, J. (1995) Victimisation of persons by fraud. *Crime and Delinquency* 41(1): 54–72. Doi: 10.1177/0011128795041001004.

Van Wyk, J. and Benson, M. L. (1997) Fraud victimisation: Risky business or just bad luck. *American Journal of Criminal Justice* 21(2): 163–179. Doi: 10.1007/BF02887448.

Whitty, M. (2013) The Scammers Persuasive Techniques Model: Development of a stage model to explain the online dating romance scam. *British Journal of Criminology* 53(4): 665–884. Doi: 10.1093/bjc/azt009.

Wolf, R. (2000) Elders as victims of crime, abuse, neglect and exploitation. In: Rothman, M., Dunlop, B. and Entzel, P. (eds) *Elders, Crime and the Criminal Justice System*, New York: Springer Publishing, pp. 19–42.

3

'GULLIBLE, GREEDY OR STUPID SURELY?' FALLING FOR CYBER FRAUDS AND SCAMS

The techniques of the fraudsters

Introduction[1]

In this chapter we examine why victims fall for scams. There is a common perception that victims must be gullible, greedy, stupid or a combination of these to fall for them. There is a dominant negative stereotype which pervades many assumptions about who becomes a victim of cyber frauds and scams (Cross, 2015, 2013) and this will be further explored in Chapter 5. However, we argue that the reality of cyber fraud victimisation paints a very different picture compared to the common misconceptions and false assumptions that currently exist. The reality is that anyone can become a victim of a cyber fraud or scam, if targeted in the right way at the right time by a highly skilled offender. This will be further developed throughout this chapter.

The ease at which some people can be deceived is apparent in the following anecdotal story by one of the authors, concerning a colleague, who like many, held a fairly typical stereotyped view towards victims of cyber fraud, but who was himself then a victim, through what he thought was an innocent and genuine approach.

> In response to the research conducted in this area by one of the authors, a colleague noted he could not believe how stupid some victims are to fall for scams. It was to him so obvious. However, a few months later the same colleague returned to the author's office to seek an opinion on whether he had become a victim himself. He had replied to an email that had noted his expertise and suggested he should be in the American 'Who's Who'. Without thinking he had replied to the email supplying his entry and the US$150 'processing fee'. This was not the genuine 'Who's Who' and the colleague had lost US$150 and was extremely worried that his credit card details would be used for further frauds.

The above example shows how the victim had fallen for a scam that successfully targeted his vulnerability, that is, drawing upon his desire (and expectation) to be recognised in such directories. In addition, the setting of the fee was small enough to seem plausible and not too high as to raise any suspicions, and of course receiving a legitimate looking email. Each of these three factors contributed to the success of this approach by the offender to this particular victim. These are just some of the many tactics used by fraudsters to trap their victims and will be further explored throughout this chapter.

In a small number of circumstances, it is likely that fraud victims could be understood as gullible, greedy and naïve persons, but our research dispels this myth, rather arguing that the vast majority are not and the reason many are susceptible to them results from the various techniques (such as social engineering and grooming) used by the fraudsters. It is too easy to blame the victim for their own victimisation and argue that they should have seen it coming and should have known better. This ignores the role of the offender and also underestimates the highly skilled and tech savvy nature of many criminals. This chapter will examine the wide range of tactics used by offenders in attempting to defraud individuals, illustrating this with real case studies of actual frauds from the authors' own research as well as other global examples. It will start by looking at the general research in this area, before moving on to examine the diversity of frauds, the selection techniques, perpetration strategies and tactics used by offenders to avoid detection.

Falling for frauds and scams

Given the huge cost of fraud to society and the large numbers of victims affected, it is surprising to note there has been limited research exploring the reasons how and why people become victims (see for example, Button et al., 2009; Button et al., 2014; Langenderfer and Shimp, 2001; Office of Fair Trading, 2009; Shichor et al., 2001; Whitty and Buchanan, 2012; Whitty, 2013a; 2013b). In the UK, the Office of Fair Trading commissioned research into this issue undertaken by psychologists at the University of Exeter (Office of Fair Trading, 2009). This involved 30 victims and near victims (those closely involved in the scam such as a relative but who were not actual victims) of predominantly traditional (offline) mass marketing frauds, which included advanced fee, lottery, psychic and investment frauds, to name a few. The research found two main reasons victims responded to scams, which were: appeals to trust and authority, and visceral triggers. This study also identified a series of error-inducing triggers (to push victims into responding) and some of the most significant were: scarcity cues (emphasising a personal offer with a time limit to respond); induction of behavioural commitment (series of small steps towards victimisation); disproportionate size of reward (a high value reward for small investment); and a lack of emotional control (some were less able to control their emotions and were more open to persuasion).

Further to this, Whitty and Buchanan (2012) focused purely upon romance scams perpetrated online. Their study comprised three distinct phases, the first using a survey of 1,193 participants across two websites, an online dating site (n=796) and a victim support site (397) for those who had experienced romance fraud. The second phase examined an analysis of 200 victim accounts of their victimisation, submitted to an internet support site. The third phase, conducted 20 in-depth interviews with victims, some who were recruited through completion of the initial survey, and others who were referred from the (former) Serious Organised Crime Agency (SOCA) based on their known victimisation. The only significant finding of the first phase noted those with high romantic beliefs as being at greater risk of victimisation, and this also held for the second phase. Among other findings, some of the persuasive techniques were also noted such as: profiles of fraudsters providing stereotypical traits likely to appeal to prospective lovers, the use of fictitious authority figures to persuade the victims, and the gradual grooming of the victim, amongst others (Whitty, 2013a; Whitty and Buchanan, 2012). This led Whitty (2013b) to put forward a seven-stage process entitled 'the scammers persuasive techniques model'. This model attempts to identify the various stages of the offence and how the offender successfully grooms a person into sending money and consolidates their ongoing victimisation.

Lastly, the work of Button et al. (2014) drew upon interviews and focus groups with 63 (15 via interviews and 48 via focus groups) victims of online fraud to note a wide range of reasons people fall for scams, including the diversity of scams, small amounts of money sought, mass targeting, visceral appeals, embarrassing frauds and grooming, to name some.

While few in number, these existing studies contribute important insights into the processes and ways in which people become victims of fraud. The remainder of this chapter will draw upon these and many other studies which have touched upon this issue to further elaborate on the tactics and methods used by offenders to successfully target victims.

Diversity of frauds and scams

In Chapter 2 the huge diversity of frauds and scams was illustrated. It was shown there is a multiplicity of frauds and that everyone has a weakness or vulnerability that could exploited by a skilled offender. This is an important tactic of the fraudsters, particularly as they seek to modify and develop new approaches targeted at particular segments of society. Indeed, Chapter 2 also illustrated some of the more popular scams which are particularly associated with certain segments of the population. Thus, the diversity and range of scams increases the likelihood of, and potential for, most people to be targeted or come across a fraudulent or scam approach. Like the academic discussed in the beginning of this chapter, his weakness was his expectation and desire that he should be noted as a worldwide expert in his field and therefore should be included in America's 'Who's Who'. However, that same person as a non-gambler would be very unlikely to fall for a lottery scam, or, as someone who does not dabble in the stock market, would also be unlikely to fall for an investment scam. This illustrates the infinite number of 'plotlines' available to offenders, which use a diverse number of scenarios to target individual victims (Cross and Kelly, 2016). In this way, it is important for offenders to be able to modify their methods and tactics to better target certain groups or individuals to increase the likelihood that they respond positively to an approach. It can be argued that there is a fraud for everyone, and it is up to the offender to decide on how to best match a potential victim with an appropriate fraudulent pitch. This diversity, however, builds upon a wider range of established tactics, which will now be explored. These will be divided between the victim selection techniques and the detection avoidance strategies (Button et al., 2009).

Victim selection techniques

The first part of the offender's strategy is to identify potential victims. The tools used to achieve this can range from one-to-one, mail, telephone, email, through to websites, social networking sites and advertisements. Some of the methods linked to these will now be explored.

Potential victim lists

Potential victims can be contacted in a number of ways. As previously cited, mass marketing approaches are common, with offenders sending out bulk letters and emails, as well as texts and phone calls. These are often sourced from legitimate customer lists that are available to all genuine businesses for their own marketing purposes. In addition, the availability of open source information, such as telephone directories, lists of shareholders, names of company directors, can also be used as another means to reach potential victims, as can legitimate marketing lists sold to businesses for specific market segments. For example, fake lottery scams may use known lists of consumers who participate in lotteries and other gambling activities. Unfortunately, fraudsters may also purchase so-called 'suckers' lists which contain the details of those who have previously fallen for a scam (Shover et al., 2003; Smith et al., 1999). Their title is crude but reflects a list of known victims often created by offenders and sold or traded to other offenders, in an attempt to revictimise the person through a recovery scheme or an entirely different approach. Email addresses can be harvested from across various sites on the internet, such as chatrooms, mailing lists and websites, by dedicated software programs or by malware. Offenders can then target these addresses through the use of spam emails. Offenders can also use methods that generate mass marketing approaches that go to multiple email addresses, for example, identity thieves undertaking phishing attacks.

Case study 3.1 'Suckers' lists'

Trading Standards officers in Northern Ireland secured a 'suckers' list' of over 1,000 people living in the province. The list was sold by criminal gangs and included a list of people who had previously fallen for scams. (Magee, 2015)

Case study 3.2 'Suckers' lists'

Officers from the National Trading Standards Scams Team identified the details of almost 200,000 people who appeared on 13 different 'suckers' lists' which were seized by those investigating fraud operations. Analysis to date had suggested that 10,843 people were known victims who had lost over £13 million in total. (Hyde, 2015)

Social networking

There are a growing number of frauds that use social networking sites to identify potential victims. The most significant example of this is romance-related frauds. As cited in the opening chapter, dating and romance frauds use the guise of a genuine relationship between the offender and victim to build a high degree of trust and rapport. This then leads victims into a false sense of security in the relationship and exploits their desire to be in such a relationship. When asked to send amounts of money at some point, many will comply without thinking. In many cases, stolen and fictitious identities are placed online by offenders (through social media sites or specific dating sites) and used to lure and target potential victims into these false relationships. The huge growth in social networking sites has also created many more opportunities. For instance sites such as LinkedIn have been used to target those seeking new job opportunities with career-oriented frauds and to trick people into downloading malware. Job seekers are also the targets by identity thieves, who advertise fake job opportunities or host job search seminars, with the intention of gaining resumés and financial details from applicants, and subsequently using their identity for criminal purposes.

Case study 3.3 Using social media to target victims

The West Australian Department of Commerce reported an increase in employment scams between 2014–2016. Offenders are using sites such as Gumtree and Facebook to advertise fraudulent job opportunities to unsuspecting victims. (Cox, 2016)

Case study 3.4 Using social media to target victims

A West Australian man, Brandon Nunn, had his identity stolen after responding to a job advertisement. Thinking that the opportunity was genuine, Nunn sent through his passport, driver's licence, tax file number and forklift ticket. This is enough information for offenders to open up new accounts and lines of credit in his name. (Moodie, 2016)

Affinity groups

A common selection technique of Ponzi (a false investment scam) schemes is to target affinity groups. These are groups who have some common bond or link, for example, they work together, attend the same place of religious worship, or are members of clubs. The tactic is to get one person hooked who then discusses their above average returns with the aim that they will spread the word leading to further recruits. Affinity frauds leverage the established levels of trust that group members have with each other as well as the social capital in existence. Evidence from the USA has suggested a disproportionate number of these frauds occur amongst church-affiliated groups (Ganzini et al., 1990). The Madoff Ponzi scheme is a good example of a fraud that utilised the close groups of the rich and famous.

Targeted advertising

Some fraudsters use more straightforward traditional tactics. They advertise their false schemes in publications, on legitimate websites such as eBay or even set up

Case study 3.5 Madoff Ponzi Scheme

In 2009 Bernie Madoff was sentenced to 150 years in jail after having been found to have run the largest Ponzi scheme in US history. A Ponzi scheme is a fraudulent investment scam where investors are promised very high returns and the fraudster uses new members of the scheme to fund the returns for the older entrants, but ultimately relying on investors who remain in the scheme accumulating 'paper' gains. Ultimately the scheme collapses or the fraudster disappears with the monies. On paper, Madoff's fraud amounted to $65 billion, but the actual losses were around $20 billion to victims. Madoff used his impressive reputation to lure in thousands of investors from the rich and famous. His scheme collapsed in 2008 as the financial crisis took hold and investors sought to remove their cash from the scheme but the demands exceeded by far what was left in the coffers. (Justice, 2009; Yang, 2014) websites. The above example of Brandon Nunn, who was a victim of identity theft as a result of employment fraud, illustrates this, with the fake advertisement posted on a legitimate job search website. Modern advertising using the web and texting are also used.

Perpetration strategies

Once the fraudster has identified the potential victims the next stage is to convince them of the proposed scheme and encourage them to part with the money or information required to complete the scam. Many of the scams under consideration in this book require the fraudster to have good general business skills and contacts (Levi, 2008). To set up a mass marketing operation, using mail, the web or telephones, requires good organisational and administration skills. To secure appropriate lists, scripts for scams and other required tools may also require good networks, frequently involving other criminal groups. Once monies are received, skills in laundering it or access to networks that can help, are also required. It is therefore important that successful offenders hold these organisational and entrepreneurial skills. Indeed Button et al. (2009) described many fraudsters operating in this area as 'scampreneurs'. These skills along with a variety of other techniques are used to maximise the success of the fraudsters and are detailed below.

Small amounts of money and mass targeting

Many frauds operate on the basis of mass targeting and seeking only small sums of money from the victim. By asking for a small amount of money, this seeks to avoid raising any suspicions by potential victims. Initial requests for a large amount of money may operate as a red flag for a person concerned that it is fraud. This was exemplified in the opening of this chapter, where the victim was asked to pay US$150. This amount of money appeared commensurate and genuine for the underlying reason as to why it was needed. Clearly modern forms of communication such as email, text messages, and the internet have enabled industrial scale targeting for very low costs and this underpins the prevalence and success of mass marketing techniques. However, it is important to recognise that traditional methods are also still used by fraudsters and are still successful in their own right at soliciting fraud victims. For example, the traditional mail system is still used by fraudsters to send letters and promotional literature relating to scams. Fake lotteries are very common and many specifically target pensioners. Given the preference for many older people to communicate via these more traditional methods of physical mail and letters when they receive a professional looking letter inviting them to join a lottery or stating they have won a prize, this successfully appeals to their specific vulnerability. In many instances, these lotteries or prize draws require a fee to release the winnings and this can be very successful in eliciting positive responses, through the sending of money.

Similarly the use of the telephone to target victims is also used. Again, many telemarketing schemes attract older victims, although there is a current popularity with telephone scams that seek remote access to one's computer in order to obtain personal information.

Many share sale scams (or boiler room frauds as they are often known) still work on the basis of the fraudster cold calling targets and using their sales patter to try and sell the victim worthless investments (as well as many other products and services). Advertisements posted in newspapers or magazines have also been used by fraudsters in an attempt to reach potential victims. The example of boiler room fraud illustrates the seamless use of multiple technologies (old and new) to target victims. As stated, the approach may be initiated through a telephone call to an unsuspecting victim. In response to this phone call, victims are often sent professional looking glossy brochures and marketing material for their particular investment opportunity, which contain detailed information and may mirror legitimate prospectuses. Victims are often also referred to a website, which has been created to further develop the genuine image that the offenders are seeking to portray in an effort to get the person to invest. In this regard, offenders will use all available technologies to increase the perceived legitimacy of their ruse and successfully convince victims to part with their money.

The evolution of technology has also had a large impact on the ability of offenders to perpetrate transnational offences, whereby the offender resides in one country and targets victims in a second country and may request money to be transferred to a third or fourth country. This places enormous challenges on the police in each jurisdiction to investigate, as policing is traditionally based on physical, geographical borders. This is a point that is returned to and expanded in later chapters.

The ease and low costs associated with targeting large numbers of victims has also enabled those from the poorer parts of the world to target richer countries. This is evident through an examination of the historical foundations of advance fee fraud, which traces this back to Nigeria and other West African nations. The accessibility to technology and therefore, potential victims worldwide, has seen many offenders, both individually and collectively, employ a business model which can operate and be sustained through a small percentage of hits, or those who positively respond to a fraudulent pitch. While West African countries are still seen as hot spots for offenders and fraud victimisation (Cross and Blackshaw, 2015), it is important to acknowledge that offenders reside globally, including in developed, first world, western countries, such as the UK, USA, Canada and Australia. It would be naïve to think that cyber frauds and scams are simply a West African problem or a problem of developing nations. Rather, it is a global problem.

The second aspect to this strategy is that many frauds are perpetrated on the principle of a large number of victims losing relatively small sums of money. This has multiple advantages for the fraudster. First, the small amount of money lost means that many victims will be reluctant to report the fraud, which is often a time-consuming process. Second, for those that do report, they are unlikely to receive much interest from the authorities who generally set high thresholds before they consider an investigation. Buying goods, entering lotteries, purchasing tickets for concerts and sporting events which never transpire are all common types of frauds perpetrated online where relatively small sums of money are sought. Third, in some cases the small amount lost might not even be noticed by the victim. Some frauds have involved amounts of a few pence or pounds added to the credit card bills or statements of victims, which they do not notice. These three points all illustrate some of the challenges faced by victims in reporting cyber frauds to authorities as well as the barriers to police being able to effectively respond to these criminal incidents. This is an issue that will be explored later in Chapter 7.

Case study 3.6 Fake tax demand scam in the USA

In 2014 in the USA, a scam based upon the premise that a person owed taxes was perpetrated against thousands of US citizens. Individuals were phoned and told they were speaking to representatives from the Internal Revenue Service (IRS) and that they owed money for unpaid taxes. The call number shown even mimicked the local IRS office number. The fraudsters tactics here were based upon mass targeting and impersonating an official body. (Reuters, 2014)

The industrial scale of some frauds was illustrated by Button (2012: 290) relating to one fraud investigated by the (former) Serious Organised Crime Agency (SOCA). Officers identified one fraudster operating from the USA and devising new scams on a regular basis perpetrated by direct mail. Once devised, the letter

Case study 3.7 Boiler rooms

Four hundred Australian investors contributed AUD$6 million into an investment opportunity with an index trading company, purportedly operating out of Brisbane. Potential investors were contacted via telephone and were convinced to trade large amounts of money, with the ability to log in and track their accounts online. Many of these victims had previous trading experience and were seen as savvy in this area, but were unable to identify the fraud. However, one day victims were unable to make contact with those operating the business and then discovered that they had become involved in a boiler room venture operating from the Gold Coast, Australia. Unlike many other schemes, police arrested two individuals who were prosecuted, convicted and sentenced to 10 years jail. (Robertson, 2015) and list of targets were sent to India to be printed. Thousands of letters were then shipped to the UK to enter the postal system. 'Thousands' would then fall for the scam and send monies to another country. In this particular case SOCA seized most of the letters and cheques heading to the fraudster's third country bank and contacted the victims to explain what was happening and to offer help. However, in this case and many others, the individual regularly perpetrated these mail scams.

Authority and legitimacy

Authority and legitimacy has been noted as another key trigger for victims falling for frauds (Office for Fair Trading, 2009; Whitty and Buchanan, 2012). This is achieved in a number of ways. First the scam needs to look legitimate. In this regard, a website selling bogus holidays needs to mirror websites that sell genuine holidays. Any variation may raise the suspicion of the potential victim, meaning that they decide not to participate. This also applies to scams perpetrated by mail, where letters and promotional literature are also often very professionally produced, as noted previously with boiler room schemes. Fraudsters sometimes will even locate themselves in places that provide clues to greater legitimacy, such as the City of London for investment scams.

Case study 3.8 Operation Broadway

Operation Broadway is an initiative of the City of London Police, Metropolitan Police, and City of London Trading Standards, which targets boiler room fraud, particularly focused on businesses purportedly operating out of Canary Wharf, in London. This particular area has been chosen as it is seen as one of the most prestigious business addresses available in London, and contributes to an overall impression on the authenticity and legitimacy of a company based at this address. This operation explicitly targets the technique of authority and legitimacy employed by offenders in attempting to defraud victims with fraudulent investment opportunities. (Action Fraud, 2015; Barrett, 2015)

The second aspect to this type of strategy is when the fraudster uses legitimate websites to perpetrate their fraud. For example the fraudster might set up on eBay or a similar site and sell fake or non-existent goods and services. They will often do this until they are discovered and then disappear, reforming under a new branding. In romance frauds there have been many cases of individuals setting up false profiles and using photographs of other persons as the front for their frauds. This has also occurred in the selling of holidays such as bogus villas for hire on legitimate websites. In this approach the fraudsters are relying on the victim to think that, because they are using a well-known and legitimate website such as eBay, then the vendor or person must be legitimate.

Case study 3.9 'Lorraine'

Lorraine was the victim of a bogus holiday fraud. She had seen a holiday on a website – which seemed to have all appropriate accreditations linked – and booked a £1,500 holiday for her family. Then one morning while watching breakfast television there was an item about a bogus holiday scam and she suspected it included her holiday. She phoned up the television company who advised her to contact the Metropolitan Police, which she did and who confirmed the fraud. Lorraine and their family did not get their dream holiday and suffered what was to them a substantial loss. The professional appearance of the holiday website had tricked her. (Button et al., 2009)

Case study 3.10 Car retail websites

Many victims have been caught up in fraud perpetrated through online car retails sites in Australia. Offenders will send through a fake invoice which claims that monies have been transferred to the victim and the sale is complete. The offender will then send a courier to collect the car (effectively stealing it), or demand a refund on the full transaction or an overpayment of some sort. If victims comply, they then lose those funds, as the original transaction never occurred in the first place, and victims are left out of pocket. (Watson, 2016)

The third aspect to legitimacy relates to when fraudsters pretend to be legitimate bodies. They might do this by setting up a fake website, faking logos on emails, or simply telling someone over the phone they work for an organisation that they do not. Some of the most common frauds that fall in this area are the phishing scams based upon a fake email from a bank or other financial institution, which usually contains the appropriate logos and corporate images. These emails will often appear as 'security alerts' that request the victim to send their personal information and banking details to trigger a 'resetting' of the account and the unfreezing of funds. The reality is that they have just revealed a variety of data, which can be then used to perpetrate frauds. In the UK there has also been an epidemic of banking scams based upon an individual allegedly being phoned by their bank claiming there is a security issue and then 'passed' to another department over the phone where they are then asked for sensitive information to 'secure' their account, including their PIN number. Consequently they are then told a courier will be sent to retrieve their cards. Sometimes a variation on this may also involve a person claiming to be a police officer, which moves on to the next aspect of authority and legitimacy.

Fraudsters will often impersonate persons and bodies in positions of authority/legitimacy. Most commonly this will be the police. There is extensive research showing how persons are obedient to authority, most notably the famous Milgram experiments (Milgram, 1975). In these experiments significant numbers of participants were prepared to administer potentially lethal electric shocks to a person answering questions wrongly (who was an actor faking pain noises) because a person in a white coat in a position of authority told them to do so. Many frauds involve fraudsters pretending to be police officers in emails, as well as over the telephone and rely on the victim responding to their requests for information and action. Other positions of authority are also used, such as in law firms and the security departments of banks. In these situations, the offender is relying on the person to comply with requests from the person in the position of authority. Some of the common examples of this tactic have been fraudsters who phone up potential victims claiming to be the police and stating there is a problem with their bank account, but they need information to verify who they are talking to. Another more sinister version is where individuals have been contacted and told 'child pornography' has been detected on their computer, but of a 'minor' nature and that if they pay a small penalty fee they will not be prosecuted (Button et al., 2014). The use of authority and legitimacy as a tactic by offenders to elicit success also underpins the prevalence of identity theft as a means to successfully target potential victims. By assuming the identity (either corporate or individual) of a legitimate entity, this allows the offender to craft a seemingly legitimate story, which could be verified through simple internet searches. The ability to do this can then reinforce the lies that are being told to the victim, and increase the likelihood that they will respond as directed, usually through financial transfers.

Case study 3.11 The bogus police officer

In one example of an elaborate scam in the UK, Essex Police reported the case of a man who was tricked out of £30,000 by a scam involving a 'bogus police officer'. The victim was contacted by a man claiming to be a police officer who was investigating the deposit of £30,000 of counterfeit cash into his account. The 'police officer' told him he needed to withdraw it so that it could be examined. The victim was told to phone his bank, which he did, but the fraudster used a technique such that the call did not go through to the real bank. The victim withdrew the cash and was told a courier would pick it up. The victim became suspicious, but was then told he would be 'arrested' if he did not hand over the cash, so he did. The authority and impersonation of the police officer (and bank) also combined with coercion had been the central technique in this fraud. (Essex Police, 2014)

Visceral appeals

Visceral appeal was another key finding in the Office of Fair Trading (2009) research as well as some other studies that have explored the reasons underpinning how a person becomes a victim of cyber fraud and scams (Kienpointner, 2006; Langenderfer and Shimp, 2001). As Titus (1999: 4) argues, 'the lure of something free, absurdly cheap or unrealistically lucrative is integral to many fraud 'come ons''. Appeals to basic needs and emotions, such as money, sex, love, pain, sorrow and the like, are frequently made by fraudsters. Many frauds offer instant and easy routes to large sums of money, such as through investments that will 'soar' in value, lottery 'wins' and 'inheritances' from long-lost relatives. Romance frauds are usually based upon the offer of love and/or sex to the victim. Some frauds play on one's feelings of sorrow, such as a child suffering from cancer in desperate circumstances in need of just a few pounds. Related to this is the often 'too good to be true' aspect of the fraud where there is a disproportionate relation between size of alleged reward and cost of obtaining it. However, relying on clichés such as this for prevention messages is highly problematic as will be discussed in later chapters.

Case study 3.12 'Christine'

Christine was a pensioner in her 70s with a husband who was terminally ill with Alzheimers. Her husband had received correspondence suggesting he could secure £500,000 if certain fees were paid. Christine was lured by the large sum of money and what seemed was the relative ease to secure it. After the first fee was paid by Christine, she was sucked into a succession of further payments which culminated in the loss of their £108,000 life savings. When she went to the solicitor to re-mortgage the house she was told it was a scam and told to inform the police, who investigated and eventually arrested three Nigerians, one of whom was convicted, one who fled the country and the other who was deported. Christine had fallen for the visceral appeal of easy money and, once she had paid in with the first instalment, became trapped into paying even more in an attempt to get her money back. (Button et al., 2009)

Case study 3.13 The airport conman

A man was convicted for reportedly making £15,000 a month by approaching women parking in expensive cars in the short stay carparks at international airports throughout Europe claiming he had missed his flight and was over the limit on his bank card and asking for a small sum of money (around £25) for a budget airline flight home. He was eventually caught in Munich and sentenced to 10 months in jail. The victims fell for the appeal to help someone in distress, combined with the small sum of money sought. (Brown, 2015)

Pressure and coercion

Some victims are pressured and sometimes even coerced into engaging with the fraud. There are a number of measures that fraudsters frequently use. The most common is a time pressure where the victim is presented with an opportunity but one that has a limited period of time for a response. Other victims are bombarded with pressure though repeated phone calls, large amounts of mail or frequent emails. Sometimes the victims may be pressured to comply through threats of blackmail and extortion – particularly if they have been coerced into participating in some embarrassing or possibly criminal actions – otherwise they will be reported to the police or their activities will be publicised. Further to this, there are instances where physical threats of violence to the victim or their friends and family have also been made. Smith et al. (1999: 3) found evidence of one fax to a victim of a Nigerian 419 scam:

> to inform you to produce a mandatory sum of US$35,000 only, into our account given below in Switzerland within ninety six hours, alternatively you will kidnapped and forced to commit suicide during the period of our on-coming anniversary of fifty years [sic].

Some of the clairvoyant and psychic mailing scams also play on fear by threatening bad luck, health problems and other negative consequences on those (or their families and friends) who refuse to participate. For instance one piece of scam mail, which had been used successfully by fraudsters and was given to one of the authors stated (authors' edit):

> **act quickly** because a **silent threat** is now hanging over you and it could cause you to forfeit forever an **enormous sum of money...WITHOUT MY PROTECTION ...** you could become the ... victim ... of wickedness ...

Case study 3.14 'Tom'

Button et al. (2014) noted the example of 'Tom', a middle-aged married man with children, who regularly used the internet for both work and personal reasons. He had experienced a virus on his laptop at home. One morning when he switched on his laptop he was faced with a message which read '[name of local police], you are in violation of a Great Britain law for looking at illegal child abuse images ("child porn")'. The message went on to explain how if he paid a £100 fine then no further action would be taken. Tom had not been accessing illegal pornography but paid the fine due to the concern he had that further action would be taken regardless. He became suspicious and reported it to the fraud department at the local police. He found his laptop had also been infected with a virus when he had opened the email, which took time and effort to remove.

Grooming

Grooming is another common strategy used by fraudsters. Under this tactic, fraudsters gradually build up trust and incrementally push the boundaries. Whitty and Buchanan (2012) found evidence of grooming in romance fraud, as did Button et al. (2014) with other types of fraud. As noted by Whitty (2013b) in her 'scammers persuasive techniques model', with romance fraud the relationship may begin by gradually building up trust and the fraudster may even send small gifts to further build the relationship. A point will come where the fraudster will want something back and this again may start with small sums of money, asking for a small loan. At this stage, the offender is testing the trust established between themselves and the victim and pushing the boundaries to see what is acceptable. Once the victim is hooked and the offender is confident in their ability to extract money from the victim, the boundaries are then pushed, leading to 'delayed' repayment of loans, and soliciting ever greater sums of money. This same process happens in many other types of frauds. Investment frauds may start with the 'broker' contacting the victim and discussing potential areas of investment, then returning with small investment opportunities and gradually building up to large frauds. Within the context of romance frauds, victims can also be convinced to engage in intimate or sexual acts, which are recorded by the offender and can be used against the victim to further elicit compliance, at the risk of not wanting to be exposed to family and friends.

Operating in a legal hinterland

Many of the frauds operate in a legal hinterland where the tactics they use make it difficult to unambiguously identify it as fraud. This makes some 'victims' adamant they are not victims of fraud; others, even though they recognise it probably was a fraud, less likely to report it because of the perceived ambiguity; and another group who may be conscious it is a fraud, want to report it, but because of the ambiguity face a law enforcement community unwilling to take it on or pass it on to other agencies. For example, some lotteries do pay out prizes and consequently the reaction of many police forces who receive complaints is that it is a 'civil matter' between the victim and the lottery. Some scams also have very small print contradicting the main message of the scam. Fraudsters play on this and even if the law enforcement community does become interested they claim the dispute is a civil matter and of no interest to the police (Shover et al., 2003). Again, this is further developed in later chapters.

Good sales techniques

Central to many scams of this type are the requirements for very good sales skills (Levi, 2008). Many of the 'boiler rooms' also take on the structures of legitimate call centres that deploy sales expertise according to skill. For example,

Case study 3.15 'Doreen'

Doreen was a care assistant in her 50s, married to an Englishman, originally from the Philippines. Through her colleagues at work and fellow ex-patriots she had heard of a scheme called 'Circles of Success'. She was eventually invited to a meeting at a house in an exclusive neighbourhood which entailed lots of very good food. At this meeting where she had been subjected to a hard sell she was convinced to part with her ISA (Individual Savings Account) of £3000. The 'Circles of Success' was really a pyramid scheme. She realised several weeks later and then tried to do something. Once she recognised it was a scam she was sent on a merry-go-round of different agencies, starting with Citizens Advice, who told her to report it to Consumer Direct, who then told her to go the police, who told her it was a civil matter and she should go to a solicitor. In this case the victim was attracted by the visceral appeals for the money and flawed by the legal hinterland the scam operated in for securing regulatory or police interest. (Button et al., 2009)

Shover et al. (2003) drawing upon interviews with 47 criminal telemarketers in the USA found three key types of role:

Sales agents: who make the first calls with a scripted pitch and identify potential victims.
Closers: who are more experienced then take on the role.
Reloaders: who are the most experienced and maintain contacts with those already defrauded to secure more monies from them.

Sometimes the victims, who are often vulnerable, are also subjected to high pressure sales where they are contacted multiple times with the purpose of signing them up, as cited earlier (Shichor et al., 2001). Indeed an American survey found some victims 'besieged by telemarketers' (AARP, 1996 cited in Titus and Gover, 2001: 143). Further Shichor et al. (2001) in a survey of victims of one investment scam found that 82.3 per cent had reservations about the scheme when contacted, but such was the persuasiveness of the sales agents, they still participated.

Fraud at a distance

Duffield and Grabosky (2001) have identified the importance of distance for the committing of frauds for the offender, as they are less likely to feel any empathy for the victims. Distance also serves other purposes. It presents challenges for many victims to confront the offender. They can't just pop into a local office to complain. They may find it difficult to actually contact the fraudster and if they do secure a telephone number or email address, the former may have cost implications and they may also be ignored. There is also the additional factor that for a fraudster it makes law enforcement intervention less likely as there is often a reluctance to become involved in expensive overseas investigations and this may also act as a deterrent to report or for the report to be accepted by law enforcement. The internet and modern forms of communication are very well suited to enabling frauds to take place at a distance.

Embarrassing and criminal frauds

Many perpetrators create frauds that are embarrassing or sometimes even potentially involve criminal behaviour, which reduces the likelihood that victims will report them to authorities. One of the most common embarrassing frauds is romance related. Love and sex are for most people very sensitive and personal subjects that they do not wish to share with third parties. Thus, many victims of romance frauds who have fallen in love with fake profiles are very reluctant to reveal this to third parties for fear they will be looked upon as stupid. They may have revealed very personal information in the online romance and some may have even engaged in sexual activities online. They may even have been told by the fraudster once discovered if they go to the police they may see the recorded activities they have engaged with online (Whitty and Buchanan, 2012). The barriers to victims reporting and the shame and stigma associated with cyber frauds and scams are an issue that is further explored in later chapters.

Another fraud relating to sex is fake escort sites. Some fraudsters have set up websites offering a service to bring clients to escorts for sex and friendship. Many budding escorts have paid fees, but then nothing has happened. For many victims the idea of going to the police about becoming a victim of fraud related to an activity, which is seen by many as embarrassing and in some aspects may even be illegal, is not likely. The so-called Nigerian 419 scams also play on this embarrassing theme because if they were real and a person started to engage in them, that would constitute an act of money laundering; for example, in this scam the victim is often expected to receive a large sum of illegally gained money to their account and receive a nominal fee to help 'launder' it. Going to the police to complain about this for many is not considered an option.

Case study 3.16 Bogus escorts

A gang was convicted in the UK of setting up websites offering the chance to work as 'escorts'. Over 14,000 people fell for the scam paying registration fees of £250 to £450 for which they never received any work. They were promised lucrative work in exotic locations. The gang had secured over £5 million from the scam. The techniques here involved both embarrassment, relatively small sums of money and professional looking websites. (BBC News, 2014)

It is also important to note how the illegitimate nature of some frauds also attracts some people to become involved. For instance, the very nature of the Nigerian 419 scam, which if true would be an act of money laundering, leads some to consider they are engaging in an illegal act which is why there are high rewards and it is worth the risk. At a lesser level these same decision-making strategies may also arise when a person is offered the chance to buy stolen goods. The low price for some overrides the moral qualms about purchasing such goods. Illegitimacy and the potentially high rewards for some victims not only act as means not to report once duped, they also entice some into the scam in the first place.

Embarrassing frauds can also be based upon the status of the individual too. For example many victims of investment scams are often senior businessmen very conscious of their reputation. Reporting a fraud they may have suffered, which may lead to their identification in the media or to their peers finding out is for many a price not worth paying. Thus, many victims who have their reputations to think of decide not to report. The importance of this tactic to the fraudsters is that it makes it much less likely they will be reported, investigated and therefore caught.

Case study 3.17 Bogus pills for bigger penises

In 2003 in Arizona in the USA over $74 million of assets was seized by authorities from a company which had been offering a range of pills it claimed would enlarge penises, breasts as well as many other miraculous things. The company had built its business on an avalanche of emails offering a variety of products with wonder benefits, which many fell for (Brunker, 2003). The tactics here involve mass bombardment, offering visceral appeals, for relatively small sums of money, in an embarrassing area. Many would be too embarrassed to go to the police to claim, 'my penis enlargement pills did not work!'

Identity fraud perpetration techniques

Some of the strategies used to perpetrate identity fraud will be considered in their own right in this section because the aim of these approaches is usually personal information, rather than money itself and as a consequence a different set of techniques is often used. The fraudster is seeking genuine identity documents, such as passport, driver's licence, credit card or selective personal information such as name, address, date of birth, bank account numbers, national insurance number, or tax file number, to name the most prominent. Once that information is secured the fraudster can then use it to secure legitimate documents to perpetrate a fraud or directly use the information to do so. Most commonly this might include taking out a loan in the victim's name, or buying goods and services with their banking details. Some of the most common techniques used by offenders to perpetrate identity theft will be explored below. It is important in this section to acknowledge the combination of new and old technologies used to obtain identity credentials. As seen above with various types of fraud, identity thieves can use a combination of online and offline tactics to obtain personal information that an individual would otherwise not disclose.

Redirection or stealing of mail

One of the most common techniques used in identity fraud is the redirection of the mail of a victim to a drop address (Experian, 2008). There are also more opportunistic fraudsters who simply steal mail out of letterboxes, acquire the mail of a housemate or a previous occupier of an address. This is particularly common in complexes with multiple residents, as it arouses less suspicion. As soon as the offender is able to control the mail they can then use the victim's identity to apply for credit, and organise mail order goods until the victim discovers and cancels the arrangement.

'Jackal' fraud

In this type of fraud a deceased person's identity is used to secure credit, goods and services (Experian, 2008). It is known as 'Jackal' fraud from the film 'The Day of the Jackal' where the assassin assumes the identity of a long-dead child to apply for a passport, which is then used to perpetrate further frauds.

Theft of personal information

Some identity frauds are based upon very basic strategies. For example, a wallet or purse stolen in a burglary, theft or some other crime might contain official documents that are sold to a fraudster or used by the original criminal to assume the identity of the victim for the purposes of securing credit, goods and/or services (Allison et al., 2005). A variation on this is where the information is used to create counterfeit documents, which can be used for a fraud.

'Dumpster diving'

Another relatively simple approach – although a slightly messier method – is simply stealing a person's rubbish with the hope they have left personal information in it (such as bank statements, utility bills), which can then be used to assume the person's identity for the purpose of fraud (Allison et al., 2005).

'Skimming' and 'sniffing'

'Skimming' is a more sophisticated means of stealing a person's identity whereby, when a person presents a credit or debit card to a corrupt cashier, they also swipe

Case study 3.18 'David'

David was a gentleman, aged in his 60s, who worked in the city. While on holiday in Paris during the Christmas period he was telephoned by his bank to ask if a few days earlier he had withdrawn £9,500 from one of his current accounts. He had not and the branch where this had occurred had not been a place he had ever visited. The bank informed him that the person who had withdrawn this money had used his 'passport'. David eventually got his money back from the bank but there were a number of issues which still worried him and the fraud also had an impact upon him. This was an example of someone probably using his personal information and counterfeit passport to steal money from David's account. (Button et al., 2009)

the card to copy the data on it. That can then be used to make a copy. Ideally for the fraudster there will also be some means to identify what the person's PIN number is, although this is not essential for 'card not present' transactions (Allison et al., 2005). Some criminal gangs have created sophisticated façades to be placed on automatic teller machines (ATMs) which record the details of the card and in some cases film the customer entering their PIN. Some versions simply have a person in close vicinity to try and film or note the PIN number. Compromised EFTPOS machines can also be installed in retail outlets, without the knowledge or involvement of the business owners. As a result, the details of all customers can be captured by offenders on every transaction processed by the compromised machines.

The advent and growth of contactless card payment, where the customer simply places their plastic card over a machine to authorise payment, has also created a new risk and technique fraudsters can use. 'Sniffer' technology can be purchased relatively cheaply and, if placed within a reasonable distance of a card, reveals the necessary information for a cloned card to then be manufactured and utilised for unauthorised transactions. This could be achieved by 'virtual pickpocketing' where the sniffer device is covertly placed next to the victim's wallet in their pocket or purse in their bag. Alternatively, it could be in the vicinity of a legitimate device. For instance, in a busy bar where drinks are being paid by contactless means, a bartender may hand the device reading the card over the bar and the fraudster with the sniffer could be standing at the bar with a concealed sniffer.

Social engineering

Some fraudsters will pretend to be someone they are not in order to secure bank account and other personal data and this is often known as pretext calling or more commonly as 'social engineering'. This can be done in person, over the telephone or most commonly through email. The most common approach is the so-called *phishing* email where a person receives an email from what looks to be

Case study 3.19 ATM skimming gangs

In August 2014, a Romanian gang who had targeted 36,000 victims using various technological gadgets at ATMs was convicted. The gang had manufactured spy cameras, card skimmers, card traps to enable them to clone cards with the PIN numbers written on them secured through their surveillance. (Financial Fraud Action, 2014)

their bank or some other official body, that seeks the personal information of the person. Some of the emails use the logos of the banks and look very professional. At a less sophisticated level the fraudster might just telephone potential victims pretending to be a bank to secure the information they require.

Case study 3.20 Bogus jobs

A gang was convicted in 2013 for a scam that was reported to have netted them over £1 million. The fraud started with fake adverts for jobs posted on a legitimate website. Persons responding to the adverts were sent an email with a link they were asked to click on to provide information. This also down loaded malware recording their key strokes and thus personal information. This information was used to apply for financial products in their names. This scam used legitimate websites and utilised technical expertise using malware. (Action Fraud, 2013)

Trojans, malware and spyware

The more sophisticated identity fraudsters sometimes send out 'trojans', so called because what may seem like a legitimate email, website or pop-up box actually hides a computer virus that once installed via opening a mail, clicking on a pop up or downloading a site sends data to the fraudster (for example, login names or passwords) which is then used to target legitimate accounts (Bank Safe Online, 2009). Some offenders also use social engineering techniques to trick victims into downloading malware and spyware, which is used to harvest sensitive personal information which might also be used for frauds.

Hackers

Some of the more sophisticated fraudsters may also have the capacity to 'hack' into certain organisation's computers which then gives them access to the personal data they need and can then exploit (Newman and McNally, 2005). It is commonplace for news stories to reveal new data breaches at an alarmingly frequent rate, whereby hackers have penetrated the systems of a company or government agency and compromised the personal information of customers. In some cases, millions of individuals can have their data compromised on multiple occasions through no fault of their own. In many circumstances, the victims only realise that they have had their identities stolen when they receive a statement with unauthorised financial transactions or they receive statements for good/services that they have not purchased. This is particularly problematic for victims in countries (such as Australia) where there are no mandatory data breach reporting laws that require companies to notify customers when their personal information has been exposed. The impact of identity theft as a result of hacking is explored in the following chapter.[2]

Case study 3.21 Major US health insurer

In 2015, a major US health insurer was hacked and potentially millions of its current and former customers' data (such as social security numbers, birthdates, addresses) were compromised. A few days after this incident many customers (former too) began to receive phishing emails claiming to come from the same insurer offering a credit monitoring service in recompense seeking further information. In this case the tactics started with the hack followed by the use of impersonation and legitimacy. (Feinberg, 2015)

Case study 3.22 Ashley Madison

In July 2015, hackers calling themselves 'The Impact Team' released data files on 37 million individuals who were allegedly subscribed at some point in time to the Ashley Madison website. This website is known for facilitating extramarital affairs, and therefore the association of individuals to this website as well as the personal information leaked online was of a highly sensitive nature and likely to cause maximum impact. In addition to standard items of value to identity thieves such as name and credit card details, details surrounding the sexuality and sexual preferences of users were also made public. Those who were in the database soon reported receiving emails threatening blackmail and extortion if payments were not made as well as malware appearing on websites offering to remove names from the list. (Bisson, 2015)

Corruption and incompetence

Personal information on individuals and businesses is also sometimes secured through a corrupt employee passing the information on, or occasionally just through sheer incompetence (Newman and McNally, 2005). One of the authors was involved in a study involving interviews with those convicted of occupational corruption. One of the interviewees was a call centre operative who smuggled in a pen and paper (operatives were not supposed to be able to bring in such items to work) and copied the financial and personal details of some clients. He then used those details to order goods, which were delivered to his house. Not surprisingly this fraudster was soon caught, but some more sophisticated fraudsters often secure the information on an industrial scale and sell this on.

Darkweb/net

Much information to perpetrate identity fraud is purchased on the darkweb/net. This type of fraud, because of its growing prominence, will be considered separately at the end of this chapter.

Detection avoidance strategies

The third part to the strategies of the fraudsters involves those techniques that are used to avoid getting caught. Clearly for most fraudsters there is a desire to get away with their crime and spend the money secured. A variety of strategies has been identified with regard to how fraudsters seek to avoid detection.

'Rip and tear'

Many boiler room-based fraudsters are mobile and do not stay in a location very long (Hines, 2001). They will set up in a place for a period of time and initiate intensive targeting of potential victims and then move on before the local law enforcement community become alerted to their operation. This tactic is often called 'rip and tear' (Shover et al., 2003). In some cases 'boiler rooms' will bring in local sales staff – who may not even know it is a scam (Stevenson, 1998) – and frequently these are the only staff left when the law enforcement community turn up, not the organisers who by then are long gone (Hines, 2001).

Operation from regimes with limited police interest/weak sentencing

Many of the mass marketing scams operate in countries where there is limited police interest or, if caught, the sentencing regime is light. Spain and the Marbella area is commonly cited as a source of many boiler room scams which target the UK and this is generally held to be because of a lack of interest by Spanish law enforcement. In a similar fashion, the Gold Coast is known to be the boiler room capital of Australia, operating under the perception that law enforcement bodies are unable to effectively target and dismantle their operations. They only have an interest where their own citizens are targeted and, not surprisingly, the fraudsters don't usually target their own doorstep. In the USA, many fraudsters have operated across the border from Canada where the penalties and interest of law enforcement are perceived to be lower. In Hong Kong and China, victims have been targeted by fraudsters using Indonesia and Cambodia and in South Korea from Koreans based in China (Button et al., 2014).

Making reporting unlikely

Fraudsters often pursue frauds for low sums of money that make reporting to the authorities unlikely by the victim (Hines, 2001). Indeed one of the authors was presenting to a pensioners forum on frauds and was approached afterwards by one of the audience. He explained he had received a pop-up note on his mobile phone telling him he had won a prize from Tesco (a UK supermarket chain). As he shopped there he thought it was legitimate and clicked on the link. This led to a premium rate telephone call, which cost him £6. Asked if he had reported it he replied 'it wasn't worth it for such a small loss'. As noted earlier some also pursue embarrassing and criminal frauds that make reporting unlikely. Some fraudsters also operate scams so they are, or are perceived to be, in legal hinterlands, making reports and law enforcement involvement less likely if contacted. Some frauds also pose jurisdictional challenges, meaning there might be confusion for the victim in who to report it to, or on the other side, who has responsibility for investigating it. As Starnes (1996: 206) argues 'many operators of fraudulent schemes slip through the cracks in state or federal statutes, or create new schemes to fall outside the scope of statutes'.

Fraudster networking and the 'darkweb'

This book has already alluded to a number of areas where fraudsters work together and share useful information. In Chapter 1, the issue of the 'normalisation' of fraud was illustrated where the darkweb is used to buy and sell credit card information, which can then be used to perpetrate frauds. In this chapter 'suckers' lists were identified where fraudsters sell lists of names to other fraudsters, indicating the people who have fallen for scams and might be likely to fall victim again.

The 'darkweb' or 'darknet' are terms used to describe parts of the internet that can only be accessed by special software. They are used largely to conduct illegal transactions, such as to access illegal pornography, fileshare and buy illicit items such as drugs and firearms. These parts of the internet are also being used to sell information and tools which can be used to perpetrate fraud and other economic crime. For instance, in August 2016 it was revealed that the details of 200 million Yahoo users were put up for sale on a darkweb site called the 'Real Deal'. All these details were being sold for 3 bitcoins or $1200. The details were rumoured to have been hacked by the notorious hacker Peace_of_Mind (RT, 2016). Some of the items that can be bought on such websites and are of use in fraud activities are listed below and have been sourced from Infosec Institute (2015), Levi et al. (2015) and RSA (2015).

- Credit/payment card details – CCV (Credit Card Verification – CCV is the long number, name and expiry date) and CCV2 (is the three number verification code on the back of the card). These are sold as such and the information from legitimate cards can be used to enable frauds to be perpetrated.
- DUMP information is the information from the magnetic strip of a card – this can be used to clone cards to then use to perpetrate frauds.
- Personal information (information relating to persons such as name, address, bank details, password), which enable frauds to be perpetrated. This is often termed as FULLZ – the full financial information of the victim.
- Fake documents (documents such as driving licences, passports), which can be used to perpetrate identify fraud.
- Malware (which can be used to perpetrate frauds, economic and other types of crime).
- Technological devices to enable frauds such as card coders and sniffers.

There are a large number of darkweb sites, which change as law enforcement agencies catch them up and close them down. The Infosec Institute (2015) notes that the AlphabayMarket is one of the best for fraud and, 'has a specific section dedicated to Frauds; this category includes payment card fraud, account frauds, personal information, and generic services'. It also notes that US credit/payment cards retail at between $6 and $25, whereas European cards retail at $14 to $45.

Conclusion

This chapter has examined the wide range of techniques used by fraudsters to perpetrate their frauds. Rather than victims being gullible, greedy and stupid it has shown how a sophisticated variety of techniques are used to maximise the potential success of the fraudsters. Starting from a very wide diversity of frauds, which maximises the potential number of victims, the fraudsters then use a variety of proven tactics often copied from the legitimate world of business. From using legitimate marketing lists to selling goods and services on legitimate sites, the fraudsters then use techniques such as mass targeting for small amounts of money, the use of impersonation and authority figures, through to visceral appeals to elicit positive responses from victims. There are also additional tactics used to perpetrate identity fraud, which incorporate both offline and online methods. The chapter also considered how fraudsters reduce the risk of getting caught and ended with a brief exploration of the darkweb and how that is being used to share information and sell information and tools to help perpetrate fraud.

Having established the ways in which offenders successfully perpetrate cyber frauds and scams and the complexity with which they operate, it should not be surprising that they are successful in so many situations. The following chapter moves the focus to the victim of cyber frauds and scams, and starts to unpack the devastating impact that fraud victimisation can have on an individual.

Notes

1 This chapter draws upon the article Button, M., McNaughton-Nicholls, C., Kerr, J. and Owen, R. (2014) Online frauds: Learning from victims why they fall for these scams. *Australian and New Zealand Journal of Criminology* 47(3): 391–408. Doi: 10.1177/0004865814521224.
2 In February 2017, the government passed the Privacy Amendment (Notifiable Data Breaches) Bill 2016, which establishes a (arguably limited) mandatory data breach notification scheme in Australia.

References

Action Fraud (2013) *Fraudsters Convicted for Fake Online Adverts*. Available at: http://www.actionfraud.police.uk/fraudsters-convicted-for-fake-online-adverts-nov13 (accessed 24 October 2016).

Action Fraud (2015) http://www.actionfraud.police.uk/operation-broadway.

Allison, S., Schuck, A. and Lersch, K. (2005) Exploring the crime of identity theft: Prevalence, clearance rates, and victim/offender characteristics. *Journal of Criminal Justice* 33(1): 19–29. Doi: 10.1016/j.jcrimjus.2004.10.007.

Bank Safe Online (2009) *Trojans Explained*. Available at: http://www.banksafeonline.org.uk/trojans_explained.html (accessed 18 March 2009).

Barrett, D. (2015) *Police Raid Iconic Skyscrapers in Fraud Crackdown*. Available at: http://www.telegraph.co.uk/news/uknews/crime/11482823/Police-raid-iconic-skyscrapers-in-fraud-crackdown.html (accessed 24 October 2016).

BBC News (2014) *Suffolk Escort Scam Fraudster Ordered to Repay £160,000*. Available at: http://www.bbc.co.uk/news/uk-england-suffolk-26731570 (accessed 24 October 2016).

Bisson, D. (2015) *The Ashley Madison Hack – A Timeline (updated 9/10/15)*. Available at: http://www.tripwire.com/state-of-security/security-data-protection/cyber-security/the-ashley-madison-hack-a-timeline/ (accessed 24 October 2016).

Brown, M. (2015) *Teesside conman who made £15,000 per month duping women at airports*. Available at: http://www.gazettelive.co.uk/news/teesside-news/teesside-conman-who-made-15000-9175285 (accessed 24 October 2016).

Brunker, M. (2003) *Anatomy of a Penis Pill Swindle*. Available at: http://www.nbcnews.com/id/3077050/print/1/displaymode/1098/ (accessed 24 October 2016).

Button, M. (2012) Cross-border fraud and the case for an 'interfraud'. *Policing: An International Journal of Police Strategies & Management* 35(2): 285–303. Doi: 10.1108/13639511211230057.

Button, M., Lewis, C. and Tapley, J. (2009) *A Better Deal for Victims*, London: National Fraud Authority.

Button, M., Lewis, C. and Tapley, J. (2014) Not a victimless crime: The impact of fraud on individual victims and their families. *Security Journal* 27(1) 36–54. Doi: 10.1057/sj.2012.11.

Cox, K. (2016) *Scammers Target Job Advertisements Through Social Media*. Available at: http://www.abc.net.au/news/2016-07-14/scammers-target-job-advesrtisements/7630654 (accessed 24 October 2016).

Cross, C. (2013) 'Nobody's holding a gun to your head…': examining current discourses surrounding victims of online fraud. In: Richards, K. and Tauri, J. (eds) *Crime, Justice and Social Democracy: Proceedings of the 2nd International Conference*, Crime and Justice Research Centre, Queensland University of Technology, Queensland University of Technology, Brisbane, QLD, 25–32. Available at: https://eprints.qut.edu.au/61011/ (accessed 21 October 2016).

Cross, C. (2015) No laughing matter: Blaming the victim of online fraud. *International Review of Victimology* 21(2): 187–204. Doi: 10.1177/0269758015571471.

Cross, C. and Blackshaw, D. (2015) Improving the police response to online fraud. *Policing: A Journal of Policy and Practice* 9(2): 119–128. Doi: 10.1093/police/pau044.

Cross, C. and Kelly, M. (2016) The problem of 'white noise': Examining current prevention approaches to online fraud. *Journal of Financial Crime* 23(4): Online first. Doi: 10.1108/JFC-12-2015-0069.

Duffield, G. and Grabosky, P. (2001) The psychology of fraud. *Trends and Issues in Crime and Criminal Justice*, no. 199, Canberra: Australian Institute of Criminology. Available at: http://www.aic.gov.au/media_library/publications/tandi_pdf/tandi199.pdf (accessed 21 October 2016).

Essex Police (2014) *Bogus Police Officer Cons Man Out of £30,000*. Available at: https://www2.essex.police.uk/news_features/features_archive/2014/october_2014/bogus_police_officer_cons_man.aspx (accessed 24 October 2016).

Experian (2008) *Victims of Fraud Dossier: Part IV*, London: Experian.

Feinberg, A. (2015) *Beware: Anthem Hack Victims are Getting Bombarded by Phishing Scams*. Available at: http://gizmodo.com/beware-anthem-hack-victims-are-getting-bombarded-by-ph-1684285394 (accessed 24 October 2016).

Financial Fraud Action (2014) *Crime gang jailed for ATM fraud against 36,000 victims: New technique of sidewards ATM spy cameras uncovered*. Available at https://www.financialfraudaction.org.uk/wp-content/uploads/2016/09/210814-operation-sandhaven-final.pdf (accessed 24 October 2016).

Ganzini, L., McFarland, B. and Bloom, J. (1990) Victims of fraud: Comparing victims of white collar crime and violent crime. *Bulletin of the American Academy of Psychiatry and Law* 18(1): 55–63.

Hines, J. (2001) Telemarketing fraud upon the elderly: Minimizing its effects through legislation, law enforcement and education. *Albany Law Journal of Science and Technology* 12(3): 839–862.

Hyde, D. (2015) *Con Men Keep 'Suckers List' of 200,000 Likely Victims*. Available at: http://www.telegraph.co.uk/news/shopping-and-consumer-news/11757106/Con-men-keep-suckers-list-of-200000-likely-victims.html (accessed 24 October 2016).

INFOSEC Institute (2015) *Card Fraud in the Deep Web*. Available at: http://resources.infosecinstitute.com/card-fraud-in-the-deep-web/ (accessed 24 October 2016).

Justice (2009) *United States of America versus Bernie L. Madoff*. Available at: https://www.justice.gov/usao-sdny/file/762821/download (accessed 3 November, 2016).

Kienpointner, M. (2006) How to present fallacious messages persuasively: The case of the 'Nigeria Spam Letters'. In: Houtlosser, P. and van Rees, M. A. (eds) *Considering Pragma-Dialectics*, Mahwah, N.J./London: Lawrence Erlbaum Associates, pp. 161–173.

Langenderfer, J. and Shimp, T. A. (2001) Consumer vulnerability to scams, swindles, and fraud: A new theory of visceral influences on persuasion. *Psychology and Marketing* 18(7): 763–783. Doi: 10.1002/mar.1029.

Levi, M. (2008) *The Phantom Capitalists*, Revised Edition. Aldershot: Ashgate.

Levi, M., Doig, A., Gundur, R., Wall, D. and Williams, M. (2015) *The Implications of Economic Cybercrime for Policing*, London: City of London Corporation. Available at: https://www.cityoflondon.gov.uk/business/economic-research-and-information/research-publications/Documents/Research-2015/Economic-Cybercrime-FullReport.pdf (accessed 24 October 2016).

Magee, K. (2015) *'Suckers List': Scammers Target Over 1000 People in NI*. Available at: http://www.bbc.co.uk/news/uk-northern-ireland-32705024 (accessed 24 October 2016).

Milgram, S. (1975) *Obedience to Authority*, New York: Harper Torchbooks.

Moodie, C. (2016) *Scammers Target Jobseekers on Recruitment Websites*. Available at: http://www.abc.net.au/news/2016-07-24/hold-sun-job-seekers-being-scammed-on-legit-websites/7654804 (accessed 24 October 2016).

Newman, G. and McNally, M. (2005) *Identity Theft Literature Review*. Available at: https://www.ncjrs.gov/pdffiles1/nij/grants/210459.pdf (accessed 24 October 2016).

Office of Fair Trading (2009) *The Psychology of Scams: Provoking and Committing Errors of Judgement*, London: Office of Fair Trading. Available at: http://webarchive.nationalarchives.gov.uk/20140402142426/http://www.oft.gov.uk/shared_oft/reports/consumer_protection/oft1070.pdf (accessed 24 October 2016).

Reuters (2014) *Largest Ever US Tax Fraud-Phone Scam Targets Thousands: IRS Watchdog*. Available at: http://www.reuters.com/article/2014/03/20/us-usa-tax-fraud-idUSBREA2J28W20140320 (accessed 24 October 2016).

Robertson, J. (2015) *'The Biggest Mistake of My Life': How Gold Coast Boiler Room Scams Duped Investors*. Available at: https://www.theguardian.com/money/2015/aug/17/the-biggest-mistake-in-my-life-how-gold-coast-boiler-room-scams-duped-investors (accessed 24 October 2016).

RSA (2015) *Cybercrime 2015 An Insider Look at the Changing Threat Landscape*, London: RSA. Available at: http://www.emc.com/collateral/white-paper/rsa-white-paper-cybercrime-trends-2015.pdf (accessed 24 October 2016).

RT (2016) *200 Million Alleged Yahoo User Details Up for Sale on Darknet*. Available at: https://www.rt.com/news/354245-yahoo-hack-dark-web/ (accessed 24 October 2016).

Shichor, D., Sechrest, D. and Doocy, J. (2001) Victims of investment fraud. In: Pontell, H. and Shichor, D. (eds) *Contemporary Issues in Crime and Criminal Justice: Essays in Honor of Gilbert Geis*, New York: Prentice Hall, pp. 87–96.

Shover, N., Coffey, G. S. and Hobbs, D. (2003) Crime on the line: Telemarketing and the changing nature of professional crime. *British Journal of Criminology* 43(3): 489–505. Doi: 10.1093/bjc/43.3.489.

Smith, R. G., Holmes, M. N. and Kaufmann, R. G. (1999) Nigerian advanced fee fraud. *Trends and Issues in Crime and Criminal Justice*, no. 121, Canberra: Australian Institute of Criminology. Available at: http://www.aic.gov.au/media_library/publications/tandi_pdf/tandi121.pdf (accessed 21 October 2016).

Starnes, R. A. (1996) Consumer fraud and the elderly: The need for a uniform system of enforcement and increased civil and criminal penalties. *Elder Law Journal* 4(1): 201–224.

Stevenson, R. J. (1998) *The Boiler Room and Other Telephone Sales Scams*, Chicago, IL: University of Chicago Press.

Titus, R. M. (1999) The Victimology of Fraud, Paper presented to the *Restoration of Victims of Crime Conference*, Melbourne, Australia, September 1999. Available at: http://www.aic.gov.au/media_library/conferences/rvc/titus.pdf (accessed 24 October 2016).

Titus, R. M. and Gover, A. R. (2001) Personal fraud: The victims and the scams. *Crime Prevention Studies* 12: 133–151.

Watson, M. (2016) *Warning Over Online Scammers Targeting Car Buyers and Sellers*. Available at: http://www.abc.net.au/news/2016-04-02/scammers-targeting-car-buyers-and-sellers-online/7293160 (accessed 24 October 2016).

Whitty, M. (2013a) Anatomy of the online dating romance scam. *Security Journal* 28(4): 443–455. Doi: 10.1057/sj.2012.57.

Whitty, M. (2013b) The scammers persuasive techniques model: Development of a stage model to explain the online dating romance scam. *British Journal of Criminology* 53(4): 665–884. Doi: 10.1093/bjc/azt009.

Whitty, M. and Buchanan, T. (2012) *The Psychology of the Online Dating Romance Scam*, Leicester: University of Leicester. Available at: https://www2.le.ac.uk/departments/media/people/monica-whitty/Whitty_romance_scam_report.pdf (accessed 24 October 2016).

Yang, S. (2014) *5 Years Ago Bernie Madoff was Sentenced to 150 Years in Prison – Here's How his Scheme Worked*. Available at: http://www.businessinsider.com/how-bernie-madoffs-ponzi-scheme-worked-2014-7?IR=T (accessed 3 November 2016).

4

'NOT A VICTIMLESS CRIME'

The impact of fraud upon victims

Introduction[1]

It is surprising to note that despite extensive research on crime victimisation there has only been a very small amount of research on fraud victims (Croall, 2001; Fraud Advisory Panel, 2006; Ganzini et al., 1990; Levi, 2001; Levi, 1999; Levi and Pithouse, 1992; Spalek, 1999). This literature highlights some of the devastating consequences and impacts of fraud on the victim. For some, such is the severity of the harm they experience, it has been likened to that of violent crime (Marsh, 2004). Further to this, there is evidence from some victims who express feelings in the aftermath of online fraud that they have been 'mentally raped' (Whitty and Buchanan, 2016: 180; see also Deem, 2000: 37). While the most obvious consequence is financial harm, it is important to recognise that the impacts of fraud go far beyond that of pure monetary losses. However, the financial loss can be significant. For some victims, such is the loss that they are required to sell assets (often their home), go back to work (if they were retired), or are unable to secure credit or sometimes in the worst case scenario they may even become bankrupt. This chapter will explore the impact of fraud on the victims, examining both the financial and non-financial harms experienced by these victims, and in doing so it will draw upon some of the latest research from around the world. The chapter will start with an examination of the impact of crime in general, before exploring some of the specific impacts of fraud, which have been noted in the research. Throughout the chapter case studies of real victims from the authors' research will also be used to illustrate the arguments made.

Impact of crime in general

There has been a significant body of research illustrating the impact of crime on victims (Spalek, 2006; Walklate, 2007). The more substantial research on crime in general has noted a variety of common impacts that victims suffer. Some of these common impacts will be identified below, but it is important to note that similar crimes may affect different people in different ways. A burglary of two houses, which both involve the loss of a television of similar value, will not necessarily have the same impact upon the victims. A range of factors may relate to this, including the established coping mechanisms of the person in the first place, the social capital of the victim to recover, the burden of the financial loss relative to the victim's income and their experiences in reporting to police. Overall, the heterogeneity of all victims, and fraud victims in particular, must be borne in mind through the discussion throughout this chapter. In reviewing crime victimisation broadly, Spalek (2006) notes five common themes under which a variety of further impacts are noted. Each of these is detailed in turn.

Psychological impact

There are a number of aspects linked to the psychological impact of crime. First there is the shattering of cognitive meanings, whereby existing views of the world are broken such that victims lose faith in people or certain groups (often associated with the perpetrator). Second, some victims experience a loss of self-control where they often feel any control over their lives has been taken from them. Many victims also end up blaming themselves for the crime. Another common impact is for the victim to compare their experience with others, particularly those with worse experiences, as a way of coping with their victimisation. Some victims will also use the experience to search for meaning in their lives. Finally, some victims will also experience strong feelings of retribution towards the perpetrator, although this does not hold for all victims.

Emotional impact

Spalek (2006) notes a variety of research findings relating to the emotional impacts of crime. First of all not only will many victims experience fear at the time of the incident, many will also fear further or ongoing victimisation. Many victims, particularly males, will also experience anger as a result of the crime. Some research has also shown some victims will hide and internalise emotions as a result of crimes. Victims of some crimes, particularly violent ones, sometimes also experience post-traumatic stress disorder.

Behavioural impact

Another common theme in research in general on crime victims is that the victimisation leads to changes in behaviour. Some will avoid the situation associated with the crime, such as rape victims avoiding similar places to where they were attacked. Some will completely change their lifestyle; for instance, Spalek (2006) cites the case of a woman who, while playing tennis, had a man expose his genitalia to her and as a consequence of this event she stopped playing the game.

Physical impact

Many violent crimes involve injuries to the victim, which result in the need for medical treatment. Bruises, cuts, gunshot wounds, sexually transmitted diseases, and pregnancy represent some of the physical impacts victims of violent crime experience. Nausea, headaches, fatigue may be other consequences which result from crime. Such is the impact for some victims they may resort to violence against themselves or towards those who victimised them.

Financial impact

Finally, Spalek (2006) notes the financial impact upon many victims. There is the loss that may arise from the actual crime, but also the secondary costs that arise, such as the costs of improving security, increased insurance premiums and loss of work. The Spalek (2006) review notes many general crime impacts, which will shortly be detailed for fraud victims. Some of these impacts are common, some rare. The diversity of fraud, however, ensures the impacts of this particular crime can also be very diverse, depending upon the type of fraud and the circumstances of the victim. This section, however, will also illustrate impacts that are not noted amongst crime victims in general and are specifically related to fraud victimisation. Most importantly the section will debunk the common myth that for many fraud victims victimisation has a limited impact or perhaps is even 'victimless'. The following section will start by exploring that very issue.

The 'victimless' crime?

It is critical to debunk the commonly accepted myth that many frauds are a 'victimless crime'. This view largely arises from the prevalence of credit card fraud victims who suffer a financial loss, but who then are reimbursed by their banks. It also arises from large organisational victims of fraud who are often viewed as being able to soak up 'relatively small' losses and who at times can be understood as faceless corporations. As this chapter will illustrate, those who experience unauthorised transactions on their credit cards are only one group of fraud victims, who do not comprise the majority. For the many other victims of fraud, an overwhelming majority do not get their money back. Even those who do get their money back can often suffer from a variety of impacts unrelated to financial harms. This argument also negates the organisational victim, that is, the bank or retailer, who ends up taking a financial loss as a result of the fraud and in many cases will have to pass the loss onto their customers and consumers, which further illustrates that organisations can and do suffer financial losses as a result of fraud. This chapter will demonstrate the completely devastating impacts that fraud can incur on victims, leading some to even commit suicide. As previously cited, it is incorrect to assume that fraud victims only suffer financial losses, with the reality highlighting that fraud victimisation can extend to the deterioration of physical and emotional health and well-being, depression, relationship breakdown, homelessness, unemployment and in worst case scenarios, suicide. The impact of fraud can be as severe as those who experience violent crime, however the same degree of acknowledgement and support is not apparent. This is a theme explored in later chapters.

Similar to research examining the impact on crime victims in general, for fraud victims, there is a wide range of devastating impacts that will be outlined in the following sections. However, as with other crimes, it is important to note that there is diversity in the severity of the impact experienced by fraud victims, with the dollar value of the fraud not necessarily commensurate with the impact experienced by the individual. Rather, the extent and nature of the impacts do vary according to the individual and there are some victims who have suffered significant losses for whom the impact is minimal. In one of the largest studies to date, that specifically examines fraud victims (in the UK of mass marketing frauds such as bogus investments, fake lottery, advanced fee fraud, and identity frauds), 745 victims rated different impacts upon them. The data is presented in Table 4.1 below.

The table shows that the four most significant impacts reported by fraud victims were anger, financial loss, stress and psychological/emotional feelings. However, a significant number experienced problems in relationships with their partner or family at 17.2 per cent with a further 9.1 per cent experiencing problems in their relationships with friends. Around 1 in 10 also experienced a worse

TABLE 4.1 Fraud victims' views of possible impact of fraud: 1= No effect: 7 = severe effect (Button et al., 2014: 45)

Possible effects of fraud	*Numbers*	*Mean*	*% claiming low effect: 3 or under*	*% claiming high effect: 5 or higher*
Caused feelings of anger	729	5.2	21.9%	68.40%
Financial loss	665	3.9	48.6%	45.0%
Caused feelings of stress	681	4.0	44.3%	44.3%
Caused psychological/emotional feelings	622	3.4	53.9%	36.7%
Caused problems in relationships with partner or family	548	2.1	79.6%	17.2%
Worse personal credit rating	466	1.8	84.5%	11.4%
Caused physical health problems	536	1.8	85.9%	10.8%
Loss of pension	433	1.6	88.9%	10.0%
Caused problems in relationships with friends	519	1.6	87.7%	9.1%
Caused mental health problems	499	1.5	90.8%	7.4%
Loss of home	410	1.3	95.4%	4.0%
Loss of employment	406	1.2	96.8%	2.5%
Caused feelings of suicide	487	1.2	96.3%	2.3%
Led to suicide attempt(s)	471	1.1	98.3%	1.7%

credit rating or a loss to pension. A very small number reported feelings of suicide or had attempted suicide, which is a concerning statistic. These and other consequences will now be the subject of more in-depth analysis. Throughout the chapter, case studies of real victims will be used to illustrate the impacts.

Financial impact

The diversity in fraudulent approaches and the amount of money lost by fraud victims is reflected to a large extent by the wide range of monetary values that victims suffer. Fraud losses can range from no actual financial loss (as happens in many credit card frauds where monies are often reimbursed by banks and other financial institutions) to millions of pounds/dollars. Some frauds, such as ticket frauds, are likely to yield relatively small losses to the individual as tickets generally cost in the tens of pounds/dollars. This is in contrast to investment frauds, where hundreds and thousands (or more) of pounds/dollars is not an unusual investment figure, and as a result, these types of frauds generally involve much greater financial losses to victims. As Table 4.2 shows, in the UK the average loss for a ticket fraud was £80, whereas for a pension fraud it was almost £39,000. Indeed the table illustrates the nature of diversity evident in the average losses for a selection of different types of fraud.

Further statistics from the study undertaken by Button et al. (2014) reveal that, of the 745 victims interviewed over the telephone, one in six (16%) had lost under £100, 37% had lost under £1,000 and three-quarters (76%) had lost under £10,000. At the other end of the scale, one victim had lost over a million pounds and 22 victims had lost between £100,000 and £1m. The same research also investigated the loss related to household income. This showed that many victims sustained losses that would seriously impact upon their lifestyle. For example, of those with a household income of under £10,000, eight (16%) reported a fraud loss of over £10,000, more than a year's income. Of those with a household income of £10–50K, 45 (8%) reported a loss of over £50,000, which again is more than a year's income.

The financial impact can then have secondary consequences for some victims and their way of life. For example, some victims reported having to 'downgrade'

TABLE 4.2 Selected common frauds in the UK and their average losses

Type of fraud	*Average loss*	*Country and source*
Pension fraud	£38,974	UK (Levi et al., 2015)
Investment fraud	£21,534	UK (Levi et al., 2015)
Online shopping and auction frauds	£1,700	UK (Action Fraud, 2013)
Identity fraud	£1190	UK (Action Fraud, 2011)
Bogus holidays	£889	UK (Action Fraud, 2015)
Advance fee payments fraud	£784	UK (Levi et al., 2015)
Ticket fraud	£80	UK (Action Fraud, 2010)

their lifestyle, with fewer expenses, and less foreign holidays. Others indicated that they had to work longer or re-start work because of the loss sustained to their pensions. It is not unusual for victims to lose their houses and other property as a consequence of the fraud. This can also impact on a deterioration of their credit rating or in certain circumstances even lead to bankruptcy. For example, the National Institute of Justice research on victims of fraud (consumer frauds) in the USA found 20 per cent suffered financial or credit problems as a direct result of the fraud (cited by Deem, 2000). There can also be extended impacts, or secondary victimisation, on those beyond the direct fraud victim. For example, employers and business owners who suffer fraud losses can be forced to sell or close their companies, which can lead to unemployment for those whom they have hired. There are also many issues of debt associated with those who suffer fraud. Button et al. (2010: 12) highlighted the case of Bernard, a small businessman, who had been defrauded, and as a consequence struggled to pay debts to local suppliers and was in the process of selling the family home to help achieve this. Some were not sympathetic to his plight, as he noted:

> I mean we had one guy who drove round the front lawn and chewed up the lawn when we were trying to sell the house. Another wrote c**t in big letters an hour before someone from the Middle East flew in to buy ... look at the house so I had to go out the back taking green paint and paint it. So if you look at our ... lovely 19th century stonework and there's one big yellow stripe across it covering up the word c**t [laughs], cos he believed it (that the victim had not lost large sums of money in the fraud), you know. And afterwards he said I'm sorry I did that, I let myself down.
>
> *(Bernard, small business fraud victim)*

Even where there are no actual financial losses some victims spend a great deal of time having to deal with the consequences of the fraud. For example, estimates indicate it takes an average of 48 hours for the typical victim of identity fraud to clear their name (cited in Fraud Advisory Panel, 2006). Research by Pascoe et al. (2006) has suggested that for most victims of identity fraud they can spend between 3 and 48 hours rectifying their situation (actual time taken might be over a longer period of days/weeks).

Little or no impact

While the previous research has focused heavily on those victims who suffer a varying degree of financial loss, there is also research that notes those victims who suffer very little impact as a result of victimisation (Button et al., 2009). Clearly there is a degree of relativity to this and an investment banker earning hundreds of thousands of pounds per year who suffers £50 ticket fraud will suffer a smaller financial loss compared to a cleaner earning £10,000 per year who loses £1000 on a fake lottery scam. However, this was not always the case. There were also examples of victims interviewed in the Button et al. (2009) research who had lost tens of thousands of pounds in bogus investments, but who saw the loss as part of their general approach to 'high risk' investments, and were of the belief that 'you were bound to win some and lose some'. The case studies below from the Button et al. (2014) research illustrate this. 'Doug', who was the victim of a boiler room fraud and who lost between £1 and £10,000 (exact amount not revealed on victims' request) opined that the government's economic policies had had more of an impact on his life than the fraud loss. In a similar manner, Nathan, who was an identity fraud victim whose losses were cancelled (bad debts fraudster ran up), only noted the impact of dealing with the bureaucracy of the whole situation and not any direct financial losses.

Case study 4.1 'Doug' boiler room fraud victim (between £1–10k loss)

But ... but as I say the impact on our lives, of that, is miniscule compared with what this stupid government's cost us, and is going to cost us for the rest of our lives. (Button et al., 2014: 43)

Case study 4.2 'Nathan' identity fraud victim (no financial loss)

Um, you know, the extent of the problems it's caused me, you know, isn't that great. It's just, er, you know, because it was resolved so quickly, um, you know, so the only really ... the only real sort of lasting impact is having to go through so many hoops, you know, for, for my legitimate banking and all those sorts of things. Um, but that's just there. I don't think there's any real impact to this that, you know, other than it constantly being on your mind, you know, about where stuff is. I don't know. (Button et al., 2014: 44)

Psychological impacts

Earlier in this chapter it was noted there is a wide range of psychological impacts that victims of crime generally experience. Research on fraud victims has also identified a variety of common psychological impacts and as Table 4.1 noted, three of the top four impacts identified by fraud victims in the research by Button et al. (2014) were psychological. Some of these impacts will now be explored in more depth.

Anger

Anger was the top-rated impact found by Button et al. (2014). Spalek (1999) in her study on the victims of the Maxwell pension fraud also found that 'anger' was a common emotional impact of the fraud. Not surprisingly many victims focus their anger at the perpetrators and some even express their desire to physically hurt the perpetrators. The case study box below, illustrates some of the feelings that were expressed by victims in this research (Button et al., 2009: 54–55).

Case study 4.3 Angry victims

Archie (investment fraud victim)

Um – I think the – the anger that somebody has actually done it and they've gone to long lengths to actually do it to me through trust. That I think is the thing that has really got to me.

Fred (lottery fraud victim)

Oh aye, I was … I wasn't right pleased, if I'd have got to him I'd have … he … he'd have wanted hospital treatment [laughs].

Brian (bogus tipster victim)

I got very uptight about it and ermm, lost me temper very quick and I was going round with a sore head, annoyed at everybody 'cause I'd been conned, especially when the realisation that you are being conned hits you. You know, you're wild and I really wanted to get hold of this ### #### and just batter him, I really did.

Stress

The next most significant psychological impact found by Button et al. (2014) was stress. Spalek (1999) also found the victims she interviewed who had experienced financial loss through a large Ponzi scheme, suffered stress, anxiety and fear as a result of their loss. A study of the impact of identity fraud also found some victims' emotions were affected (Pascoe et al., 2006). Some became worried about someone accessing their personal details. Others became agitated and distressed. For some, this led to feelings of violation, stress and anger (Pascoe et al., 2006). In a similar vein, research on mass marketing scams has found some victims suffer stress, anxiety and loss of self-esteem (OFT, 2006). The experience makes many victims worry about why they were targeted, some think they might be targeted again, and for others, the anxiety is focused around the resulting financial impact.

> **Case study 4.4 Stressed victim**
>
> ***Becky (small business victim of card not present fraud)***
>
> Well it's an added stress and I'm sure I've got a few more grey hairs over it, but [laughs], I've not been to the doctor for anything no.

Upset

Another significant psychological impact is the upset caused by fraud to many victims. Some victims would break into tears or experience events that highlighted the consequences of the fraud they had suffered (Button et al., 2009: 56).

> **Case study 4.5 Upset victims**
>
> ***Loraine (bogus holiday fraud victim)***
>
> I mean it did, it knocked me for six didn't it, absolutely knocked me for six. Because I think for days I was just walking around crying … But yes I was just … I am just … the thing is I know it's three years ago and I am still as angry and still sick feeling as I did, as the first day I did it. When we did the TV show (about their experience), I mean I don't know how many takes we had to do that, because I got very emotional again.
>
> ***Archie (investment fraud victim)***
>
> Um – it flattened me. I went into myself. Didn't want to discuss it. Um – and that was for a period of time when I was fairly focused on it – um – but focused inwardly as well too, and then the defence mechanisms kick in. Didn't want to get involved with the family with it at all.
>
> ***Steve (multiple fraud victim)***
>
> Yeah. It's, it's when your son says to you … 11-year-old son says to you, um, don't worry dad, I'll buy mum's Christmas present this year. I mean, er …[laughs].

Ridicule and embarrassment

Another psychological impact that deserves a section in its own right and which can be considered a secondary impact (as noted by Button et al., 2014), was the ridicule endured as the result of being a victim as well as a sense of shame and embarrassment. There are two aspects to this type of impact. First, there are victims who agree with official bodies for their fraud to be publicised in the hope it raises awareness and leads to less people falling for such scams. This may lead to some not falling for that type of fraud, but some victims may find as a consequence celebrity ridicule as members of the public often deride them (many may also secure sympathy too). Button et al. (2014: 51) illustrated this with two victims who took their fraud experiences to the media and shared them publicly. Their responses to this public 'outing' as such are reproduced below.

> If we walked into Tesco's to go shopping we would go at nine or ten o'clock at night, because it was quieter, because if went out during the day all I saw was people looking at us. People were constantly looking at us, come up to us and saying 'I'm sorry to hear about it' and bits and pieces, and Happy Birthday, and 'it's a shame', and even old people wasn't it.
>
> *(Loraine, bogus holiday fraud victim)*

> I was embarrassed by it, especially when as I say it was before I was troubled with the cancer, and I was doing my shopping in a large superstore. And people were stopping me and saying 'Oh what an idiot you've been'. How on earth did you make such a fool of yourself? And I just had to tell them it was very easy.
>
> *(Hilda, lottery fraud victim)*

The second aspect to this type of ridicule is a more localised version. Victims who reveal to family, friends, colleagues, or whose victimisation simply becomes known, often face a variety of negative reactions. Most common is ridicule at how 'stupid' could they have been to fall victim to – what to many – was an obvious scam. Alongside such ridicule many victims also are labelled 'greedy' and 'stupid'. Such reactions can also come not just from the general public, but also from the official bodies who are supposed to be looking after them. The case study of Val below illustrates this further.

Case study 4.6 'Val'

Val had invested £120,000 (her husband's inheritance) in an investment which promised a rate of return of 10 per cent, in what seemed a secure investment. Relatives also invested and a solicitor oversaw it (who subsequently turned out to be in on the scam). The 'investment' was overseen by a gentleman who was chauffeur driven in a Rolls Royce. Val realised something was wrong, when after a few weeks their 'income' payments stopped. She tried to contact the firm to no avail. After some research on the internet she eventually contacted the Metropolitan Police, and lodged a complaint. The culprits were caught, prosecuted and convicted in what amounted to a £15 million scam. However, one of her worst experiences was at the court case, which notes in her own words:

> The worst thing for us was when they did the actual court case, the judge said that we were all wealthy arrogant people that wanted to get on the bandwagon of hedge fund investment.... He did. He just said that we were wealthy arrogant people that had erm... which was annoying 'cause we weren't. We were just normal people, obviously if my husband hadn't been involved we would never have got involved in it. We probably would've gone straight to the building society, paid off the mortgage and said, end of. Instead, we thought well we could invest it, make a bit more from it, do something more for the children, that type of thing. (Button et al., 2010: 11)

Val's case also highlighted another common issue related to this, which is feelings of shame and how stupid they feel they may have been, as she noted:

> I think we both felt at the time that oh what a waste, you know, we've thrown all that money away and plus the fact that you know, you kind of think to yourself well how stupid could I be, to pour it into something like this and then not really you know, kind of think to yourself well, what an idiot. Why did I do that? (Button et al., 2009: 57)

Impact on relationships

One of the most significant impacts fraud can have is on relationships. This can happen between partners, within families and between friends. Button et al. (2014) noted three main ways that fraud damages relationships:

1. The financial impact causes stresses in relationships.
2. One partner keeps the loss secret and eventually has to reveal it.
3. Family members become distressed as a relative squanders life savings on scams and the attempts to stop them result in tension.

There have been a number of such examples which have been revealed in research. Button et al. (2014) illustrated the case of Doreen who had lost £3,000 but hadn't told her husband for fear of the consequences. She also alluded to other friends who had fallen for the same scam who hadn't told partners. She revealed:

> Some of them, also my friends, also their husbands, they didn't tell their husbands! [laughs] Because it will be a marital problem, you know, you

> know the consequences you do think there is always the consequences, you're always just thinking, not now, maybe one day but not now ... Yeah, yeah, yeah, I have to be careful, be careful because, you know the reason why people get split, one of the reasons is money.
>
> *(Button et al., 2014: 48)*

Button et al. (2014) also found another victim who was so ashamed of the fraud she hadn't told her seriously ill husband, who she was caring for.

> No, I haven't [told him]. I was so ashamed I suppose ... of the fact that I'd done it, that I didn't want anyone to know. And so I have in fact told one friend, that's all ... and I was so ashamed of the fact that I'd been so stupid.
>
> *(Button et al., 2014: 48)*

The greatest devastation Button et al. (2014) found in relationships was in families where there was a chronic scam victim. These are victims who become essentially 'addicted' to the fraud and repeatedly send money, even when family, friends and official bodies are advising them against their involvement. The consequences of such frauds often lead to large and ugly rifts in families. Family members often tell the victim that they are involved in a scam. Offenders will seek to counter these warnings through their ability to isolate the victim from family and friends as well as their ability to manipulate and coerce the victim into compliance through the high levels of trust and rapport which have been developed. For example, often the victim is led to believe by the offender that their family members want their inheritance and are not looking out for the victim's best interest. This can often lead to the victim not trusting their close family and the family members watching on in frustration as their loved one sends their money away. Button et al. (2014) noted the experience of Lisa, the daughter of a chronic scam victim.

> [I] asked him [father], begged him, pleaded with him not to send any money, but he's just ... he's even driven her (wife) to cash points to make her withdraw money because he couldn't get enough out in a day to get cash from the bank. She's just turned into a complete nervous wreck, she's sort of, you know, old, nervous issues, I've alerted their GP and the ... he has a community mental health nurse visiting them. I wondered whether my dad was ... had got some form of dementia because I couldn't understand how he could be ... have the suspicions that this is not right, investigate it ... have the suspicions verified, if you like.
>
> *(Button et al., 2014: 48)*

In another example 'John', the son of a chronic scam victim noted this impact on the relationship with his mother:

> But that day after I blew up outside the bungalow, because like I say I nearly smashed the window to get attention, and she was stood the other

> side of it. And she came out like a shock and came back to sort of reality. And I absolutely flipped, and she started laughing at me. She said 'I know it's funny isn't it'. And I mean I really did flip, and then she said a bit later to my sister, 'I think #### fell out with me'. You know, as if it had only just started to sink in. And I made my mind up then them letters wasn't going to that door, so I stopped the postman. I mean I maybe could have got arrested, but I said them letters aren't going through that door. He said 'well if you've got identification, you know, I can let you collect it.' So, and he did know us anyway, so I produced identification, and then he told me what to do and we went down to the main post office and got it sorted and got a letter. Which that was the saving grace really, but I had to go down every day and queue up, so you know … It's alright saying money isn't important, erm … you know, you've got this almost like a hatred for your own mother for a short period of time. And you say money is not important, but if you discovered she'd spent twice as much as you thought she had, you'd hate her even more. So money does come into it doesn't it. And it's not money, it's you know my father's money and …
>
> *(Button et al., 2009: 60)*

The damage to relationships as a result of victimisation was also realised by some of the victims. As Hilda, the chronic victim of lottery scams noted:

> Yes, so I didn't tell them. But one daughter still lives in Darlington, who doesn't speak to me anymore for some reason, I don't know why. But she'd seen the news and she told them in Kent, so I didn't have to tell them, she went and told them. She would enjoy doing that I think. I didn't actually tell anybody except Peter, because Peter was taking me to the building society.
>
> *(Button et al., 2009: 60)*

Physical and mental health impacts

While most fraud offences perpetrated in an online environment do not involve physical contact between the victim and the offender, this does not negate the physical impact and deterioration of physical health that can result from fraud victimisation. For some victims, the stress and effects of the fraud victimisation exacerbate existing health ailments (such as heart conditions, high blood pressure, to name a few).

There are also significant impacts on mental health experienced by the majority of fraud victims, with depression being one of the most common forms of psychological impact cited by victims. For some victims, there is also the possibility that the onset of severe psychological distress can manifest itself in the expression of physical symptoms. For example, in Spalek's (1999) study on the Maxwell pensioners fraud victims she found that some of the victims felt their husbands' deaths were accelerated as a result of the scam. In these cases, the effects of fraud victimisation were understood as a catalyst for a more rapid decline in the physical health of victims. The manifestation of physical symptoms is also evident in the work of Button et al. (2009) who found two victims reporting skin conditions in the aftermath of their experience of fraud victimisation.

Case study 4.7 The physical impact of fraud victimisation

Peter (small business fraud victim)

'But if you want to see Class A psoriasis which I didn't have before… and if there is, um, any relationship as they say there is between stress and psoriasis'.

Harold (identity fraud victim)

'Yes, um, I, um I have started suffering from a rather mild, um, skin problem called urticaria in which, um, certainly in 2003, which was just when this had gone on for six months, um, I just went all red, red rash, right down the front of my body and down my legs, itchy rash, it's called urticaria. And, um, I was given some medicine for it, pills and it knocked it out. There've been a few reoccurrences, not so severe as that first onslaught, but it's never happened before and, um, I think it's a symptom of the awful level of anxiety that I now live on'. (Button et al., 2009: 53)

As previously cited, fraud victimisation can have devastating consequences for individuals and for most, it will be apparent through a decline in their mental health, evident by some level of depression. The extent and severity of any depression can vary between victims, with some indicating a fairly short episode, which did not impact too greatly, while others report debilitating and ongoing effects. The existence of depression was also revealed in a study examining the impacts of fraud on victims of a Ponzi scheme, whereby the findings indicated that many were afflicted with depression as a consequence (Ganzini et al., 1990). The following case studies from the Button et al. (2009) research below further illustrate this.

Suicide (attempts and ideation)

It has already been ascertained that the impact of fraud for some victims can be as severe as those who experience violent crime (Marsh, 2004), while others liken it to being mentally raped (Whitty and Buchanan, 2016). The severity of depression and the effects of fraud can lead some victims to thoughts of suicide,

Case study 4.8 The mental impact of fraud victimisation

Barry (long firm fraud victim)

'Er, yeah I did. Yeah, there, there, there are … there have been sort of bouts of, er, of depression that, that were … I, I could go inside myself and, um, and, and feel sorry for myself and then I'll … I just, um … I haven't got the … more so in the earlier stages when it first happened to me, when I, when I realised that my money was, um, in jeopardy …'

Mike (multiple fraud victim)

'Er, yeah, I would say with me, yes. I've been mentally to the brink a couple of times. Yeah. So … I've always thought I'm pretty strong but, you know, um, er, it's when you have to carry the baggage of your own family, that's, that's difficult'. (Button et al., 2009: 54)

attempts at suicide and in a small number of cases, actual suicide. The extent of these feelings was noted by the Button et al. (2014) research, which found a small (but significant) number of the 745 victims they interviewed had thought about or attempted suicide: 2.3 per cent and 1.7 per cent respectively. Clearly for some victims, who have lost life savings or feel they have been completely humiliated as a result of the fraud, the impact can lead to such thoughts and actions. In one article in the UK tabloid *The Daily Mail*, of several hundred victims of a pension's fraud scam in which many had lost their pensions it was claimed four victims had committed suicide (Levy, 2015). The cases of William Foxton, Leslie Fountain and Philip Hunt below reveal three tragic cases. Mr Foxton lost his life savings, Mr Fountain thought he had won a significant sum, which would have cleared his debts, and Mr Hunt had not only lost a significant sum of money, but the 'woman' called 'Rose' he thought he was in love with. In all three of these cases the fraud played significant parts in their decision to commit suicide. Sadly, there are also many other documented cases worldwide, where victims of fraud have seen the decision to end their life as the only appropriate course of action (see Cross et al., 2014). The need to support fraud victims to avoid this outcome is further explored in Chapter 6.

Damaged reputation

The research by Button et al. (2014) identified a number of secondary impacts, which can result as a consequence of a fraud. One of these related to damaged reputation or fears concerning potential damage to reputation. This largely

Case study 4.9 Suicide of fraud victims

William Foxton

William Foxton, who was a £100,000+ victim of the Maddoff Ponzi scam committed suicide by shooting himself with a pistol in a public park. The victim faced financial ruin and bankruptcy as a result of the losses and it is thought that this is the reason he decided to take his own life. (*Telegraph*, 2009)

Leslie Fountain

Leslie Fountain was a technician in a good job at a university who had run up debts of £25k. He fell for a fake lottery in which he thought he had won $1.2 million. This was a scam and when he discovered this he committed suicide by setting himself alight. The inquest heard that he had spent the night before his death trying to access his winnings and had become increasingly frustrated. (BBC News, 2004)

Philip Hunt

Philip Hunt was a lonely divorcee who fell in love with a woman called 'Rose' over an internet dating site. He was told by her she was very rich and that if he could help her transfer $2.9 million from Nigeria to the UK they could start a new life together. He spent £82,000 from his life savings, running up debts and re-mortgaging his house to help facilitate her movement to the UK. Mr Hunt committed suicide by jumping in front of a train and police found a final text message to 'Rose' on his mobile phone near his body which said, 'I'm cold, lonely and depressed, I'm so lonely without you tonight. Going to meet my maker'. (Brooke, 2010)

relates to victims of identity fraud who fear or experience someone using their identity in a negative way. One of the most disturbing examples in this research was the case of Harold, who was a semi-retired man in his 50s living on his own in London. In 1999 he received a credit card bill with an item for $202.20 which was nothing to do with him. Three months later another unauthorised transaction appeared on his bill. Harold asked for his card to be changed, which it was. Three years later the police 'burst' into his house at 5am to arrest him on suspicion of downloading child pornography. His house was searched and his computer seized. Harold lived in an affluent suburb of London and his neighbours soon found out what had happened. Six months later his computer was returned and his bail cancelled. In the meantime, however, serious damage had been done to Harold's reputation. As he noted:

> And then another person in the street who said, um, 'oh well, there are those who talk about no smoke without fire'. You know these sort of comments add up and someone else, more recently who I had regarded as a friend, but I've – I won't see him again, um, although I've known him for 25 years, um, he made a flippant comment about 'well there must have been something', um, I rang him up about that later and gave him a thorough, not a talking to, but a very mildly expressed explanation and said 'look you don't seem to understand, these are the facts' and I told him what had happened and he said I was being flippant. I was just being flippant. I mean like a woman for example whose husband was an old friend of mine and they had three children, I know them all, I met them in Clapham at a private view in a house, and I noticed certain caginess and as I went up to greet them all I noticed the mother moving her children away from me like that. I didn't – I didn't really sort of want to believe consciously that I was believing my own eyes. I just thought well she's being sort of funny or something.
>
> *(Button et al., 2010: 9)*

Clearly there is a risk with identity fraud that the offender's actions will damage the victim's credit rating. However, for some victims the fears extended beyond this. Some identity fraud victims are high achieving individuals who are very preoccupied with their reputations and there is a fear that the fraudsters could do something in their name which damages their reputation. The example of 'David' in the case study box reveals this very clearly.

Case study 4.10 'David'

David was a gentleman, aged in his 60s, who worked in the City of London. While on holiday in Paris during the Christmas period he was telephoned by his bank asking if a few days earlier he had withdrawn £9,500 from one of his current accounts. He had not and the branch where this had occurred had not been a place he had ever visited. The bank informed him that the person who had withdrawn this money had used his 'passport'. David eventually got his money back from the bank but there were a number of issues which still worried him and the fraud also had an impact upon him. One of the most significant, was the damage to his reputation as the quote from his interview below, illustrates:

> And **it drives you mad**. Do you know one of the worst things about it is? What you worried about Mr ####, you've got your money back! In other words, you're not a victim. We the bank, are the victim. ####! It's not like that! I mean somebody out there is pretending to be me. I'm sorry, that upsets me, you know! If I was some … if I was drinking paraffin under an arch at a bank station,

I wouldn't give a toss about that. But actually I've worked hard to build up my reputation, to build up my business, to … I've worked hard with the reputation of the firms I run here, the charity that I run here and I'm very bothered that there's some #### out there who is running around, pretending to be me. (Button et al., 2010: 6)

Fear of violence and other negative consequences

Following on from the actual ridicule and embarrassment that many victims fear will happen to them, there is the potential for far greater consequences to occur, such as violence. Smith et al. (1999) have noted how threats of violence can often form part of Nigerian 419 scams. Generally, violence and threats of violence are rare in frauds, but there are some cases in which it is used and in some cases victims fear violence. In other cases victims are threatened with other negative actions. For example those who have been involved in scams such as 419s which, if real, would amount to money laundering, are sometimes threatened with potential police action. Similarly some victims who have been defrauded as a result of seeking to engage in embarrassing activities, such as becoming an escort or seeking penis enlargement, may fear exposure and potential embarrassment. Some romance fraud victims who have engaged in sexual acts online or who have sent intimate pictures are often threatened with them being published (Whitty and Buchanan, 2012). Indeed it was revealed that in Wales about 50 individuals a year are blackmailed after being tricked online into sending intimate pictures (McCarthy, 2014).

Case study 4.11 Blackmail and extortion

A Nigerian man was convicted of online romance fraud in a US court, after it was established that he had created several fake dating profiles and established relationships with several women across the USA. One in particular, was coerced into performing intimate sexual acts on camera, and this footage was then used against her to extort further money. (US Department of Justice, 2016)

Victims of cyber fraud can also be unknowingly recruited as money mules or drug mules by their offenders. In many cases, the requests to transfer money, or collect a package, is part of the plotline used by the offender, and at the time they employ it, they have developed a high level of trust and rapport with the victim, to ensure compliance. However, if caught by authorities, the consequences can see victims arrested, prosecuted and incarcerated for their actions. The following case studies document various victims who have been caught up as both money or drug mules.

Case study 4.12 Money mules

A Tasmanian woman caught up in a romance fraud, was charged by police with laundering over AUD$3 million of funds for an international organised crime syndicate. She was asked to transfer funds which arrived in her account, to other bank accounts overseas. Despite transferring such a large amount of money, the woman only took AUD$3,000 for herself. (Shannon, 2016)

Case study 4.13 Drug mules

New Zealand woman Sharon Armstrong, who was the victim of romance fraud, was asked by her partner to collect a briefcase of documents from Argentina, on her way to meet him in London. After collecting the briefcase, Armstrong was detained by customs officials on her departure from Buenos Aires. The briefcase that she was carrying contained over 5 kilograms of cocaine, and she was arrested, prosecuted and found guilty of attempting to traffick drugs. She was sentenced to 4 years and 10 months in an Argentinean jail but was deported back to New Zealand after 2 and a half years. (Bavas, 2016; Harley, 2012; Sullivan, 2016)

Fraud offences generally differ from other criminal acts as they involve deception rather than direct physical harm, as witnessed in those involving violence against the person. In the context of cyber frauds and scams, in the majority of cases, the victim and the offender will never meet. While this may reduce the likelihood of a physical threat to the victim, it is important to note that the physical threat invoked by some offenders can be perceived as authentic and have real consequences for victims. This was evident in the work of Cross et al. (2016) whereby two women who were both romance fraud victims, sold their properties and moved houses in response to the fear and anxiety they held towards their physical safety in the aftermath of their victimisation. Further to this, there was another victim who had received death threats against him and his wife, after he had posted information about the offender online once he realised he had been defrauded.

Sadly, there are also circumstances where the physical safety and well-being of fraud victims is compromised through travelling to meet with their offender/s. Cross et al. (2014) detail a small number of case examples, where victims have needed to be rescued by police after being kidnapped by offenders. In one of the most tragic cases, 67-year-old Australian grandmother, Jette Jacobs, travelled from Perth to South Africa to meet with her Nigerian boyfriend and was found dead a few days later.

Case study 4.14 Fear to physical safety

I just kept thinking that I am on my own. I come home at night, I don't know if he is out there. I don't know who he is. That is what drove me to leave that place ... I moved because I was thinking that I can't stay there ... At night I started to leave my lights on at home. I started to get panicky because he knows the time I come home. (Female romance fraud victim (interview 41))

I actually got some death threats. We [my wife and I] left the country over it for a while. It got pretty serious ... I got phone calls ... They put a note in my yacht: 'We know where you live. We know where your wife lives. We know what your wife's phone number is' ... I had an SMS from them as well: 'Last warning'. (Male investment fraud victim, (interview 63)) (Cross et al., 2016: 30–31)

Case study 4.15 Compromising physical safety

A US investment fraud victim travelled to Benin to meet with individuals he had met online. He was soon kidnapped and a ransom was requested for his release. However, combined efforts of the Benin Police and the FBI were able to rescue him and subsequently arrest those involved in his kidnapping. (BBC News, 2012)

A South Korean lottery fraud victim travelled to South Africa with his daughter to claim his prize. Both the man and his daughter were taken hostage by their offenders, who demanded a ransom of $10M (or £6.5M). After being alerted to this, South African police raided the house and secured the release of both hostages without incident. (Smith, 2012)

Australian woman and romance fraud victim Jette Jacobs, travelled to South Africa to meet with her Nigerian boyfriend, Jesse Omokoh. After spending a few days in her apartment, she was found dead, allegedly murdered by Omokoh, who fled back to Nigeria. Investigations undertaken between South African and Nigerian Police led to the arrest and charging of Omokoh with Jacob's murder. She had been defrauded of approximately AUD$90,000. (*The Australian*, 4 February, 2014)

These cases highlight the fact that despite the online nature of many frauds, and the perceived geographical distance between the victim and the offender, there are still many ways in which the physical safety and well-being of the victim can be compromised, through threats made against them by offenders,

TABLE 4.3 Change in victims' behaviour as a result of the fraud (Button et al., 2009: 61)

Type of change reported	*Number*	*Per cent*
No change reported	190	25.5%
A lot more cautious with regard to investments/purchases generally	164	22.0%
A lot more careful in response to approach to invest, especially by phone	111	14.9%
More careful in using credit card, especially online	102	13.7%
Specific preventative action taken to avoid future frauds	97	13.0%
Behavioural change such as frequent anger, loss of trust, addiction to junk mails, agoraphobia, rudeness	86	11.5%
Increased awareness of fraud context and greater security	28	3.8%
Loss of money has meant living more frugally (usually in retirement)	8	1.1%
Total changes reported by victims	586	
Total victims reporting changes in behaviour	555	74.5%
Total number of telephone interviews	745	

or through genuine physical harm incurred by victims travelling to meet their offenders. For some, these decisions can prove fatal.

Change in behaviour

As noted in the start of this chapter, a common impact of crime victims in general is that it leads to changes in behaviour related to the victimisation (Spalek, 2006). The OFT study of mass marketing fraud found over half the scam victims studied had changed their purchasing and payment behaviour as a result of the fraud (OFT, 2006). Button et al. (2009) found that, amongst the 745 victims interviewed over the telephone, around three-quarters (74.5%) said that victimisation had changed their behaviour. Table 4.3 summarises the different changes that were mentioned by victims. The most common changes were being more cautious in relation to investment and purchases, particularly using credit cards, which could be seen as a positive too. However, some were more negative such as loss of trust, rudeness, agoraphobia and living more frugally.

Conclusion

This chapter has explored the impact of fraud on victims. It has dispelled the myth of a 'victimless' crime and shown the extensive range of impacts that occur on individuals who experience such crimes. The impacts were shown to include financial loss, psychological impact, ridicule, embarrassment, impact on relationships, physical and mental health problems, damaged reputation and suicide, to name most. The chapter has also throughout used the testimony of real fraud victims to illustrate the damage done.

Note

1 This chapter draws upon the article Button, M., Lewis, C. and Tapley, J. (2014) Not a victimless crime: The impact of fraud on individual victims and their families. *Security Journal* 27(1) 36–54. Doi: 10.1057/sj.2012.11.

References

Action Fraud (2010) *Scam Ticket Warning.* Available at: http://www.actionfraud.police.uk/scam-ticket-warning-may10 (accessed 24 October 2016).

Action Fraud (2011) *Identity fraud continues to rise with 4 million victims in UK alone – Yet consumers continue to be complacent with their ID.* Available at: http://www.actionfraud.police.uk/Identity_fraud_continues_to_rise_with_4_million_victims_in_UK_alone (accessed 24 October 2016).

Action Fraud (2013) *Christmas Shoppers Warned Take Care with Online Shopping.* Available at: http://www.actionfraud.police.uk/christmas-shoppers-warned-take-care-with-online-shopping-nov13 (accessed 24 October 2016).

Action Fraud (2015) *Fraudsters are Conning Travellers Our of £2.2 Million a Year.* Available at: http://www.actionfraud.police.uk/news/fraudsters-are-conning-travellers-out-of-2.2-million-a-year-apr15 (accessed 24 October, 2016).

Bavas, J. (2016) *Romance Scam: Victim Tricked into Drug Trafficking Speaks Out.* Available at: http://www.abc.net.au/news/2016-05-30/romance-scam-woman-shares-story-of-being-conned-jailed/7456300 (accessed 24 October 2016).

BBC News (2004) *Suicide of Internet Scam Victim.* Available at: http://news.bbc.co.uk/1/hi/england/cambridgeshire/3444307.stm (accessed 24 October 2016).

BBC News (2012) *Benin: US 'Internet Scam Victim' Freed by Police.* Available at: http://www.bbc.com/news/world-africa-18293883 (accessed 24 October 2016).

Brooke, C. (2010) *Lonely Divorcee Kills Himself After Falling for £82,000 Dating Con.* Available at: http://www.dailymail.co.uk/news/article-1247774/Divorcees-train-suicide-82-000-internet-date.html (accessed 24 October 2016).

Button, M., Lewis, C. and Tapley, J. (2009) *A Better Deal for Victims*, London: National Fraud Authority.

Button, M., Lewis, C. and Tapley, J. (2014) Not a victimless crime: The impact of fraud on individual victims and their families. *Security Journal* 27(1) 36–54. Doi: 10.1057/sj.2012.11.

Button, M., Gee, J., Lewis, C. and Tapley, J. (2010) *The Human Cost of Fraud: A Vox Populi*, London: Centre for Counter Fraud Studies and MacIntyre Hudson. Available at: http://www.port.ac.uk/media/contacts-and-departments/icjs/ccfs/cost-of-fraud.pdf (accessed 24 October 2016).

Croall, H. (2007) Victims of white collar and corporate crime. In: Davies, P., Francis, P. and Greer, C. (eds) *Victims, Crime and Society*, London: Sage, pp. 78–108.

Cross, C., Richards, K. and Smith, R. (2016) *Improving the Response to Online Fraud Victims: An Examination of Reporting and Support*, Criminology Research Grant Final Report. Available at: http://www.crg.aic.gov.au/reports/1617/29-1314-FinalReport.pdf (accessed 21 October 2016).

Cross, C., Smith, R. G. and Richards, K. (2014) Challenges of responding to online fraud victimisation in Australia. *Trends and Issues in Crime and Criminology*, no. 474, Canberra: Australian Institute of Criminology. Available at: http://aic.gov.au/publications/current%20series/tandi/461-480/tandi474.html (accessed 21 October 2016).

Deem, D. (2000) Notes from the field: Observations in working with the forgotten victims of personal financial crimes. *Journal of Elder Abuse and Neglect* 12(2): 33–48. Doi: 10.1300/J084v12n02_05.

Fraud Advisory Panel (2006) *Improving the Investigation and Prosecution of Serious Fraud*, London: Fraud Advisory Panel.

Ganzini, L., McFarland, B. and Bloom, J. (1990) Victims of fraud: Comparing victims of white collar crime and violent crime. *Bulletin of the American Academy of Psychiatry and Law* 18(1): 55–63.

Harley, A. (2012) *Sharon Armstrong Sentenced for Cocaine Smuggling in Argentina*. Available at: http://www.newshub.co.nz/nznews/sharon-armstrong-sentenced-for-cocaine-smuggling-in-argentina-2012032416 (accessed 24 October 2016).

Levi, M. (1999) The impact of fraud. *Criminal Justice Matters* 36: 5–7.

Levi, M. (2001) White collar crime victimisation. In: Shover, N. and Wright, J. P. (eds) *Crimes of Privilege*, Oxford: Oxford University Press.

Levi, M. and Pithouse, A. (1992) The victims of fraud. In: Downes, D. (ed.) *Unraveling Criminal Justice*, London: MacMillan.

Levi, M., Doig, A., Gundur, R., Wall, D. and Williams, M. (2015) *The Implications of Economic Cybercrime for Policing*, London: City of London Corporation. Available at: https://www.cityoflondon.gov.uk/business/economic-research-and-information/research-publications/Documents/Research-2015/Economic-Cybercrime-FullReport.pdf (accessed 24 October 2016).

Levy, A. (2015) *Suicides of Four Victims in Pensions Fraud Scam*. Available at: http://www.dailymail.co.uk/news/article-3066637/Suicides-four-victims-pension-fund-scam-Dozens-marriages-said-collapsed-families-lose-homes-scandal.html (accessed 24 October 2016).

Marsh, I. (2004) *Criminal Justice: An Introduction to Philosophies, Theories and Practice*. London: Routledge.

McCarthy, J. (2014) *The Teenagers Falling Victim to Internet Sex Scams – and the Welsh Web Warrior Who is Fighting Back on Their Behalf*. Available at: http://www.walesonline.co.uk/news/wales-news/teenagers-falling-victim-internet-sex-7623687 (accessed 24 October 2016).

Office of Fair Trading (2006) *Research on Impact of Mass Marketed Scams*, London: Office of Fair Trading.

Pascoe, T., Owen, K., Keats, G. and Gill, M. (2006) *Identity Fraud: What About the Victim*, Leicester: Perpetuity Research and Consultancy International.

Shannon, L. (2016) *Tasmanian Woman Charged Over '$3m Money laundering Operation'*. Available at: http://www.abc.net.au/news/2016-04-20/money-laundering-charges-against-tasmanian-woman/7341188 (accessed 24 October 2016).

Smith, D. (2012) *South African Police Rescue Asian Pair Kidnapped in 419 Scam*. Available at: https://www.theguardian.com/world/2012/jan/13/south-african-police-419-scam (accessed 24 October 2016).

Smith, R. G., Holmes, M. N. and Kaufmann, R. G. (1999) Nigerian advanced fee fraud. *Trends and Issues in Crime and Criminal Justice*, no. 121, Canberra: Australian Institute of Criminology. Available at: http://www.aic.gov.au/media_library/publications/tandi_pdf/tandi121.pdf (accessed 21 October 2016).

Spalek, B. (1999) Exploring the impact of financial crime: A study looking into the effects of the Maxwell scandal upon Maxwell pensioners. *International Review of Victimology* 6(3): 213–230. Doi: 10.1177/026975809900600304.

Spalek, B. (2006) *Crime Victims*, Basingstoke: Palgrave.

Sullivan, R. (2016) *Sharon Armstrong Spent Two Years in an Argentinian Jail After Being Caught in an Online Dating Scam*. Available at: http://www.news.com.au/lifestyle/sharon-armstrong-spent-two-years-in-an-argentinian-jail-after-being-caught-in-an-online-dating-scam/news-story/200a2a7e68566f203fc76fbf10174a96 (accessed 24 October 2016).

Telegraph (2009) *Bernard Madoff Fraud Victim Committed Suicide to Avoid Bankruptcy Shame*. Available at: http://www.telegraph.co.uk/news/uknews/5503929/Bernard-Madoff-fraud-victim-committed-suicide-to-avoid-bankruptcy-shame.html (accessed 24 October 2016).

The Australian (2014) *Nigeria 'Scammer' Orowo Jesse Omokoh Held Over Death of Australian Jette Jacobs*. Available at: http://www.theaustralian.com.au/news/nation/nigeria-scammer-orowo-jesse-omokoh-held-over-death-of-australian-jette-jacobs/story-e6frg6nf-1226817168140 (accessed 24 October 2016).

US Department of Justice (2016) *Nigerian Scammer Convicted of On-line Romance Fraud*. Available at: https://www.justice.gov/usao-sdil/pr/nigerian-scammer-convicted-line-romance-fraud (accessed 24 October 2016).

Walklate, S. (2007) *Imagining the Victim*, Maidenhead: McGraw Hill/ Open University Press.

Whitty, M. and Buchanan, T. (2012) *The Psychology of the Online Dating Romance Scam*, Leicester: University of Leicester. Available at: https://www2.le.ac.uk/departments/media/people/monica-whitty/Whitty_romance_scam_report.pdf (accessed 24 October 2016).

Whitty, M. and Buchanan, T. (2016) The online dating romance scam: The psychological impact on victims – both financial and non-financial. *Criminology and Criminal Justice*, 16(2): 176–194. Doi: 10.1177/1748895815603773.

5

BLAMING THE VICTIM

Introduction[1]

Despite the substantial impact that fraud can have on individual victims, many who experience fraud have the additional burden of being blamed (either directly or indirectly) for their own circumstances. It was well established in the previous chapter, the severity and extent to which online fraud can devastate a person's life. Unfortunately, many victims also experience additional trauma at the hands of their family, friends, and the criminal justice system more broadly. A persistent and strong attitude of victim blaming, evident with respect to online fraud victims, exacerbates the harm that has already been experienced. This chapter will explore the negative consequences that victim blaming has in relation to online fraud victims. It explores the early work of scholars in developing victim typologies and illustrates how these have been used to hold victims responsible and accountable for their own actions. In addition, this chapter will examine the negative stereotype of fraud victims, which asserts victims as greedy, gullible, uneducated and somewhat deserving of their victimisation. This chapter will use a number of case studies to highlight the operation and effects of victim blaming, and will also draw directly from research undertaken by the authors on this topic.

An introduction to victimology

Since the emergence of 'victimology' in 1940 (Burgess, Regehr and Roberts, 2013: 76), there has been a substantial amount of focus on the role of the individual victim and their part in causing or contributing to their victimisation (Dignan, 2005; Walklate, 2012). Many of the victim typologies that have been established derive from victim precipitation theory, which focuses heavily on the level of guilt and responsibility borne by victims in contributing to their victimisation (Wilcox, 2010). Many of these typologies can be viewed as a continuum of blame, from the completely innocent to the fully culpable. Collectively, many victim typologies reinforce the perception that victims should be able to avoid victimisation, through modifying and regulating their own actions and interactions with potential offenders (Wilcox, 2010). For example, Mendelsohn proposed one of the earliest victim typologies, which ranged from those who are completely innocent, those with minor guilt and responsibility from their own ignorance, those who are as guilty as the offender and share equal responsibility, those who are slightly guiltier than the offender (in terms of provocation), those who are exclusively responsible for their victimisation, and lastly, imaginary victims, who suffer no actual harm but falsely accuse another party (Burgess et al., 2013: 77). Subsequent victim typologies have maintained this focus on the degree of guilt and responsibility of the victim, including Fattah's five categories of victims, from the non-participating victim, to the predisposed victim, the provocative victim, the precipitating victim and the false victim (Burgess et al., 2013: 76).

Another type of victim typology focuses on the relationship between the victim and offender, and is evident in the work of von Hentig who put forward 13 victims, based on their degree of culpability exhibited in the incident (Dignan, 2005: 32). Furthering this, Schafer put forward a typology that sought to combine the work of Mendelsohn and von Hentig, and proposed seven victims – unrelated victims, provocative victims, precipitative victims, biologically weak victims, socially weak victims, self-victimising victims and political victims (Burgess et al., 2013: 80). Schafer's typology draws attention to the previously mentioned idea of victim precipitation, which explicitly attributes a level of blame to the victim for their victimisation and therefore implies that victims can take actions to prevent their victimisation (Burgess et al., 2013: 80).

Holding individual victims responsible for their own circumstances and therefore ascribing blame and guilt to them has not decreased over the past decades, with many still having the strength and momentum to explain today's incidents of crime victimisation. This has been particularly the case for victims of family violence, rape and sexual assault, and while there has been a large amount of critique levelled towards victim-focused explanations in these contexts (see Bieneck and Krahé, 2011; Suarez and Gadalla, 2010; Thapar-Björket and Morgan, 2010) on the basis that they perpetuate the idea of 'victim blaming', both the discipline and society has been unable to eliminate this influence entirely. This is particularly evident in the case for victims of online fraud.

The ideal victim

Nils Christie (1986) wrote a seminal piece entitled 'The Ideal Victim'. In this, he argues that 'being a victim is not a thing, an objective phenomenon. It will not be the same to all people' (Christie, 1986: 18). This alludes to a broader argument whereby he states that the 'victim' label is not given to all victims equally, and that there are factors surrounding both the individual themselves, the offender and the situation, which contribute to one being afforded 'victim' status. He proposed the concept of the 'ideal victim', who 'when hit by a crime – most readily [is] given the complete and legitimate status of being a victim' (Christie, 1986: 18). The example proffered by Christie was a little old lady, who was robbed by a man, as she was on her way home during the day after caring for her sick sister. The five attributes seen to be of importance to this example are as follows:

1. The victim was weak (sick, old or very young people are particularly suited as ideal victims).
2. The victim was carrying out a respectable project – caring for her sister.
3. She was where she could not possibly be blamed for being – in the street during the daytime.
4. The offender was big and bad.
5. The offender was unknown and in no personal relationship to her.

(Christie, 1986: 19)

The strength of this example lies in a combination of the personal characteristics of the victim with the circumstances surrounding the offence. There is no notion of culpability or responsibility for the woman, and therefore she is afforded 'victim status' without question.

The influence of the 'ideal' victim is evident in current understandings of fraud victims. Unfortunately, this operates to counter the narrative, whereby fraud victims are seen in contrast to that of the ideal victim. The following section breaks down some of the negative stereotypes and misconceptions that surround online fraud victims.

The stereotype of online fraud victims

The key element to any fraud offence is that of deception and it can be difficult for an outsider to understand how a victim can be deceived into sending large amounts of money from an online solicitation. On this basis, there is strong discourse that attributes blame and responsibility toward victims of online fraud and believes that they should be held accountable for their actions (Cross, 2013). At the most basic level it can be argued that, without their participation, no victim would be defrauded, online or otherwise. However, this fails to acknowledge the complexity of how many victims are targeted and the highly skilled offenders who manipulate and exploit victims through sophisticated social engineering techniques (Drew and Cross, 2013). Many offenders successfully identify the weaknesses and vulnerabilities of potential victims, create a situation that appeals to this weakness or vulnerability, and therefore increase the likelihood of a positive response and compliance by the victim (Drew and Cross, 2013). The victim believes in the legitimacy of the situation that is presented to them, and is unable to distinguish the fraudulent nature of the communication until it is too late.

The stereotype of fraud victims as greedy, gullible, uneducated and somewhat deserving of their victimisation can be seen to stem from the previous discussions on victim typologies and the ideal victim. In the case of online fraud victims, they are held as responsible and culpable for their victimisation, given their actions in sending the money to the offender in the first place. They are understood to be complicit in the offence. On this basis, online fraud victims are seen to be in opposition to the 'ideal' victim outlined by Christie (1986). Far from being blameless and innocent, these individuals are seen as collaborators in their own downfall, and therefore deserving of neither victim status nor sympathy.

There is a common perception that victims of online fraud are motivated by greed, and this personal attribute works to alienate victims from the notion of an ideal victim, or any victim status. This was particularly strong in research undertaken by Cross (2013) with a group of seniors (aged 50 years and over) who had received fraudulent email approaches, but not responded. They put forward the following observations of victims.

> The Nigerian scams, I mean the structure of the messages you know are clearly absurd, I've heard people say especially the police it's just pure greed that draws them in and I would imagine it is just pure greed.
>
> *(Elliott, 72 years)*

> There is that incredible sense of greed that we all have when we think we can get something for nothing.
>
> *(Vince, 58 years)*

> Apart from my first thought that you have got to be a bloody idiot, all they can see is money. A quick way of getting money and all they can see if I do this I will get money and nobody will know about it.
>
> *(Roberta, 69 years)*

These comments indicate a belief that greed is the driving factor in the decision to respond to a fraudulent email request, and focus strongly on the actions of the individual victim. This is further illustrated through the following comment.

> Nobody's making you do it are they. Nobody is holding a gun to your head saying you've got to do this. No it's irresponsible, they thought it through, they must be thinking they are getting something for nothing. Could be the old greed thing, I don't know. Everybody wants to win the lotto.
>
> *(Russell, 66 years)*

There is a clear sentiment that those who respond to fraudulent approaches are driven by greed as the overriding force. What is interesting to note, is that this was also evident in those who had responded to a fraudulent email approach, albeit with personal details, rather than sending money. The two following quotes come from seniors who responded, but still held these same beliefs around the greed of victims.

> Greed, opportunists but I think something for nothing sort of thing they still believe in the free lunch or whatever it is, that we've been told does not exist. Is it greed, well maybe that's a bit harsh, I think people get involved to see if there's really something in it for them … Yeah I think that [it is] greed and I think people perhaps go down those paths, thinking that they're going to get all that money.
>
> *(Nicholas, 62 years)*

> They are greedy. They are out for money that they don't earn, they didn't earn. The money that they shouldn't claim and really if they respond to them, they are being dishonest.
>
> *(Cynthia, 65 years)*

This presents a tension between the actions of some individuals in their responding to fraudulent approaches and their attitudes towards others who respond. While neither Nicholas nor Cynthia sent money, the use of personal information can be as valuable as cash, and can be used to perpetrate identity theft in an effort to convert the stolen identity to cash. It also illustrates the dilemma whereby Nicholas and Cynthia believe in the greed of other victims, but do not perceive their own actions in the same way. While they construct other respondents to be greedy, they disassociate themselves from the same discourse.

The pervasiveness of the victim-blaming discourse, particularly as it relates to the concept of greed, is evident in the views of victims themselves. Within this same study, Cross (2013) highlights how even those who were victims and in some cases lost over a couple of hundred thousand dollars, still framed their involvement in the approach through the lens of individual greed. The following comment is from Patrick, who was involved in an inheritance fraud and while not sending large amounts of money, flew overseas and put his life in physical danger as well as losing the costs associated with his travel.

> In the back of your mind is probably that bit of extra money, that dollars and cents. We are ruled by the dollars and cents in the world and you know yourself if you haven't got money, or you are out of work, no one wants to know you … But down the road we are only human beings and we think, yeah, righto, we are going to get a bit out of it and in the meantime we get burnt trying to get that extra dollar that we think we can. That's why we go and buy lotto tickets … that bit of greed we get, and it depends how much [we] hunger for it and if you don't look at the dollars and cents behind yourself, you are just gone.
>
> *(Patrick, 61 years)*

These comments indicate a level of greed present, albeit in a weaker and less direct form compared to those quoted earlier. However, another victim, Hazel, reiterated the strong greed narrative associated with her own victimisation. She was involved in an investment fraud, which saw her lose over AU$300,000 as well as involve some of her friends in the scheme. In reflecting on how she became a victim, she put forward the following.

> I think it is greed. I really think it is greed … It is absolute greed. And even to get a million dollars is not easy out here unless you win lotto so you are driven by greed. And anyone who says anything else is a liar. You just think oh no, it will work out. All along, because you are told the money will go in your account, you think they can't dud you because the money has got to go in your account. But they do dud you because the money never gets into your account.
>
> *(Hazel, 64 years)*

This quote illustrates the fact that personal experience does not necessarily counter the greedy stereotype which is prevalent amongst those within this study. Rather, both victims and non-victims alike put forward arguments which subscribe to the idea that online fraud victims are greedy. This focuses very heavily on the personal attributes of an individual and consequently understands victimisation to be victim driven. It also implies that victims are to blame for their own circumstances, in what can be seen as a direct result of their own motivations.

There was only one victim in this study by Cross (2015), who explicitly sought to challenge the greed narrative associated with online fraud victimisation.

INTERVIEWER: There are others as well who have said that responding to these types of emails, you are trying to get something for nothing, so to speak, despite the fact that you have sent a lot of money, how would you respond to that type of statement?

MARTHA: Getting something for nothing? No one can get something for nothing. I mean anyone has to pay for something. You can't get something for nothing. You have to pay. You order something over the internet and you have to pay for it. It is the same type of thing. You are getting all this money so you have to pay for all the certificates and everything. I mean if I ordered another birth certificate over the internet I still have to pay for it.

(Martha, 63 years)

Martha was the victim of an inheritance fraud and this comment points to the expectation on her behalf that costs would need to be paid in order to claim the inheritance. This was the vulnerability that offenders seized upon with success over a period of time. While this comment does not counter the greed discourse which was prominent across the rest of the study, it does provide an insight into the thought processes of a victim involved in such a situation. It may also assist with understanding how victims can be defrauded over a long period of time, months and even years in some cases.

In addition to the perception that online fraud victims are greedy, is an assumption that they are also more gullible and less educated than those who do not respond. The following quotes are from seniors who did not respond to a fraudulent approach and were asked to reflect on why others might respond.

> Obviously if you reply to one, you are an idiot as far as I am concerned. They are pretty bloody ridiculous … But I can't believe that people are so dumb? What do you do with them?
>
> *(Henry, 60 years)*

> I suppose I have been aware of this [fraudulent emails] for a long time and the scams I mean you would be an unintelligent dope if you didn't because there has been plenty in the newspaper and plenty on television about [it].
>
> *(Audrey, 60s)*

> I reckon that it is so obvious and so obviously false that I now know that what I am about to say is wrong, but my thinking was nobody would be stupid enough to respond to that surely, but apparently they do.
>
> *(William, 73 years)*

These comments demonstrate how the focus of victimisation is placed squarely on the decisions and actions of the victims themselves. There is a distinct notion that the victim should have been able to identify the approach as fraudulent, and as a result, should have been able to avoid victimisation.

Overall, the negative stereotype of online fraud victims as greedy, gullible, uneducated, and therefore responsible and somewhat deserving of their victimisation was clearly evident in the study of Cross (2015, 2013). It is clear that notions of individual guilt and responsibility fall on the shoulders of the victims themselves, rather than the offenders who perpetrate these offences. In this way, categories within the victim typologies that point to individual culpability are most prevalent in understanding online fraud victimisation. In addition, fraud victims are seen to have violated the 'ideal' victim status. This arises out of their perceived cooperation in the offences (through sending their money/personal details) and a belief that they should have known better than to put themselves in that situation. As Christie (1986: 25) notes, 'victims that merge with offenders make for bad victims'. In this regard, those who experience online fraud are seen as 'bad victims'.

There are substantial consequences, which evolve as a result of the dominant victim-blaming attitude towards online fraud victims. It is to these impacts that the chapter now turns.

The consequences of the victim-blaming attitude

As noted in earlier chapters, fraud has one of the lowest reporting rates across all crime categories. Studies across the United Kingdom, United States of America, Canada and Australia estimate that less than a third of all victims report fraud victimisation to authorities (Mason and Benson, 1996; Schoepfer and Piquero, 2009; Smith, 2007; Smith, 2008a; Titus, Heinzelman and Boyle, 1995). There is also evidence to suggest that reporting of online incidents occurs at an even lower rate than fraud in an offline environment (Smith, 2007; Smith, 2008b). In seeking to understand the reasons behind non-reporting, the sense of shame and embarrassment on being a victim and a fear of how others will react to this is one of the most pressing challenges for victims. This largely stems from dominance of the victim-blaming attitude established in the previous section.

For many victims of online fraud, the impact of the fraud is only one of the issues that they face in the aftermath of their victimisation. In addition to dealing with the financial and non-financial losses (as outlined in Chapter 4), victims must also navigate the often difficult and traumatic road of disclosure to family, friends and third parties, such as law enforcement. Given the strong victim-blaming attitudes that are in existence, this compounds the harm already being experienced. In examining how this operates, the following section explores the role of humour, and its use as a means to reinforce the individual culpability of online fraud victims, and both minimise and trivialise subsequent victimisation.

There is a wealth of literature, which examines the role that humour and laughter play in the well-being of individuals, particularly their ability to cope with stress, anxiety and negative situations (for some examples see Capps, 2006; Fox, 1990; Lefcourt and Martin, 1986; Moran and Hughes, 2006; Nezlek and Derks, 2001). This research concludes that humour reduces the impact of stress (Capps, 2006: 396) and that 'a sense of humour permits one to better cope with the aversive experiences of life' (Lefcourt and Martin, 1986: 63). Therefore humour can be understood as an effective coping mechanism (Nezlek and Derks, 2001: 395) and such research has been particularly focused in examining the ways in which emergency service personnel and others in highly stressful occupations (such as social work and counselling), cope with the trauma and negativity that they witness on a daily basis (Moran and Hughes, 2006; Rowe and Regehr, 2010).

In the context of emergency service personnel (such as police, fireman and emergency department workers), there is recognition of a particular type of humour, known as black humour or gallows humour, which serves as a means of 'venting their feelings, eliciting social support through the development of group cohesion and distancing themselves from a situation, ensuring that they can act effectively' (Rowe and Regehr, 2010: 450). This type of humour is neither understood nor appreciated by those outside these occupations, however its operation is an important way of enabling these individuals to process their experiences and gives them the ability to distance and protect themselves from such high levels of trauma (Rowe and Regehr, 2010: 455–456). There is also emerging research into the area of disaster response, which argues that black humour can be understood as a more general phenomenon rather than simply within the realm of emergency personnel (Ellis, 2003). While Cross (2015) argues that the seniors within the current research sample cannot be compared to the emergency service personnel or those experiencing a major disaster, it was posited that the research does provide a platform through which to understand how humour operates in the context of online fraud.

At an individual level, when asked about their response to a fraudulent email, several seniors who had not responded to a fraudulent email, detail laughter and disbelief as their key reactions.

INTERVIEWER: What do you think when you read a [fraudulent] email like that?
ROBERTA: Give me a break. Whoa. Oh yeah, I suppose some idiots might believe that ...You have got to be kidding.

(Roberta, 69 years)

INTERVIEWER: What did you think when you read that [fraudulent] email?
ESTELLE: Laughter, I knew exactly what it was.

(Estelle, 64 years)

> The first time or two you think this is just too silly for words ... Because they're just so ridiculous.
>
> *(Prue, 72 years)*

> Some of them are a good read as far as a bit of a laugh, so you might forward them on sort of thing, other[wise] they are just an out and out hoax.
>
> *(James, 67 years)*

On the basis that humour is understood as a defence mechanism in the context of online fraud, humour allows seniors to distance themselves from the possibility that they may be vulnerable to potential fraudulent attempts. By joking about the perceived trivial nature of the fraudulent email attempts, it allows seniors to avoid having to think of themselves as potential victims. This can also be seen to extend to both family and friends.

INTERVIEWER: Do you speak about these emails with your friends or family?
LILLIAN: Oh yes, I say to them I have won another hundred thousand dollars today and they say good on you. They wouldn't reply either, I am sure, none of my friends or family would reply to anything like that. I don't know.

(Lillian, 75 years)

Rowe and Regehr (2010: 459) argue that humour can enhance social cohesion and promote social support. In addition, Pogrebin and Poole (1988) argue that humour promotes solidarity through the acknowledgement of a common perspective. Collectively humour is used to bond people together in differentiating themselves from those who respond, and this is notably evident through laughter and jokes. Seniors are able to do this because there is a common acceptance that fraudulent emails are absurd.

INTERVIEWER: So what did you think when you received the email?

BRUCE: Not another one of these! No my comment was, you wouldn't want to believe this dear, but I have won another $6m!

INTERVIEWER: So you spoke to [wife] about it?

BRUCE: Yes I just called out and laughed...

...

INTERVIEWER: So you have spoken to your friends about these types of emails?

BRUCE: Oh yeah. We always laugh about them.

(Bruce, 66 years)

...

INTERVIEWER: So when you received these emails, did you speak to [husband] about them?

BESSIE: We were going through them and saying 'oh there's another one' and [husband] was saying 'oh just delete it'. That was it. You would just delete it and just move on. You would just have a look and say here we go again... [You] just shake your head, you think it is silly. It's like getting the junk mail in your letterbox, you sort out what you want... but the rest just goes in the bin without you even looking at it, the rest just goes in the bin.

(Bessie, 62 years)

While each of the previous comments have been provided by those who had not responded to a fraudulent email, the use of humour was also observed to extend to those who had responded and in some cases, were victims. This was across both individual and collective settings.

INTERVIEWER: So what did you think? Can you talk me through what you thought when you read it [lottery email that he didn't respond to]?

WALTER: No, I laughed. I regarded it as a hoax.

(Walter, 60 years)

> I like to open it [fraudulent email] and read it and [husband] and I have a laugh over it, about all the mistakes in it and the offer of millions of dollars. But that is all. Then I delete them, but it annoys me that I am having my email channels clogged up with this sort of rubbish.
>
> *(Cynthia, 65 years)*

Both Walter and Cynthia responded to a fraudulent email request (Walter, who lost both personal information and money as the result of a fraudulent job opportunity and Cynthia, who lost personal information pursuing an illegitimate inheritance), yet both of them still attribute the same level of hilarity to other fraudulent emails. However, humour in the context of online fraud does not only appear through jokes made by seniors about the types of fraudulent emails they have received, but it also is evident through the manner in which the emails are trivialised and dismissed by many individuals.

INTERVIEWER: So have you spoken of these types of email to friends or family? Does it come up in conversation?

CARL: Not me, I think [wife] more so. I find it's just a nuisance; I couldn't be worth having a conversation about it.

(Carl, 66 years)

INTERVIEWER: Do you talk about these types of emails with your friends or family?

LEE: Yeah, sometimes we do. Because early in the stages they were all coming from Nigeria and now they're all over the world you know, it's only recently China's come into it yeah.

ANNA: So we sort of laugh a bit about it you know, take it as oh well they're at it again, but it's sad that people still look at it and get caught.

LEE: We only see them as nuisance.

(Anna and Lee, 50s)

In the context of online fraud, framing their own perceptions and conversations in a joking and playful manner allows seniors to reinforce to themselves and each other they are not vulnerable to victimisation, that they are different to people who respond, or in the case of respondents, different to other people who respond. The ability of seniors to openly joke about online fraud with each other only occurs because there is a consensus about the image of an online fraud victim. As has been illustrated, this differentiation or 'othering' exists in a social context of greed, gullibility and responsibility. In this way, humour can be seen to operate as a tool to reinforce this negative and disapproving portrayal of their actions. Moreover, by perpetuating a victim-blaming discourse, the use of humour has the potential to isolate online fraud victims and prevent them from disclosing to family, friends and authorities.

The use of humour in this way sets up additional barriers for victims to disclose to their family, friends and third parties. Many victims are afraid of how others will react to their situation. Cross (2015) demonstrated that while some victims were able to disclose to family and friends, they still internalised the shame and stigma associated with the consequences of their behaviours and were also met with derision.

INTERVIEWER: So did you tell any of your friends or family about this?
ELSIE: I told my family about this. I haven't told anybody else, because it is too embarrassing.

(Elsie, 81 years)

INTERVIEWER: So did you tell your family about it?
RICHARD: Yeah.
INTERVIEWER: And how did they react when you told them?
RICHARD: All laughed, but also disappointed.

(Richard, 71 years)

INTERVIEWER: Have you told anybody about what has happened to you? Did you tell your wife or your sons or anyone like that?
CONRAD: ... I have told a few other people but not many. I don't particularly want to let everyone know that I am a fool.

(Conrad, 76 years)

Elsie, Richard and Conrad were each able to disclose their victimisation to family or friends, however, all had internalised their own culpability in their victimisation. In terms of derision the family's laughter at Richard's situation is a prime example of how humour manifests itself towards victims of this type of crime. While humour can be a common response to a traumatic event and a coping mechanism of a person confronted with a negative event, in this case, humour is also used to reinforce disappointment. Interestingly, the examples of Elsie, Richard and Conrad, are also worth discussing because each were victims of a phishing email, whereby they sent credit card details, bank account details or a small amount of money to offenders. In terms of online fraud, phishing was viewed as a lesser type of fraud in Cross (2015) as there is a greater acceptance about how a person can become such a victim. It is also the case that compared to other victims in this research, who sent hundreds of thousands of dollars overseas, the experiences of Elsie, Richard and Conrad were quite minor, since each was able to take swift action to stop further losses, through means such as cancelling credit cards and changing passwords. Thus, while the victim-blaming discourse was still evident, the context of the victimisation meant that disclosure was not as potentially devastating for these victims.

In contrast, other victims had revealed limited details of their experiences to family and friends. For example, Ruth had told her daughter incomplete details of her involvement in a romance fraud and felt anxious about discussing the finer points during the interview.

INTERVIEWER: So how much money do you think you sent across?
RUTH: A lot. I will tell you the amount when my daughter is not around.

(Ruth, 53 years)

For Ruth, disclosing to her family the full amount of money she had lost carried with it too many risks, which included not only embarrassment and stigma in the eyes of her daughter, but also challenges to her capacity to maintain an independent lifestyle. Being the victim of online fraud was seen as indicative of decreasing mental capacities and in this sense, demonstrates the victim-blaming discourse at its most extreme. This was a fear for a number of elderly victims who were not able to disclose to anyone.

INTERVIEWER: Did you ever tell anybody while you were sending the money?
JUDITH: No.
INTERVIEWER: Did you ever discuss it with any of your family or friends?
JUDITH: No I was too ashamed.
INTERVIEWER: Have you told anyone since this happened?
JUDITH: … No I have not because it is still an embarrassment to me. I am starting to accept that it is my fault and I have been gullible and I have been caught out and it is just something that I have got to accept that my hard earned money is gone.

(Judith, 60 years)

INTERVIEWER: Have you told anybody about what has been happening?
MARTHA: No.
INTERVIEWER: No?
MARTHA: No. No one knows. No one knows. I dare not tell anyone because they will turn and say well you are a stupid idiot and they will walk away from me and I don't want that, I don't want that … so no one knows what is going on.
INTERVIEWER: What about your son?
MARTHA: No.
INTERVIEWER: How do you think he would react?
MARTHA: He would disown me. He would disown me and I wouldn't see my grandchildren ever again. That is why I can't tell him. He would hit the roof. It is me only that knows. No one else.

(Martha, 63 years)

The examples of Judith and Martha highlight the fear and isolation that many victims feel. For both of these women, there is no foreseeable way in which they feel they can tell their family or friends what has happened and seek the support they need. The establishment of the victim-blaming discourse and its reinforcement through the use of humour by others has a number of consequences for victims. First, it acts as a barrier to disclosure. Based on the small amount of available research, the well-being of victims and their recovery is premised on the level of support and encouragement they receive from their support network. In the case of many online fraud victims, their ability to use their support network is disabled through fear and shame. This leads to the second consequence, which is the isolation accompanying the victim-blaming discourse. This is augmented by the prevalence of humour as derision and diminishes further the capacity for disclosure, as illustrated by the comments of those who had not responded to a fraudulent email, detailed below.

INTERVIEWER: Do you know of anyone who has responded?
SAMUEL: No. Not personally, no. I think they would all know my views about it so strongly that unless it was over a beer, I don't think anybody would tell me.

(Samuel, 82 years)

ROBERTA: I actually haven't spoken to any of my friends about these emails. I just look at them and think, yeah ok. Stupid. Stupid people answer them obviously. Otherwise they wouldn't keep sending them.

(Roberta, 69 years)

PRUE: I suppose, most of our friends are quite cluey or if they got caught they would never say [laughs], I'm sure they wouldn't.

(Prue, 72 years)

EDWIN: I don't know of anybody within our village here that has been caught, but if they have, they probably wouldn't say so ... The person isn't going to say 'I was stupid and I did something silly,' you know, so whether in fact the odd person does get caught, we wouldn't know.

(Edwin, 79 years)

These comments are largely premised on an attitude that does not attribute any degree of sincerity towards victims of fraudulent emails. For the most part, these comments are fairly dismissive of the emails and fail to acknowledge the possibility that someone they know may respond and need support. Such attitudes then contribute to the barriers experienced by individuals who find themselves victims of fraud.

Based on the degree of victim blaming that exists towards those who respond, many victims perceive a strong, negative reaction from family and friends if they were to disclose details of their victimisation. As the following excerpts demonstrate, this level of anxiety is not necessarily irrational.

INTERVIEWER: How would you react say, if one of your children came to you and told you they had responded to one of these emails and lost a substantial amount of money?
GLADYS: I would probably say how stupid were you?
HARRY: I don't think any of them would because we have told them about this. We warned them.

(Harry and Gladys, non-respondents, 65 years)

INTERVIEWER: So say your husband or one of your friends came to you and told you that they had responded to one of these emails and lost a substantial amount of money how do you think that you would react?
FELICITY: Honestly I'd think what an idiot.

INTERVIEWER: Yes?
FELICITY: I would.

(Felicity, non-respondent, 59 years)

INTERVIEWER: Hypothetically, if one of your children or if [wife] came to you and told you that they had responded to one of these emails and they had sent a lot of money, how do you think you would react to that?
HENRY: I would probably blow my tool big time. I mean once it is done there is not much you can do about it. I would just say, you are an idiot, you are going to do your dough.

(Henry, non-respondent, 60 years)

In addition to these types of responses, there was also a strong element of disbelief on the part of non-respondents that anyone in their family or friendship circles could actually become a victim of online fraud.

INTERVIEWER: Hypothetically, if one of your friends or family told you they had responded and they had sent a lot of money, how do you think you would react to that?
RUSSELL: I would be just surprised for starters, but I'd doubt if it would happen. I don't think any of them are that stupid. Or hope not. But no I can't see them doing it, I would be very surprised. Shocked actually. I couldn't see them being that stupid.

(Russell, non-respondent, 66 years)

INTERVIEWER: If one of your friends came to you and told you that they had responded to one of these emails and had sent a lot of money, how do think you would react to that?
MILDRED: If they had lost it … I would be horrified – but I can't imagine any of them doing it.

(Mildred, non-respondent, 80 years)

There was only one response that avoided the victim-blaming discourse evident across others' comments, and advocated a subtler approach.

INTERVIEWER: If a friend or family member told you that they had responded to one of these emails and that they'd lost a lot of money, how do you think you would react to that?
FRANCIS: You've got to be in their position see, you got to answer very carefully, I would be sympathetic and understanding and advise them to go to the appropriate people and tell them what's going on, even if it does make you feel very bad and whatever … appropriate authorities need to be aware of it.
INTERVIEWER: So would that be like banks or Police or …?
FRANCIS: That's exactly right, yes.

(Francis, non-respondent, 53 years)

While the response given by Francis was not the dominant reply, it does provide evidence that challenging the pervasiveness and negativity of the victim-blaming discourse is possible.

It is interesting to note that the experience of victimisation did not necessarily temper the negativity towards other victims of online fraud. Conrad is a unique example in the study of Cross (2015). He was initially interviewed as someone who had received fraudulent emails but had never responded to them. Like many of those above, Conrad held a belief that victims were somehow different.

> Well maybe they are a little bit more deficient than I am in the grey matter? I am not sure but they [victims] must respond otherwise why would they [offenders] keep on doing it?
>
> *(Conrad, 76 years)*

However, in the weeks following his interview, Conrad responded to a business investment invitation and lost a small amount of money. When interviewed a second time and asked whether this had changed his initial views on victims, he did not demonstrate a softening in his ideas.

INTERVIEWER: Having become a victim yourself, have your attitudes towards those who do respond changed? So last time you were fairly strong against people who had responded …

CONRAD: Against those ones that you know, well to me, they were evidently, it would have to be a con job. Particularly some of those, Mr So and So is visiting from Hong Kong and he died over here and his bank account he opened here has so much in it and his name is similar to yours and some such thing… Well to me, they are so evidently a con. But this other thing, unfortunately it wasn't.

(Conrad, respondent, 76 years)

There is clearly a strong discourse focused on victims of online fraud, which is premised on guilt and blaming the individual for their own actions. The majority of seniors interviewed were unrepentant in their views towards victims and expressed strong judgemental attitudes towards any potential victim. This presents as a difficult barrier for many victims to overcome, and reinforces the failure of victims to disclose the incident to those around them.

For some victims, the anxiety associated with how their families will react is very real. This can be exacerbated for older victims of online fraud, who fear that their victimisation will be seen as a sign that they have lost competency, and may compromise their ability to maintain financial and physical independence. In a study interviewing volunteers who provide telephone support to older fraud victims across Canada, Cross (2016) noted the following examples.

> Family members can cause a big problem … I have been told that sons have been very, very hard on mothers because they feel they are losing their

> capacity, mental capacity, emotional capacity, everything … I've had it to the point where they've [sons] taken away their banking privileges, they've taken away their mail privileges, they limit, they limit them to very little outside access, and they cut off their telephone calls too. They will actually block telephone calls … So, all of a sudden the victim is cut off from everything, from all communication.
>
> *(interview 4)*

> I said 'have you got close friends and relatives that you can talk to?' 'I can't tell my kids that, they'll put me away in a nursing home'.
>
> *(interview 17)*

These two examples provided by volunteers who work with older fraud victims, illustrate the potential consequences faced by older victims in disclosing to their family about what has happened. Not only do these victims fear the shame and stigma associated with being a victim of fraud, but it also has the additional threat of being judged and labelled as having lost or impaired capacity. This was an additional source of stress and anxiety and contributes to the non-disclosure and isolation experienced by many victims.

In addition to online fraud victims experiencing stigma from their families and friends, there is evidence to demonstrate that their interactions with the criminal justice system are a further source of trauma. This is particularly focused on the reporting experiences of victims, in seeking to lodge a complaint with police in response to their incident. For many victims, they experience direct victim blaming about what has occurred. For example, Button et al. (2009: 37) documented the unsympathetic response received by investment fraud victims, first by the police, and second, by the criminal justice system itself in England.

> And even when I've spoken to, the police at times about it the, vocal reaction was like, 'Well, you're the mugs with your money, you're the fools with your money. It's your fault'. And it seems to be that … was the general way they felt it… they are speaking to me. It's like, well, you know, you're the fool mate. And I… there wasn't a great deal of seemingly sympathy. And that, that's just the feeling I got from the, the vocal type of reaction… It just didn't seem to me that they seemed to care. It was like, oh, if we catch him we catch him, if we don't, too bad.
>
> *(Roger, investment fraud victim)*

> The worst thing for us was when they did the actual court case, the judge said that we were all wealthy arrogant people that wanted to get on the bandwagon of hedge fund investment … He did. He just said that we were wealthy arrogant people … which was annoying 'cause we weren't. We were just normal people. Obviously, if my husband hadn't been involved we would never have got involved in it. We probably would've gone straight to the building society, paid off the mortgage and said, end

> of. Instead, we thought well could invest it, make a bit more from it, do something more for the children, that type of thing.
>
> *(Val, investment fraud victim)*

Both of these excerpts illustrate the negativity surrounding the victimisation of each person respectively. A similar situation was reported by Cross et al. (2016: 10) in a similar example in Australia.

> I said it was an investment fraud and she [police] said she had much more important things than that to deal with. [She said] 'We have people robbed at knife point'. I said [I had been defrauded of] $20,000. She said, 'But you gave it away sir', and I said, 'I didn't give it away, it was an investment'. She said it was voluntary and I gave it away. I ended up phoning up a few times but got nowhere.
>
> *(Investment fraud victim)*

> I expect [the police] to be sympathetic, but these two police guys – they just laugh[ed]. I was humiliated. They tell me, I submitted a police report, and I made a statement and they tell me, '[Victim's name], we cannot do anything about this with you and your lover boy in [overseas country], you just write to [Federal consumer protection website] Scamwatch'.
>
> *(Romance fraud victim)*

The treatment of online fraud victims within the fraud justice network is overwhelmingly negative, with the large majority of victims experiencing some degree of victim blaming. This leads victims to suffer additional trauma, first at the hand of the offender/s, and second, as the result of the current fraud justice network. The stigma and high levels of victim blaming associated with online fraud are relevant factors to the known levels of under-reporting for this particular crime type.

Conclusion

This chapter has examined the negative stereotype that surrounds online fraud victims and positions them as greedy, gullible, uneducated and somewhat deserving of their victimisation. Founded upon victim typologies that ascribe blame and responsibility to victims in certain circumstances it was argued that online fraud victims violate the notion of the ideal victim put forward by Christie (1986). This stems from their involvement in the crime, through the sending of money or personal details to offenders. However, this ascription of individual culpability ignores the role of the offender and their ability to skilfully manipulate and exploit potential victims.

Overall, online fraud victims are not readily given the status of 'victim', rather, they encounter strong victim-blaming attitudes by family, friends, law enforcement and other agencies. There is also evidence to suggest that victims internalise this guilt and blame themselves for their situation. The role of humour was also examined as a means of reinforcing notions of blame, through seeking to trivialise victimisation. The establishment of victim as 'other' was also illustrated through comments of seniors, who did not believe that they themselves, their family or their friends, could possibly become victims of online fraud. This is problematic for victims of fraud in their confidence and ability to disclose to those around them and seek the support they need. It is also problematic in terms of prevention, which is explored in further chapters.

Note

1 This chapter first appeared as Cross, C. (2015) No laughing matter: Blaming the victim of online fraud. *International Review of Victimology* 21(2): 187–204. Doi: 10.1177/0269758015571471.

References

Bieneck, S. and Krahé, B. (2011) Blaming the victim and exonerating the perpetrator in cases of rape and robbery: Is there a double standard? *Journal of Interpersonal Violence* 26(9) 1785–1797. Doi: 10.1177/0886260510372945.

Burgess, A., Regehr, C. and Roberts, A. (2013) *Victimology Theories and Applications*, 2nd edition, Burlington: Jones and Bartlett Learning.

Button, M., Lewis, C. and Tapley, J. (2009) *A Better Deal for Victims*, London: National Fraud Authority.

Capps, D. (2006) The psychological benefits of humor. *Pastoral Psychology* 54(5): 393–411. Doi: 10.1007/s11089-005-0007-9.

Christie, N. (1986) The ideal victim. In: Fattah, E. (ed.) *From Crime Policy to Victim Policy*, New York: St Martins Press, 17–30.

Cross, C. (2013) 'Nobody's holding a gun to your head …': Examining current discourses surrounding victims of online fraud. In: Richards, K. and Tauri, J. (eds) *Crime, Justice and Social Democracy: Proceedings of the 2nd International Conference*, Crime and Justice Research Centre, Queensland University of Technology, Queensland University of Technology, Brisbane, QLD, 25–32. Available at: https://eprints.qut.edu.au/61011/ (accessed 21 October 2016).

Cross, C. (2015) No laughing matter: Blaming the victim of online fraud. *International Review of Victimology* 21(2): 187–204. Doi: 10.1177/0269758015571471.

Cross, C. (2016) 'They're very lonely': Understanding the fraud victimisation of seniors. *International Journal for Crime, Justice and Social Democracy* 5(4): Online first. Doi: 10.5204/ijcjsd.v5i4.268.

Cross, C., Richards, K. and Smith, R. G. (2016) The reporting experiences and support needs of victims of online fraud. *Trends and Issues in Crime and Criminology*, no. 518, Canberra: Australian Institute of Criminology. Available at: http://aic.gov.au/publications/current%20series/tandi/501-520/tandi518.html (accessed 25 October 2016).

Dignan, J. (2005) *Understanding Victims and Restorative Justice*, Berkshire: Open University Press.

Drew, J. and Cross, C. (2013) Fraud and its PREY: Conceptualising social engineering tactics and its impact on financial literacy outcomes. *Journal of Financial Services Marketing* 18: 188–198. Doi: 10.1057/fsm.2013.14.

Ellis, B. (2003) Making a big apple crumble: The role of humor in constructing a global response to disaster. In: Narvaez, P. (ed.) *Of Corpse: Death and Humor in Folklore and Popular Culture*. Logan: Utah State University Press, pp. 123–140.

Fox, S. (1990) The ethnography of humour and the problem of social reality. *Sociology* 24(3): 431–446. Doi: 10.1177/0038038590024003005.

Lefcourt, H. and Martin, R. (1986) *Humor and Life Stress: Antidote to Adversity*. New York: Springer-Verlag.

Mason, K. and Benson, M. (1996) The effect of social support on fraud victims' reporting behaviour: A research note. *Justice Quarterly* 13(3): 511–524. Doi: 10.1080/074188296 00093071.

Moran, C. and Hughes, L. (2006) Coping with stress: Social work students and humour. *Social Work Education* 25(5): 501–517. Doi: 10.1080/02615470600738890.

Nezlek, J. and Derks, P. (2001) Use of humor as a coping mechanism, psychological adjustment, and social interaction. *Humor* 14(4): 395–413. Doi: 10.1515/humr.2001.011.

Pogrebin, M. and Poole, E. (1988) Humor in the briefing room: A study of the strategic uses of humor among police. *Journal of Contemporary Ethnography* 17: 183–210. Doi: 10.1177/089124188017002003.

Rowe, A. and Regehr, C. (2010) Whatever gets your through today: An examination of cynical humor among emergency service professionals. *Journal of Loss and Trauma: International Perspectives on Stress and Coping* 15: 448–464. Doi: 10.1080/15325024. 2010.507661.

Schoepfer, A. and Piquero, N. (2009) Studying the correlates of fraud victimisation and reporting. *Journal of Criminal Justice* 37: 209–215. Doi: 10.1016/j.jcrimjus.2009.02.003.

Smith, R. G. (2007) Consumer scams in Australia. *Trends and Issues in Crime and Criminal Justice*, no. 331, Canberra: Australian Institute of Criminology. Available at: http://www.aic.gov.au/media_library/publications/tandi_pdf/tandi331.pdf (accessed 21 October 2016).

Smith, R. G. (2008a) Coordinating individual and organizational responses to fraud. *Crime Law and Social Change* 49: 379–396. Doi: 10.1007/s10611-008-9112-x.

Smith, R. G. (2008b) Raising public awareness of consumer fraud in Australia. *Trends and Issues in Crime and Criminal Justice*, no. 349, Canberra: Australian Institute of Criminology. Available at: http://www.aic.gov.au/publications/current%20series/tandi/341-360/tandi349.html (accessed 21 October 2016).

Suarez, E. and Gadalla, T. (2010) Stop blaming the victim: A meta-analysis on rape myths. *Journal of Interpersonal Violence* 25(11) 2010–2035. Doi: 10.1177/0886260509354503.

Thapar-Björkert, S. and Morgan, K. (2010) 'But sometimes I think … they put themselves in the situation': Exploring blame and responsibility in interpersonal violence. *Violence against Women* 16(1) 32–59. Doi: 10.1177/1077801209354374.

Titus, R., Heinzelman, F. and Boyle, J. (1995) Victimisation of persons by fraud. *Crime and Delinquency* 41(1): 54–72.

Walklate, S. (2012) Who is the victim of crime? Paying homage to the work of Richard Quinney. *Crime Media Culture* 8(2): 173–184. Doi: 10.1177/1741659012444433.

Wilcox, P. (2010) Theories of victimisation. In: Fisher, B. and Lab, S. (eds) *Encyclopedia of Victimology and Crime Prevention*. Thousand Oaks: Sage, pp. 977–985.

6

'FORGOTTEN VICTIMS'

Supporting those who experience fraud

Introduction

Compared to many other victims of crime, fraud victims have not experienced the same support and interest of agencies (Button et al., 2009; Cross et al., 2014). There are several factors which impact on the recognition of fraud victims as legitimate victims and their ability to access general support services. This chapter examines the concept of providing support to fraud victims and the type of support required by fraud victims. To begin, it outlines the main challenges that currently prevent victims from seeking support services. Second, it will highlight some of the main support needs that are largely unmet. Lastly, it will provide some examples from across the world where this is beginning to change. It will present examples of the limited but diverse support mechanisms available to victims and highlight some good practice in some countries. Examples such as face-to-face support groups and telephone counselling services will be outlined. Before these issues are considered, however, the chapter will address some of the barriers to supporting victims.

Problems with supporting victims: getting support

As previously detailed in Chapter 4, the impact of fraud on individual victims can be devastating. Despite the widely held belief that fraud is a 'victimless' crime and not as serious as other types of crimes, the research suggests a different reality. Instead, there is evidence to suggest that the impact from fraud can be as severe as that felt by those who experience violent crime (Marsh, 2004) and has a wide range of financial and non-financial consequences. Unlike other types of crime, victims of fraud in many countries are often not able to access the victim support services that could assist with their recovery. There are several complex issues which contribute to the lack of support services available. These will be covered in turn.

As previously stated, fraud has one of the lowest reporting rates across many crime types. Studies across the UK, USA, Canada and Australia have estimated that less than one-third of all fraud is reported to authorities (Mason and Benson, 1996; Rebovich and Layne, 2000; Schoepfer and Piquero, 2009; Titus et al., 1995). This is thought to be even less for fraud perpetrated in an online environment (Smith, 2007, 2008). If a person does not report their incident, this reduces the likelihood that they will be given access to any victim service. While there are limited support services available (explored further in this chapter), those which do exist generally have law enforcement as a point of referral. With such low rates of reporting, it is inevitable that the majority of victims will not be able to access any support services available.

There are other factors which relate to the low reporting of fraud which can also be seen to contribute to an inability of victims to gain support. This includes a lack of acknowledgement or recognition that victimisation has occurred. For many individuals, there is uncertainty as to whether a crime has occurred and therefore it may be dismissed. For others who believe that a crime has occurred, in attempting to report the incident, they are often told that there is no crime and therefore they are not victims (Cross et al., 2016a, 2016b). Therefore, despite the significant impact that they have experienced, they are unlikely to further attempt to access any support mechanisms if what they have experienced is ignored, minimised or trivialised.

The negative reporting experience of fraud victims is another critical factor that inhibits victims from seeking support (Cross et al., 2016a, 2016b). As previously stated, fraud is unique compared to other crimes, whereby in most countries there is a network of agencies in addition to law enforcement, who are able to take a complaint. However, there is strong evidence to suggest that the existence of multiple agencies actually hinders the ability of victims to report their situation, as agencies will often avoid responsibility and pass a person from one department to another. Termed the 'merry-go-round' effect, there is strong evidence to demonstrate the negative reporting experiences faced by many fraud victims (Button et al., 2009). The level of frustration in not having an agency acknowledge what has occurred or take a complaint can re-traumatise victims and exacerbate the severity of harm they have already experienced (Cross et al., 2016a, 2016b).

Further to the negative reporting experience, there is a pervasive belief that fraud is somewhat of a 'victimless' crime (Gee in Button et al., 2010). There is also a tendency to disregard the effects of fraud on an individual, and assume that there are simply monetary costs which victims need to move on from. This attitude can be very destructive for victims, who can experience a diverse range of impacts across a spectrum, from minimal financial losses to severe, life destroying consequences, whereby the person either attempts or completes suicide (Cross et al., 2016a, 2016b). The impact of fraud on victims will differ depending on a variety of factors, and the amount of money is not necessarily the defining characteristic. In addition, there are certain types of fraud which are more devastating than others. For example, romance fraud victims suffer a 'double hit' of victimisation, where they must grieve the loss of the relationship as well as any financial loss incurred (Whitty and Buchanan, 2016). For some victims, the loss of the perceived relationship is actually more difficult to deal with than the financial losses incurred (Cross et al., 2016a).

The negative stereotype of fraud victims combined with the shame and stigma associated with fraud victimisation further impedes victim's access to support (Cross, 2013; 2015). For many victims, the prospect of disclosing their victimisation to family and friends is surrounded by fear of how they will react. For many victims this is not unfounded, with family and friends reacting very negatively towards the victim. An unwillingness to share their experiences with others means that many victims will suffer the effects of their victimisation in silence and in isolation. In many circumstances, the offender has specifically sought to isolate the victim from their usual support network in an attempt to maintain the relationship with the victim and enable their exploitation of the victim financially. In these circumstances, it is then very difficult for victims to re-establish their relationships with family and friends to gain the support they need once the fraud is over.

The stigma associated with fraud victimisation can be exacerbated for older victims of fraud, in that victims are afraid to tell their family about their experience because they are afraid of how their family will react. In many cases, the older person may have lost a large amount of money, which is the inheritance of their child/ren. As a result, there is a lot of guilt experienced by older victims at having lost the inheritance and a subsequent anxiety around telling their child/ren what has occurred (Cross et al., 2016a).

In addition, older victims are fearful that the fraud victimisation will be understood as an indicator that they have lost the capacity and the ability to take care of themselves both physically and financially. Older victims are terrified that they will lose their financial independence, and that their child/ren will remove this. It is important to realise that online fraud victimisation is not necessarily an indicator of diminished or impaired capacity. The types of fraudulent approaches which are directed at older persons can be very sophisticated and complex, and can be specifically targeted to the individual circumstances. There is usually a grooming process involved, where the offender/s will seek to establish high levels of trust and rapport with the victim in order to manipulate and exploit them. The development of this relationship (romantic or otherwise) is the key for offenders to get financial rewards and they will do whatever is needed to ensure compliance. This can make it very difficult for third parties (such as family, friends, or law enforcement) to break that relationship.

The fear of how family will react to the news of fraud victimisation is real, and in some cases, this has manifested itself in abuse. The following excerpt is from a volunteer who provides telephone support to older fraud victims in Canada and illustrates this point.

> Family members can cause a big problem, can be a real hardship for the victim, especially where there are mothers and sons involved … I have been

> told that sons have been very, very hard on mothers because they feel they are losing their capacity, mental capacity, emotional capacity, everything. And so if sons are, are very hard on them, and they can be belligerent, I've had, I've had calls like that, they can be really cross to mothers and belittle them and make them feel very, very small and unworthy, and so I've had them, I've had it to the point where they've taken away their banking privileges, they've taken away their mail privileges, they limit, they limit them to very little outside access, and they cut off their telephone calls too. They will actually block telephone calls … So all of a sudden the victim is cut off from everything, from all communication and it's very hard on us [older people], very demeaning and, so that victims find that very, very difficult (volunteer).
>
> *(Cross, 2016b: 12)*

This quote illustrates the severity of consequences that an older person can experience as a result of disclosing their victimisation to family members, in this case, their children. While this specific example was from Canada, it is not uncommon in other countries. Cross et al. (2016a) detail other examples where an older fraud victim has told their family what happened, and as a result, have been cut off and disowned in response. In one case, a woman was forced to live in her car for several months, as she had no options and her family would not provide her with any support (Cross et al., 2016a). Given the high levels of fear and anxiety around disclosing, the majority of older victims choose not to tell their family or anyone else about what has happened (including professionals such as doctors, counsellors and psychologists). This means that they suffer in silence and isolation and the impacts of the fraud can be exacerbated without any ability to access either formal or informal support. Unfortunately, there are several circumstances where family members have reacted very negatively towards an older fraud victim and this perpetuates the lack of reporting and disclosure of this particular crime type.

The last significant barrier to accessing victim support rests with legislative definitions of 'victim' and the eligibility criteria used to access services in the aftermath of crime. For example, within the majority of Australian states and territories, statutes covering victim support services stipulate that only victims of 'violent crime' are eligible. For example, section five of the *Victims of Crime Assistance Act 2009* (Queensland) defines a victim as one,

> Who has suffered harm (a) because a crime is committed against the person; or (b) because the person is a family member or dependant of a person who has died or suffered harm because a crime is committed against that person; or (c) as a direct result of intervening to help a person who has died or suffered harm because a crime is committed against that person.

However, the Act further defines the eligibility of those to receive financial assistance in section 21, which stipulates 'this chapter establishes a scheme for the payment of financial assistance … to a victim of an act of violence'. This means that fraud victims, who by definition are categorised as victims of non-violent crime, despite potentially experiencing similar levels of harm, are not able to access any assistance to fund services such as counselling or financial counselling. Queensland is not the only jurisdiction to define a victim in this way, and preclude their eligibility to receive any financial assistance in the aftermath of their victimisation. This lack of recognition within legislation reinforces the belief that fraud victims suffer minimal losses, which do not deserve any state-funded assistance. This is despite the research that suggests evidence to the contrary (Marsh, 2004). Similarly, in England and Wales only victims who have experienced violence/injury are able to claim compensation through the Criminal Injury Compensation Authority (Button et al., 2009).

Overall, there are many barriers which hinder the ability of fraud victims to access support services. The low levels of reporting, an inability or unwillingness to acknowledge victimisation, the negative reporting experience, the shame and stigma associated with fraud victimisation, a perception that fraud is an indicator of diminished or impaired capacity, and legislative restrictions on what constitutes a 'victim' all contribute to the lack of access and inability of fraud victims to seek both informal and/or formal mechanisms of support. Sadly, for those victims who do attempt to seek support, the experience can often be detrimental and further exacerbate the level of harm already experienced. As detailed, it is not uncommon for victims of fraud to detail incidents of victim blaming or denial of the reality of what they have experienced. In these instances, victims are left further frustrated and incur an additional trauma from the reporting experience itself (Cross et al., 2016a).

The needs of fraud victims

It is clear that there is a complex array of factors that prevent many fraud victims from accessing support services to assist in the aftermath of their victimisation. While there has been much research which has established the needs of other categories of victims, there has been little research which has explored the specific needs of fraud victims (see Button et al., 2009; Cross et al., 2016a; Kerr et al., 2013). In the research by Button et al. (2009) on various victims of frauds, a variety of needs were identified by them, as set out in Table 6.1. Not surprisingly one of the highest-rated needs (second) with 96.8 per cent indicating five or more (on a scale of one to seven) was getting their money back. The top need, however, at 97 per cent was the fraudster being found guilty, and third at 95 per cent was tougher penalties, followed by getting the case investigated at 94.2 per cent. Also high at 92.1 per cent was hearing progress on their case and the fraudster being dealt with in another way (alternative sanction) at 91.3 per cent. These needs could all be grouped around justice-related needs.

Other high scoring needs were single point of contact and place to secure information at 91.2 per cent and 86.1 per cent respectively; combined with a

TABLE 6.1 What victims wanted as response to their experience of fraud (Button et al., 2009: 69)

Characteristic of response	*Numbers*	*% giving a response of 3 or less*	*% giving a response of 5 or more*	*% giving a response of the maximum 7*
A sympathetic and understanding response	687	9.0%	83.0%	Less than 50%
Having someone to listen to your experiences	674	25.2%	63.0%	Less than 50%
A single point of contact	682	4.3%	91.2%	55.10%
A single point to secure information	671	9.0%	86.1%	50.50%
Getting your money back	685	1.0%	96.8%	91.70%
Getting your case investigated	691	2.9%	94.2%	77.00%
Hearing progress on your case	689	4.5%	92.1%	57.30%
Fraudster being found guilty	693	1.9%	97.0%	81.50%
Tougher penalties for fraudsters	675	1.8%	95.0%	78.70%
Fraudster being dealt with in another way	665	4.5%	91.3%	71.60%
Getting support to get over the fraud	624	32.0%	58.0%	Less than 50%
Support in giving evidence in court	564	10.6%	83.7%	Less then 50%
Face-to-face help from Victim Support	593	38.6%	48.6%	Less than 50%
Names of other victims to develop mutual support	652	46.8%	40.6%	Less than 50%
Getting advice on not being a victim again	682	11.1%	81.2%	Less than 50%
Receiving general information on scams, etc.	686	9.9%	83.8%	Less than 50%

sympathetic and understanding response at 83 per cent. The same score was also achieved for getting support for giving evidence in court. Also scoring in the 80s were getting advice on not being a victim and general information on scams. Some of these broader issues will be considered below. It is of course important to note the needs of victims will vary even amongst those experiencing the same fraud with similar losses.

The following provides an overview of some of the most significant needs expressed by fraud victims to assist with their recovery.

A formal response through the criminal justice system or other relevant system

Some of the most important needs relate to justice and the desire for their case to be investigated, the offender caught and an appropriate sanction applied. As will be noted later in this book fraud offences are particularly blighted with the problem of attrition where many offences even when reported are not investigated or even if they are, do not result in a criminal prosecution and conviction. For many fraud victims this is a devastating finding, particularly when they may think they have evidence which will help identify the fraudster and/or other useful leads. Given the opportunities for civil and regulatory action, which often exist, this often further adds to the frustrations. Such needs were noted by interviewees in the research by Button et al. (2009: 77):

> then Trading Standards said they couldn't do anything because they didn't have enough resources. So he (the father) said, well I've given you evidence that I've been the victim of the scam, you're telling me somebody else has and you're not going to do anything about it. So then he had a loss of confidence in Trading Standards, what's the point in talking to them, they can't do anything, they won't do anything.
>
> *(Lisa, daughter of chronic scam victim)*

> So the police pretty powerless, couldn't really do anything, which is horrendous. I mean this guy had actually paid in a cheque. You would have thought when I notified ##### went into the bank and said right this is fraudulent and they said oh well we've got a copy of him actually paying in a cheque here last week, and they must have CCTV, they must be able to go and do something about it, but no they had nothing, and the police didn't. Here we are, the police … Erm … we have reviewed the crime but so far there is not enough evidence to continue further enquiries. Not enough evidence, I've got correspondence here with you know paper and papers and papers, we've got proof that they've been into #### and paid the cheques in, erm … I don't know what more they need really, anyway.
>
> *(Dean, identity fraud victim)*

Getting money back and/or compensation

Many identity fraud victims do get their money back if it is clear they showed no negligence, but for most other victims this is not likely. However, it is not surprising that victims articulate a need to get their money back or some kind of compensation. As has already been noted in this chapter, often when there are compensation schemes fraud victims are excluded. There are, however, often opportunities for the criminal courts to mandate compensation if the offender is caught and they have assets, or if that is not feasible, for the victims to pursue civil litigation against the offender or some other body that may have been negligent and which contributed to the fraud being successful. For example, it has been reported that over 25,000 claims from victims of the Madoff Ponzi investment fraud have been validated for compensation, with many securing their original investment monies from assets confiscated from Madoff by the prosecutors (Madoff Victim Fund, 2016).

Prevention advice and information

It is well known that victims of fraud are highly likely to be targeted in the future for additional fraudulent schemes or for recovery schemes. Victim's details can end up on what are known as 'suckers lists', which is a list that contains the details of known victims and is traded by offenders (Cross et al., 2014). This then provides a foundation for other offenders to target victims with new types of schemes (for example, an investment fraud victim may be approached to invest in a similar or different but equally fraudulent scheme). Recovery schemes are different, in that the victim is approached by an offender purporting to be able to assist them with the recovery of their lost funds (FTC, 2016). For example, a victim may be approached by 'law enforcement' stating that the offenders have been arrested and are awaiting prosecution. However, in order for the police to continue with the investigation, the victim will need to pay an additional amount of money to fund the legal proceedings. In addition to advice specific to their fraud, victims often want general information about scams and support services and groups that might be of use to them. A very strong theme is also the desire for information on what is happening with their case. This is further illustrated by Button et al. (2009: 72–73) in some of the extracts from interviews with fraud victims below.

> There may be other scams coming up which you don't know, not just financial, it could be anything, eh, yes, it would help because that would stop further scams, you know, being created and also stop people from sending their own hard earned money to these scams.
>
> *(Participant 7, Focus Group 2)*

> Just basically an update really. Either by telephone or by letter explaining what's been going on and sort of ... so at least you know that it's still being pursued.
>
> *(Roger, investment fraud victim)*

> I think they could have informed me of what they were doing about it, with the addresses that I gave them. I couldn't have given them any more information than I did actually, what they did want was the actual cheques that I'd sent.
>
> *(Hilda, victim of lottery fraud)*

In some countries the fragmented response to supporting and dealing with fraud cases leads to confusion in who to go to and different and sometimes conflicting messages being given by agencies. In the research by Button et al. (2009) a recurring theme was a single point of contact and reporting. This research, along with other developments, was central in leading to the establishment of Action Fraud, which will be discussed in more depth later in Chapter 7.

Formal and informal support

In one of the only studies to explicitly examine social support as it relates to fraud victimisation, Mason and Benson (1996: 520) found that 'friends and family members strongly influence how fraud victims respond to their victimisation'. This reflected an increase in reporting to police resulting from encouragement by family and friends to come forward, compared with a marked decrease which resulted from discouragement by family and friends (Mason and Benson, 1996: 520). The results of this study indicate how vital informal support can be to fraud victims, as well as illustrating the harm caused by the ongoing effects of victim shaming and blaming which currently exists with this category of crime victims.

In addition to seeking informal support, victims may also find benefits in pursuing formal support means. Given the large degree of depression experienced by the majority of fraud victims, counselling or therapy with a psychologist or counsellor may be required to work through the psychological and emotional trauma experienced during and after the fraud incident. In particular, for the victims who express suicidal tendencies and ideation, their ability to seek professional support is critical to self-care and potential for recovery. Whereas, others may need more practical support, such as financial counselling. Despite the substantial financial losses incurred by online fraud victims, there is no present study that seeks to examine this particular area and so therefore a large gap exists in the current literature.

For many individuals, their victimisation places a great strain and tension on relationships with their family and friends. This can occur during the fraud (for example, if the victim is the main provider and loses money without saying why, or if the victim borrows money from others to continue their involvement), as well as after the fraud has been recognised and ended. The shame and secrecy of victimisation can have a detrimental impact on a wide range of relationships (spouse, parent, child/ren). Therefore, it may be advantageous to undertake relationship counselling to better understand how each of the parties is feeling and coping with the fraud. For some, the fraud victimisation may have been a symptom of a bigger issue, but for others the fraud victimisation may be the catalyst for the initial relationship breakdown.

The prospect of having to give evidence in court also spurs the needs of some of these victims who want a variety of support. This might include support on the process and what is likely to happen on the day, through to actual support on the day of the appearance when the victim might be particularly in need of support before and after giving evidence (Button et al., 2009).

Other needs

For many fraud victims, there is a strong need to simply be acknowledged as a victim, and for there to be recognition of what has happened to them. It is the inability of victims to receive this from agencies and family or friends, which can easily exacerbate the level of harm experienced by individuals. The ability of victims to tell their story is also an important factor.

The existence of a victim-blaming attitude towards fraud victims is common and is very unhelpful for victims. Many individuals already feel an internal sense of shame and embarrassment at having been defrauded in some way, and it is futile for others to reinforce this. Rather, victims need empathy and a reaction bereft of judgement.

An ideal response to fraud victims' needs

Fraud victims are not a homogenous group, therefore it is difficult to advocate for a singular or unified approach to providing victim support. Many factors will impact on the extent and severity of the harm incurred. Regardless of this, there are victims' charters implemented in various jurisdictions, which clearly articulate how victims are to be treated within the criminal justice system. For example, within Australia, each jurisdiction has a victim charter of some sort, which is generally enshrined in legislation. In 2013, the Australian government released a *National Framework of Rights and Services for Victims of Crime*, which set out five basic principles (said to mirror those in existing state-based victim charters). These five guiding principles were 'respectful and dignified treatment; information and access; justice and fair treatment; financial assistance; leadership and collaboration' (Standing Council on Law and Justice, 2013: 4).

It is clear from the existing research in Australia (see Cross et al., 2016a, 2016b) that online fraud victims are not being afforded treatment as stipulated in the National Framework, nor the victim charters (or equivalent) of each state or territory. This is evident in the large degree of direct victim blaming experienced, as well as the inability of victims to lodge a complaint and be taken seriously in the first place. The most recent research by Cross et al. (2016a) highlights the overwhelmingly negative experiences of online fraud victims at the hands of the current fraud justice network and the additional trauma incurred through attempting to report online fraud offences to authorities. Rather than being treated with respect and dignity, too often victims gave harrowing accounts where they were shamed, humiliated, ignored and their complaint was trivialised, minimised or not even acknowledged.

In England and Wales there have been a series of charters and codes for victims with the *Domestic Violence, Crime and Victims Act 2004* establishing the first statutory code. The latest version of this is the 'Code of Practice for Victims of Crime' of 2015 (Ministry of Justice, 2015). This sets a series of entitlements for victims, depending upon the severity of the crime, covering information about the case as it progresses (from investigation through to the court hearing), access to specialist services, the right to have a victim statement read to the court before sentencing, the right to opt into a victim contact scheme (where information is provided when the offender is due for parole release) to name some. Evidence from the research by Button et al. (2009) found the requirements at the time were not always being met for fraud victims (particularly on information updates). The establishment of Action Fraud has done much to fill many of the gaps that did exist and some bodies such as the Serious Fraud Office, who also had gaps, have done more to support victims since 2009 (Serious Fraud Office, 2016).

Those who experience online fraud have a variety of support needs that are currently not being met. While there are limited examples of support services dedicated to fraud victims (detailed in the following section), it should also be apparent that some of the needs of online fraud victims are comparable to the needs asserted by other types of crime victims. For example, the frequent levels of depression experienced by those in the aftermath of fraud may not be too dissimilar to that experienced by other crime victims. The grieving of a failed relationship in the example of romance fraud can be understood within existing frameworks of counselling offered by professionals to those in a similar situation outside of a fraudulent context. Consequently, fraud needs to have a greater recognition across society and within existing victim support services.

The misconceptions surrounding the perceived trivial nature of fraud and discourse of victim blaming need to be countered with the reality of fraud victimisation, and this needs to occur within professional circles as well as the wider society. The actual level of harm incurred through online fraud needs to be better understood and articulated. In this way, victims of fraud deserve to be able to access existing support services and professionals who can assist with their recovery, and in the absence of dedicated support services for this particular type of victim, it may be beneficial to integrate some of these needs into existing support mechanisms in place for other crime victims across the system.

Best practice examples from across the world

While the previous section examined the lack of support services currently available for victims of online fraud, there are limited examples from jurisdictions across the world, where the specific needs of fraud victims have been recognised and a support programme has been established. The following section provides details on a number of these programmes, and where possible, provides evidence of the positive impact that they are having for fraud victims.

Action Fraud and Victim Support (UK)

Within the UK, all victims of crime can access support through Victim Support, which is a national charity, largely staffed by volunteers. For those who are reporting fraud, as part of the reporting process in Action Fraud, all victims are asked about the severity of the impact of their crime as well as asking whether or not they would like to be referred to Victim Support for further assistance. If an individual consents to this process, the referral is made to Victim Support. Referrals can also be made to Victim Support for those who have reported fraud to their local police station. Victim Support initiates contact with the victim through a phone call (or letter if phone contact cannot be established), and has the ability to offer both emotional support and practical help. If required, face-to-face support can be organised through a network of agencies across the UK. The volunteers have the ability to meet with victims and provide ongoing support and assistance on a case-by-case basis. There are offices located throughout the UK, which increases the accessibility of victims to this service. It is important to note that fraud victims can also access Victim Support without a referral from either Action Fraud or local police. Action Fraud also provides a variety of services to victims and to those seeking information. These include:

- Referrals to relevant bodies (such as Victim Support, credit reference agencies, legal support, Cifas);
- Advice on preventing fraud and cybercrime;
- Fraud alerts; and
- Website with extensive resources.

Senior Support Unit (Canada)

The Senior Support Unit (SSU) is a telephone service which provides support to older victims of fraud (typically those aged 50 years and older). It is based at the Canadian Anti-Fraud Centre (CAFC) offices in North Bay, Ontario. The CAFC is a collaboration of the Royal Canadian Mounted Police (RCMP), Ontario Provincial Police (OPP) and the Competition Bureau Canada (CBC), and is the central reporting agency for fraud across Canada. It was originally established in 1993, as 'Project PhoneBusters' by a local member of the OPP with a colleague in the RCMP in North Bay, Ontario. It was initially solely focused on telemarketing fraud, which was prevalent in the local area at the time (CAFC 2015). However, as the extent of the fraud problem increased in prevalence and severity 'Project PhoneBusters' became the 'PhoneBusters National Call Centre' (PNCC) in 1997, which covered all of Canada, and 'SeniorBusters' was launched to provide support to older victims of fraud (CAFC 2015). In 2006, the PNCC was formally recognised as the central reporting agency for fraud across Canada, and in 2010 it was renamed the Canadian Anti-Fraud Centre, the name under which it operates today (CAFC, 2015). SeniorBusters changed its name to the SSU in 2014 and remains in operation today.

The SSU comprises approximately 50 volunteers who are all seniors themselves (CAFC, 2015). These volunteers provide telephone support to older victims and those identified as vulnerable to fraud. Volunteers receive referrals through complaints lodged to the CAFC by the victim, family members, or third parties. Once a referral is made to the SSU, a volunteer will call the person and offer support, advice and information. They may also refer the victim to other services or agencies if required (CAFC, 2015). The majority of referrals are from individuals who have reported a fraud and recognise that they have been victims. However, there are instances where a referral can come from a third party who is concerned for an individual. Depending on the circumstances of the victim, volunteers may continue calling on a regular basis until victims do not wish to receive further phone calls. This may last weeks, months or even years. The volunteers do not hold qualifications as counsellors or psychologists, rather they seek to provide peer support and an empathetic listening ear to other seniors who have experienced fraud. Volunteers may also perform data entry duties to assist with the collation of financial intelligence relating to fraud victims, rather than perform 'callbacks' (calling the victims of fraud). SSU volunteers provide support to victims across Canada, and some volunteers have the capacity to engage victims in both English and French.

Cross (2016a) examined the benefits of volunteers providing telephone support to older fraud victims, from the perspective of the volunteer themselves. Volunteers identified three aspects to their role: providing advice and warnings; providing a listening ear; and providing reassurance. In terms of their perceived impact on the victims they spoke with, this was overwhelmingly positive. Volunteers were able to detail instances where the victim was openly appreciative of their phone call.

> In most situations, people are willing to listen, they want to tell you their story, they accept the advice and they'll say, 'Thank you for caring, thank you for calling me, thank you for checking up on me'.
>
> *(Interview 14)*

> Most of them are quite thankful when you call them back, yep. I had two today, 'Thanks for calling, we're very glad you people are doing these things'.
>
> *(Interview 8)*

> Most of them are really appreciative that we've called them. Really appreciative. It's unbelievable. Some of them are crying, like, 'I had no idea'.
>
> *(Interview 11)*

In addition to general feedback, volunteers expressed specific cases where they felt their intervention was of benefit to the victim. This is illustrated in the following excerpt:

> One lady I just spoke of she wasn't, she wasn't alone and I dealt with her for almost a year and a half, just called her on a regular, weekly basis and her husband stopped talking to her, her family wouldn't talk to her, she kept hanging up on me … After about three months she finally said, 'yes, thank you for calling me, I've been so lonesome' … And she says, 'if I should hang up' she says, 'don't be alarmed it just means my husband came in'… After about a year and a half … she said to me, 'Well, thank you so, so much'. She was very, very kind about thanking me and couldn't express her appreciation. She [said], 'my husband's talking to me again'. Now she had lost her whole life savings and they had nothing.
>
> *(Interview 2)*

This demonstrates how the needs of fraud victims can change over time, and therefore their support needs will also need to be modified to suit the current situation. For this particular woman, once her husband started talking to her again, she no longer needed the support of the SSU volunteer. It also highlights the tension and stress that victims can experience within their own families and the isolation that many experience as a result of fraud.

Despite the general positivity, it must be acknowledged that there were circumstances where the support offered by SSU volunteers was not needed nor welcomed.

> Most are quite free to talk. There's other people that just hang up, say they've got call display and they're prepared, but most of them want to tell their story.
>
> *(Interview 19)*

> But then, you know, there are some people, they're very suspicious, very sceptical.
>
> *(Interview 14)*

> [There was] One woman last week who really cut me off … She was not trusting at all of a call coming in. She said, 'It's all been resolved and there really isn't anything left to discuss'. What do you do? Not much.
>
> *(Interview 7)*

Again, this highlights the different needs and wants of fraud victims, and mandates the need for a flexible approach to providing support to these individuals. While it was argued that the SSU volunteers provide a much-needed avenue of support for many older fraud victims across Canada, it must form part of an overall approach to victim support services.

Further to this, there are limitations to this model of support. The first is the referral mechanism of the CAFC. In order to receive a phone call from an SSU volunteer, the individual must have recognised their victimisation and made a report through the CAFC. Given the known under-reporting of fraud victimisation, this means it is likely that only a very small number of actual victims are reporting through the CAFC and are able to access the support required. Second, the use of telephone support may not always be appropriate in all circumstances (as demonstrated above). Volunteers may not always be the right person to provide support to a victim, dependent upon circumstances. There are likely to be instances where the expertise of a professional is required to engage a victim and assist with recovery.

Despite these limitations, the example of SSU provides an optimistic view of how volunteers can be used to provide telephone support for older fraud victims and highlights aspects for further discussion and action (Cross 2016a). The existing study indicates that there are positive outcomes to this type of support and advocates its merit for potential consideration and implementation into other jurisdictions.

Face-to-face support groups (Australia)

Within Australia, there has been the emergence of face-to-face support groups specifically targeted to victims of fraud. The first was established in Brisbane, Queensland, in late 2010. It was initiated by the Queensland Police Service (QPS) as recognition that fraud victims were unable to receive the support they needed from any mainstream victim services. The stated aim of the group is to 'help [victims] recover from what is not just a financial loss but a personal and emotional loss … This group encourages members to work through the feelings associated with being a victim of crime to becoming a survivor' (QPS, 2016). The main purpose of the group is to enable victims to come together in safe environment and to be able to share their story and speak openly about their experiences, and the consequences of their victimisation. The group provides a forum through which support can be gained through peer support, from those who have also been in their situation and therefore have a more nuanced understanding of the difficulties and challenges faced by fraud victims. The group is facilitated by members of the QPS, who provide a meeting space and organise guest speakers as required. The group has been meeting once a month since its commencement in 2010, and is open to victims as well as family members and friends of fraud victims.

The benefits of this group to those who have attended have been immense. While to date, there has been no formal evaluation of the support group, the benefits of the group are reliant upon anecdotal evidence received by the participants. In 2014, the television programme *Insight* aired an episode that focused specifically on the fraud victims support group. The following comments are taken from that episode and illustrate many of the positive sentiments expressed by those involved with the group.

> 'A lot of us, when we first come in, we feel stupid, we feel that we have been so vulnerable'.
>
> *(victim)*
>
> 'When we had the first meeting here, the room was full of sad people, there was a lot of pain in this room. It didn't take us very long to get over the pain'.
>
> *(victim)*
>
> 'You get to meet the different people, they take you under their wing, they have a little bit of a talk to you, you come again, and then you can't wait after that to come to the meetings because you come away, you are in amongst friends'.
>
> *(victim)*
>
> 'We have a laugh and a joke and you try to put a smile on other people's faces'.
>
> *(victim)*
>
> 'It is a big step to go out to people you don't know and let them know that you have become a victim … It's about helping each other in a non-judgemental way, and giving support to each other, realising that we have been through this together and by sharing your burden, it halves your burden' (police officer).
>
> *(SBS Insight, 2014 cited on QPS, 2016)*

In a similar vein to Queensland, the West Australian Police (WAPOL) and West Australian Department of Commerce commenced Project Sunbird in 2012 (explored in further detail in Chapter 8). This is a targeted approach to reducing online fraud victimisation in Western Australia. As part of this, a face-to-face support group was established in late 2014, called Relate Offline. This support group is based on the Queensland model, whereby it is facilitated by WAPOL who provide a meeting space and coordinate meeting times. The group is being led by a volunteer romance fraud victim, who is committed to improving the support options available to fraud victims. The group meets on a monthly basis and consists of approximately a dozen members. A formal evaluation is currently being undertaken to assess the impacts of the group as a face to face support mechanism as well as any avenues for improvement.

As witnessed with the telephone support model, there are limitations to face-to-face support groups. These primarily revolve around geographical location. The existing face-to-face support groups are very small in nature and restricted to a particular location, both run out of a police building. Fraud victimisation can occur across all geographical areas, urban, regional and rural, and therefore it is unlikely that this support model would be sustained outside of an urban centre in its present form, simply for logistical reasons. The hosting of a meeting in a police specific location may also act as a deterrent for victims seeking support and who may feel more comfortable in a more neutral environment.

Think Jessica (UK)

Think Jessica is a charity founded in 2007 by Marilyn Baldwin, whose mother had become a chronic scam victim losing thousands of pounds over five years and who had struggled to find support. Jessica received over 30,000 letters and became convinced by the scammers that her family were jealous of her forthcoming wealth, leading to tensions in family relationships and, because there was no diagnosed mental condition, the family were powerless to intervene. The charity seeks to raise the profile of victims of fraud and raise the profile of the dangers of postal, telephone and online scams to professionals, victims and families of victims. Think Jessica has a website with extensive resources (http://www.thinkjessica.com/), pursues poster campaigns and has produced DVDs. The founder, Marilyn Baldwin, is also a regular in the media and uses this to further raise the profile of the issue (Think Jessica, n.d.).

TransUnion (USA)

TransUnion has established a Fraud Victim Assistance Department, which is dedicated to assisting those who have experienced credit card fraud (in both offline and online contexts). It was established in 1992 and works with a range of agencies including law enforcement, to investigate and prevent credit card fraud. For those who have been affected, TransUnion can identify relevant accounts and provide advice on who to contact to reduce the harm incurred.

There are many other services similar to TransUnion across different countries, which seek to assist victims of credit card fraud with identifying and rectifying fraudulent credit transactions and accounts. One of the criticisms of this particular form of assistance is that it places the responsibility and onus of future prevention on the individual victim, through their need to place credit alerts on their name and accounts.

iDcare (Australia and New Zealand)

iDcare is the national support service for victims of identity theft across Australia and New Zealand. It operates out of the Sunshine Coast, Queensland, and comprises a small group of paid professional staff complemented by volunteers. It was established in 2014 and has been growing in demand since its inception.

Individuals can contact iDcare via an online form or through a call centre. Those who work at iDcare have a variety of qualifications, including counselling, psychology, information security, education, accounting, and programming. iDcare operates a National Case Management Centre, whereby it works with individuals who have had their credentials compromised. In addition, iDcare works with government agencies and businesses to prevent and respond to data breach incidents. Case managers at iDcare will formulate a response plan for the individual/organisation, which is tailored to their unique circumstances, and offer assistance on how best to respond to a compromise or misuse of personal information.

iDcare differentiates between personal credentials that have been compromised and those which have been compromised and subsequently misused. This is an important distinction and influences the advice and response plan tailored by the organisation for individuals. Similar to previous support services, iDcare relies upon the individual to recognise that there has been a breach of their personal information as well as report it.

Conclusion

This chapter has examined the various needs of fraud victims and outlined the current challenges that exist for these individuals in seeking to access relevant support services. Despite the lack of services which exist for fraud victims on a broad scale, this chapter has also highlighted some case studies from across the world which are seen to be best practice examples of what dedicated and specialised support can look like for fraud victims. It is recognised that the level and severity of harm on an individual as the result of fraud can differ greatly. However, it is argued that there is a need to give greater recognition and acknowledgement to the needs of fraud victims and seek to provide accessible services to those who require it. The examples outlined in this chapter are a sign of optimism for fraud victims worldwide, in that there are a number of dedicated services, which are emerging and which could be expanded to encompass a larger number of fraud victims. Further research and evaluation is required in this area.

References

Button, M., Lewis, C. and Tapley, J. (2009) *A Better Deal for Victims*, London: National Fraud Authority.

Button, M., Gee, J., Lewis, C. and Tapley, J. (2010) *The human cost of fraud: A vox populi*, London: Centre for Counter Fraud Studies and MacIntyre Hudson. Available at: http://www.port.ac.uk/media/contacts-and-departments/icjs/ccfs/cost-of-fraud.pdf (accessed 24 October 2016).

Canadian Anti-Fraud Centre (2015) *About the CAFC*. Available at: http://www.antifraudcentre-centreantifraude.ca/about-ausujet/index-eng.htm (accessed 21 October 2016).

Cross, C. (2013) 'Nobody's holding a gun to your head …': Examining current discourses surrounding victims of online fraud. In: Richards, K. and Tauri, J. (eds) *Crime, Justice and Social Democracy: Proceedings of the 2nd International Conference*, Crime and Justice Research Centre, Queensland University of Technology, Queensland University of Technology, Brisbane, QLD, 25–32. Available at: https://eprints.qut.edu.au/61011/ (accessed 21 October 2016).

Cross, C. (2015) No laughing matter: Blaming the victim of online fraud. *International Review of Victimology* 21(2): 187–204. Doi: 10.1177/0269758015571471.

Cross, C. (2016a) 'I'm anonymous, I'm a voice at the end of the phone': A Canadian case study into the benefits of providing telephone support to fraud victims. *Crime Prevention and Community Safety* 18(3): 228–243. Doi: 10.1057/cpcs.2016.10.

Cross, C. (2016b) 'They're very lonely': Understanding the fraud victimisation of seniors. *International Journal for Crime, Justice and Social Democracy* 5(4): Online first. Doi: 10.5204/ijcjsd.v5i4.268.

Cross, C., Richards, K. and Smith, R. (2016a) *Improving the response to online fraud victims: An examination of reporting and support*, Criminology Research Grant Final Report. Available at: http://www.crg.aic.gov.au/reports/1617/29-1314-FinalReport.pdf (accessed 21 October 2016).

Cross, C., Richards, K. and Smith, R. G. (2016b) The reporting experiences and support needs of victims of online fraud. *Trends and Issues in Crime and Criminology*, no. 518. Canberra: Australian Institute of Criminology. Available at: http://aic.gov.au/publications/current%20series/tandi/501-520/tandi518.html (accessed 25 October 2016).

Cross, C., Smith, R. G. and Richards, K. (2014) Challenges of responding to online fraud victimisation in Australia. *Trends and Issues in Crime and Criminology*, no. 474. Canberra: Australian Institute of Criminology. Available at: http://aic.gov.au/publications/current%20series/tandi/461-480/tandi474.html (accessed 21 October 2016).

Federal Trade Commission (2016) *Refund and Recovery Scams*. Available at: https://www.consumer.ftc.gov/articles/0102-refund-and-recovery-scams (accessed 25 October 2016).

Kerr, J., Owen, R., McNaughton Nicholls, C. and Button, M. (2013) *Research on sentencing online fraud offences*, London: Sentencing Council. Available at: https://natcen.ac.uk/media/205369/research_on_sentencing_online_fraud_offences.pdf (accessed 25 October 2016).

Madoff Victim Fund (2016) *Spring 2016 Update*. Available at: http://www.madoffvictimfund.com/ (accessed 25 October 2016).

Marsh, I. (2004) *Criminal Justice: An Introduction to Philosophies, Theories and Practice*. London: Routledge.

Mason, K. and Benson, M. (1996) The effect of social support on fraud victims' reporting behaviour: A research note. *Justice Quarterly* 13(3): 511–524. Doi: 10.1080/07418829600093071.

Ministry of Justice (2015) *Code of Practice for Victims of Crime*, London: Ministry of Justice. Available at: https://www.gov.uk/government/uploads/system/uploads/attachment_data/file/476900/code-of-practice-for-victims-of-crime.PDF (accessed 25 October 2016).

Queensland Police Service (2016) *Fraud Support and Recovery Group*. Available at: https://fraudandcybersafety.com.au/support_and_recovery/ (accessed 25 October 2016).

Rebovich, D. and Layne, J. (2000) *The national public survey on white collar crime*, Morgantown: National White Collar Crime Centre. Available at: https://www.ncjrs.gov/pdffiles1/Digitization/181968NCJRS.pdf (accessed 25 October 2016).

Schoepfer, A. and Piquero, N. (2009) Studying the correlates of fraud victimisation and reporting. *Journal of Criminal Justice* 37: 209–215. Doi: 10.1016/j.jcrimjus.2009.02.003.

Serious Fraud Office (2016) *Victims and Witnesses. Our Commitment to You*, London: Serious Fraud Office. Available at: https://www.sfo.gov.uk/publications/information-victims-witnesses-whistleblowers/ (accessed 25 October 2016).

Smith, R. G. (2007) Consumer scams in Australia. *Trends and Issues in Crime and Criminal Justice*, no. 331, Canberra: Australian Institute of Criminology. Available at: http://www.aic.gov.au/media_library/publications/tandi_pdf/tandi331.pdf (accessed 21 October 2016).

Smith, R. G. (2008) Raising public awareness of consumer fraud in Australia. *Trends and Issues in Crime and Criminal Justice*, no. 349, Canberra: Australian Institute of Criminology. Available at: http://www.aic.gov.au/publications/current%20series/tandi/341-360/tandi349.html (accessed 21 October 2016).

Standing Council on Law and Justice (2013) *National Framework of Rghts and Services for Victims of Crime 2013–2016*. Available at: http://www.victimsupport.org.au/UserFiles/File/SCLJ_Framework-2013-16.pdf (accessed 25 October 2016).

Think Jessica (n.d) *About Us*. Available at: http://www.thinkjessica.com/ (accessed 25 October 2016).

Titus, R., Heinzelman, F. and Boyle, J. (1995) Victimisation of persons by fraud. *Crime and Delinquency* 41(1): 54–72.

Whitty, M. and Buchanan, T. (2016) The online dating romance scam: The psychological impact on victims – both financial and non-financial. *Criminology and Criminal Justice*, 16(2): 176–194. Doi: 10.1177/1748895815603773.

7

POLICING AND PUNISHMENT FOR CYBER FRAUDS AND SCAMS

Introduction

In November 2014, Europol helped to coordinate a global action against airline ticket fraud. The action also involved Interpol and Ameripol, and 60 airlines across 45 countries and 80 airports, as well as the law enforcement from the relevant countries the action included the involvement of several major credit card companies and the International Air Transport Association. The action resulted in 118 arrests and 281 suspicious transactions being identified (Europol, 2014). This action illustrated many of the themes regarding the policing of fraud, which will be developed in this chapter. It demonstrated the wide range of bodies involved from many countries. It illustrated both the national and the international and the private for profit and not-for-profit sectors. For the many victims of credit card fraud who experience an unaccounted-for airline ticket on their statement which was the main target of the action, most would not realise the complexity and diversity of those who are involved in policing such a crime. Unfortunately such actions are not common enough and this, along with several other themes will be developed in this chapter.

The chapter will commence with a consideration of what is policing, and from that illustrate that the process of policing involves a very diverse set of organisations originating from the public, private and voluntary sectors. The chapter will focus upon those bodies, drawn from these sectors, which take an interest in fraud. It will do so using a classification which draws out from the general state police bodies and bodies from hybrid, private, voluntary and finally international policing. The chapter will go on to examine some of the challenges such mixed provision creates, before exploring a case study of good practice in policing in this area. The chapter will then move on to examine the punishment of fraudsters. It will note the problem of attrition, before examining some victims' views and expectations regarding punishment. The chapter will then explore criminal, civil and regulatory penalties that are used to deal with fraud before concluding.

Policing, pluralisation and fraud

Policing is much broader than the police. As Mawby (2003: 15) succinctly puts it,

> there is a marked difference between 'policing' as a process and 'the police' as an organisation. Policing, a term we might apply to the process of preventing and detecting crime and maintaining order, is an activity that might be engaged in by any number of agencies and individuals.

Policing as a process is therefore clearly undertaken by a wide range of individuals and organisations that go beyond 'the police' in the public, private and voluntary sectors. It is also important to note Crawford's additional insight (2003: 137), that 'policing may also be the product of new technologies ...' It would also be wrong to restrict policing to purely criminal acts, which some definitions imply. The importance of also considering order maintenance illustrates the wider reach and perhaps the definition offered by Jones and Newburn (1998: 18–19), which specified organised forms of 'rule of law enforcement', is a more useful phrase, particularly when considering the much more ambiguous position of many frauds. Extracting these policing key functions in relation to fraud in this book, it is important to note that policing encompasses:

> Organised responses to breaches of the law and this may include civil and regulatory as well as criminal.
>
> Those organised responses involve prevention activities and investigations of suspected breaches with the purpose of pursuing sanctions where possible.

This chapter will illustrate the very wide range and diverse types of organisations engaged in the policing of fraud. It will also demonstrate how researchers have neglected this aspect of policing. It will do so by largely using England and Wales, although examples from Australia, the USA and other countries will also be used.

Over the last three decades there has been a growing recognition amongst academics that the state police constitute only part, albeit a significant part, of the broader 'picture' of policing. Long established pockets of policing; changing structures in society, such as the growth of mass private property; combined with new public policy trends such as 'privatisation'; have resulted in a substantial complexity of policing provision drawn from the state, private and voluntary sectors (Johnston and Shearing, 2003; Loader, 2000; Shearing and Stenning, 1982). Much of the literature on policing has tended to focus upon the most visible and commercial elements of change, such as uniformed private security personnel patrolling public streets, guarding shopping centres, and escorting prisoners (Crawford et al., 2005; Cunningham et al., 1990; Sarre and Prenzler, 2011). There has, however, been a wide range of other areas of policing identified and classified. Button (2002) noted the following key areas of policing, drawing upon the others' research, as set out in Table 7.1.

TABLE 7.1 Classification of policing

State general police
Hybrid policing
Central and decentralised public policing bodies
Specialised police organisations
Non-private security policing bodies
Private
Voluntary policing

The state general police are the most visible and obvious policing body, whose functions vary from country to country but usually provide the uniformed presence on the streets, investigate most volume crimes and respond to many emergencies and incidents. In England and Wales, the Metropolitan Police in London undertake this role; in Sydney, the New South Wales Police Force and in New York, the New York Police Department. These bodies generally deal with fraud too and some have specialist sections, but as this chapter will later reveal, the priority and resources given to it is often low compared to other volume crimes.

'Hybrid' policing can be defined as 'those public and private bodies that are neither the public police, private security nor some voluntary initiative' that are engaged in policing (Button, 2002: 12). The 'hybrid' policing sector can be broken down into three further sub-categories. First there are central and decentralised public policing bodies, which are state bodies who have policing functions. For instance, in the United Kingdom there is a body called the Health and Safety Executive, which polices health and safety crime. As will be shown shortly, there are a number of bodies in countries that fit this category and which deal with fraud. Second, there are specialist police organisations. These are bodies that resemble the state police, but which operate in a specific area of responsibility. For example, in most countries the military have their own police, in the UK there is a specific police force for nuclear installations, called the Civil Nuclear Constabulary. Like the state general police they may deal with fraud-related cases. The final part of hybrid policing is the not-for-profit private bodies which are involved in policing in many countries. Charitable bodies involved in countering animal cruelty are the most prominent of these, such as the Royal Society for the Prevention of Cruelty to Animals (RSPCA), which investigates and prosecutes persons who have committed acts of cruelty against animals in England and Wales. There are, however, charitable bodies which also becoming involved in fraud-related cases, which again will be explored shortly.

The third significant contribution is the private sector, which encompasses a variety of commercial organisations that provide policing services for fees, with the aim of making a profit, or departments within organisations providing security/policing functions. There is a wide range of commercial bodies that offer fraud-related services, generally more for organisations rather than individuals. Again this chapter will explore some of these. Finally, there is voluntary policing.

This can be divided between that which is sanctioned by the state and that which isn't. The latter is vigilantism and this chapter will show small pockets of this in relation to fraud. State sanctioned voluntary policing tends to be initiatives that allow citizens to volunteer and support the police, such as the Special Constabulary in England and Wales. Again there are a variety of schemes that fit this category and which have been targeted at fraud.

Some of the more symbolic police functions, which have seen significant hybrid, private and voluntary involvement, have captivated the interest of a significant number of academics, such as patrol (see for example Crawford et al., 2005; Noaks, 2000; Rigakos, 2002; Sarre and Prenzler, 2011). The fragmented response to fraud, however, has been much less researched (Button, 2011). Thus, it is important to first consider the generally very thin blue line of state general police resources dedicated to fraud.

State general police dedicated to fraud

A study published in 2015 found only 624.3 police officers (and civilian investigators) dedicated to fraud in England and Wales, which represented 0.27 per cent of police personnel (Button et al., 2015a). Of course, the official police position would be that any police officer would be capable of dealing with a fraud-related case, but the reality would be that for many police officers fraud would be a very low priority and for a significant number of officers they simply would not have the capability to investigate a fraud-related case (Fraud Review Team, 2006; Levi, 1987; Loveday, 2016). The general state police resources in England and Wales are very thin. This is also the case in many other countries.

Table 7.2 identifies the main state general police-type organisations that serve the general public in dealing with fraud. In England and Wales there are

TABLE 7.2 The main general police bodies in England and Wales who deal with fraud

England and wales
Forty-three police forces based upon geographical area. Most have an economic crime unit, but not all. As noted earlier these account for a very small percentage of police personnel. Some forces also have cyber crime units, which would also deal with cyber frauds, amongst other cyber crime.
City of London Police has significant role as the lead police force on economic crime, it hosts the National Fraud Intelligence Bureau and Action Fraud.
The Dedicated Card and Payment Crime Unit is a private-funded police unit drawing on City of London Police and Metropolitan Police officers.
National Crime Agency (which is essentially a national police agency focused upon serious and organised crime) hosts an Economic Command and the National Cyber Crime Unit, both of which deal with certain types of fraud.
Serious Fraud Office is a national policing body focused upon very serious high value fraud.

43 police forces based on geographical areas and most (excluding four) have some form of economic crime unit (Button et al., 2015a). These vary in size and will deal with a wide variety of crimes that fall under this umbrella term, which go beyond the scope of this book, such as occupational frauds and bribery cases. They will generally have a healthy number of fraud and cyber fraud-related cases. Some police forces also have cyber crime units, which also become involved in fraud-related cases. The Metropolitan Police, since the Button et al. (2015a) research was conducted, has established a unit called FALCON, dedicated to online crime and fraud, which is well resourced and with an aspiration of 500 officers (although it is not known what the current staffing is). As the risk of online crime grows, this is likely to be replicated by other forces (Ring, 2014).

It is also important to note the City of London Police and their very important role in fraud. They are the national lead force and take the lead on certain investigations. They host Action Fraud, which, as previously detailed in Chapter 6, is the national reporting body for fraud. Thus, unlike other volume crimes, an individual can only report a fraud to Action Fraud and not to the local police force. Linked to Action Fraud, the City of London Police host the National Fraud Intelligence Bureau. They receive all the reports from Action Fraud, as well as a variety of other bodies and use that intelligence to produce cases ready for investigation, which are then disseminated to the most relevant body. Unfortunately, because there are so many fraud cases and only limited fraud investigative resources, many of the cases they allocate are never investigated. The Dedicated Card and Payment Crime Unit is a private-funded police unit from the financial services sector, drawing on City of London Police and Metropolitan Police officers. Their focus is upon the crimes in their name and, as such, many individuals who suffer identity frauds or other plastic payment-related frauds, may have this body investigating their case.

It is also important to note the National Crime Agency (NCA) in England and Wales. This is essentially a national police force focusing upon serious and organised crime. Much of the work is not related to fraud. However, the NCA hosts two important bodies in the overall policing of fraud. First there is the Economic Crime Command, which deals with fraud alongside money laundering, counterfeit currency and international corruption. With fraud, the NCA (and its predecessor the Serious and Organised Crime Agency) has been involved in investigating and disrupting a variety of mass marketing frauds operating across borders. It is important to note it also deals with frauds beyond the scope of this book, which are serious and involve organised criminals. The other significant part of the NCA of relevance to this book is the National Cyber Crime Unit, which leads the UK and supports other bodies in the response to cyber crime. As noted earlier in this book cyber crime is broader than cyber fraud, but clearly many frauds are perpetrated in this way, which is why this is also an important body to note.

The final significant body in England and Wales is the Serious Fraud Office. This body deals with serious and complex cases of fraud and bribery. It tends to have a small caseload of complex cases (dozens per year) and although it does deal with fraud cases, which are the focus of this book, it tends to deal with cases involving large occupational frauds, or corporate frauds, for example.

Within Australia, there are seven state and territory police with the Australian Federal Police (AFP) assuming federal jurisdiction. The AFP also provides state policing services to the Australian Capital Territory. Within many of these states, police agencies will have a dedicated fraud squad, however it may co-exist with another area of policing, such as cyber crime. For example, the Queensland Police Service has a Fraud and Cyber Crime Group, and likewise, the South Australian Police have a Major Fraud section within a Commercial and Electronic Crime Branch. Fraud offences are usually dealt with at a state level, as they are found within state legislative criminal codes. The AFP will only investigate fraud claims if the alleged victim is a Commonwealth government department or authority. However, the AFP does have a High Tech crime unit, which deals with offences contained in the Commonwealth *Criminal Code Act 1995*, that encompasses computer intrusions; unauthorised modification of data (including the destruction of data); distributed denial of service attacks using botnets; and the creation and distribution of malware (AFP, n.d.).

The establishment of ACORN in November 2014, was an important step to improving the overall response to cyber crime in Australia, which includes the cyber frauds and scams of interest to this book. However, there are still critiques against state and territory police agencies concerning their response to cyber frauds and scams. For example, the Queensland Government commissioned an inquiry into Organised Crime in Queensland in 2015. The report considered a variety of offences, which were related to organised crime, including fraud. The findings of this report were highly critical of the level of resources allocated to the investigation of fraud and financial crime in Queensland, and consequently, were critical of the lack of response offered by police in terms of investigating offences. For example, the report stated,

> The Gold Coast now appears to be a hub of on-shore boiler rooms. This is a problem that has been known to the Queensland Police Service for some years, but despite that, the issue has not been prioritised nor has the QPS been resourced sufficiently to deal with it.
>
> *(Queensland Organised Crime Commission of Inquiry, 2015: 373–374)*

Overall, this is indicative of the systemic and historical lack of resources and priority given to fraud offences in many jurisdictions, including Australia. There are signs which show this attitude is changing, with several police jurisdictions in Australia taking the initiative to contact victims prior to them attempting to report. This will be covered in further detail later in this chapter.

Hybrid policing

Frauds are also the responsibility of a variety of bodies that fall within the hybrid policing category. If this book was considering the full range of frauds, this would be a much more lengthy section. The focus on the frauds within this book, however, means there is a smaller number. Table 7.3 notes some of the most significant bodies in England and Wales under consideration. Trading Standards officers employed by local authorities are the most important to note. In England and Wales, under the national government sits a variety of local government authorities and depending upon the area hosts trading standards groups in country councils or unitary authorities (a type of council in England and Wales). They deal with a variety of frauds, but they regularly become involved in cases of businesses that engage in fraudulent trading. Trading Standards have limited powers but do conduct investigations and pursue sanctions through the civil and criminal courts. They also usually pursue preventative work in the community, such as prevention and awareness campaigns against frauds and scams.

The protection of consumers from unfair and/or misleading trading practices is not just the responsibility of local government trading standards officers. There are a variety of central government regulators that have regulatory (and sometimes criminal) enforcement functions, which leads them to deal with scams against the general public. Ofcom is a government body which regulates TV, radio and video on demand sectors, fixed line telecoms, mobiles, postal services,

TABLE 7.3 Significant hybrid policing bodies dealing with fraud in England and Wales

England and wales
Central and decentralised public policing bodies
• Competition and Markets Authority
• Financial Conduct Authority
• Gambling Commission
• Insolvency Service Companies Investigation Branch
• Local authority trading standards
• Medicines and Healthcare Products Regulatory Agency
• Ofcom (regulates postal services, telecommunications, television, radio broadcasters and some advertising)
• Ofgem (regulates energy providers)
• Ofwat (regulated water companies)
Specialised police organisations
• British Transport Police
Not-for-profit private policing bodies
• Advertising Standards Authority
• Cifas
• Financial Fraud Action UK
• Phonepayplus

Case study 7.1 Trading Standards prosecute money launderer

In May 2016, a man was convicted in Chester of money laundering £34,000 through his bank on behalf of rogue traders/scammers as a result of an investigation by the City's trading standards officers. (Elams, 2016)

plus the airwaves over which wireless devices operate. There are a number of areas where it can become involved in the policing of fraud that uses these mediums to promote scams. In 2008, Ofcom fined ITV over £5 million for abuses in premium telephone line competitions where viewers paid to enter competitions by phoning in were not entered, amongst other breaches (Conlan, 2008). This particular area of concern is now the responsibility of a specialist contracted regulator, Phonepayplus, which will be considered shortly. More recently, in July 2015 Ofcom fined a company £200,000 for mis-selling landline telephone lines (Ofcom, 2015). Ofwat, which regulates water utilities companies has also in the past dealt with misleading returns that have resulted in overcharging of customers.

A very important body to note in this area is the Insolvency Service Company Investigations Branch. They deal with various modes of misconduct by company directors, of which a significant number relate to fraud and scams perpetrated by companies. Possible outcomes of their investigation can include disqualification of the Director or referral for criminal prosecution or regulatory action to a relevant body (Insolvency Service, 2016). Many of the referrals are made to another hybrid policing body known as the BIS Criminal Enforcement Team, which was part of the Department for Business, Innovation and Skills (which has recently become the Department for Business, Energy and Industrial Strategy). They conduct criminal investigations and in 2014–15 successfully prosecuted 156 persons (BIS Enforcement Team, 2016).

The Financial Conduct Authority (FCA) is the regulatory body for the financial services sector. Part of its regulatory function means it regularly becomes involved in investment frauds targeted at consumers. As such it conducts criminal, civil and regulatory investigations as well as pursuing a variety of preventative work. For example, the FCA runs a list of unauthorised firms who offer investment services, which are not regulated and/or have been proven to have offered fraudulent investments (see https://www.fca.org.uk/consumers/unauthorised-firms-individuals). The Competition and Markets Authority has responsibility for consumer protection, amongst a variety of other functions and has pursued enforcement actions to protect consumers. Any scam which involves gambling may also involve the government regulator in the UK, the Gambling Commission. The Medicines and Healthcare Products Regulatory Agency regulates medicines and healthcare products and as a consequence sometimes deals with fraud-related behaviours involving the advertising and sale of such products.

Case study 7.2 Regulatory criminal action for fake Viagra

In 2007 a woman was jailed for 2½ years after being found guilty of offences related to the sale of false drugs, such as Viagra. Packaging them in her garden shed, the woman sold over the internet to customers largely in the UK and USA. The case was investigated jointly with the Medicines and Healthcare Products Regulatory Agency and the City of London Police. (BBC News, 2007)

There are various specialised policing organisations in the United Kingdom, but most of them serve a particular organisation and sector, thus when they do deal with fraud they generally deal with frauds against the particular organisation, rather than against the general public. The only specialist police organisation that deals extensively with the public is the British Transport Police, which serves the privatised rail companies and London Underground and it has dealt with cases of ticket fraud against the public, although again much of the fraud it deals with is occupational fraud by employees of the rail companies.

The not-for-profit policing organisations in England and Wales dealing with frauds against the general public are also smaller than those dealing with the totality of fraud. Premium rate telephone calls are a particular area where scams occur and Ofcom has a contracted-out, not-for-profit regulator, Phonepayplus, which deals with breaches of the regulations by operators, investigates them and punishes them where proven. For example, in 2014 a Birmingham company, Subhan Universal Limited, was fined £6000, reprimanded and ordered to refund monies to those who had complained after it was found to have set up false telephone lines for viewers hoping to vote in television contests such as 'Britain's Got Talent' and 'I'm a Celebrity get me out of here'. Viewers thought they were voting in the real ITV contests, but were not (Jones, 2013). These regulators tend to be much more focused upon prevention and thus not clearly full policing bodies (i.e. they don't investigate and pursue sanctions). These were considered in more depth in the prevention chapter so other than noting the role of Cifas in preventing identity fraud against the general public and Financial Fraud Action UK in preventing banking fraud as private not-for-profit bodies, little more will be said. The Advertising Standards Authority (ASA), which is a private not-for-profit body, also has a role as some frauds involve advertising. The ASA does investigate some cases and pursue sanctions through its own procedures, which it has delegated authority to deal with in some cases. However, its reach regarding fraudsters using advertising is pretty weak (see Case study 7.11).

Similar to the state police bodies, within Australia there are consumer protection agencies across a state and federal level. At the Commonwealth level, the Australian Competition and Consumer Commission 'promotes competition and fair trade in markets to benefit consumers, businesses, and the community' (ACCC, n.d.). The ACCC is a regulatory body with specific powers of enforcement regarding competition, fair trading and consumer protection laws under the *Competition and Consumer Act 2010*. Regarding cyber frauds and scams, while the ACCC does not necessarily have enforcement powers which can target the offenders who perpetrate these offences, it has a very strong presence promoting education and awareness campaigns across the media to target consumers and potential victims. The *Scamwatch* website is hosted by the ACCC and provides a comprehensive amount of detail regarding the number of different types of frauds and scams in existence.

Each state and territory also has a consumer protection department, whose functions include investigating frauds and scams. Similar to the ACCC, each department has enforcement powers under their relevant legislation, however these are often limited or non-existent in terms of specifically targeting the online fraud victimisation of persons in their jurisdiction.

The Australasian Consumer Fraud Taskforce comprises 22 government regulatory agencies and departments in Australia and New Zealand, who work collaboratively with private, community and non-government agencies to prevent fraud. Again, while this body does not have enforcement powers of its own, the main focus is on the promotion of awareness to potential victims across both countries.

Within the United States, there are a number of bodies which have substantial powers of investigation and arrest regarding fraud. For example, the US Postal Inspection Service (USPIS) is a federal law enforcement agency, whose mission is to 'support and protect the U.S. Postal Service and its employees, infrastructure, and customers; enforce the laws that defend the nation's mail system from illegal or dangerous use; and ensure public trust in the mail' (USPIS, n.d.). The USPIS has the authority to target offenders who are using the mail service to 'defraud, endanger, or otherwise threaten the American public' (USPIS, n.d.).

There are several other agencies with an interest in cyber frauds and scams across the USA. This includes the Homeland Security Investigation unit within the US Immigration and Customs department, and the Criminal Investigation Command within the US Army. The variety of agencies involved in the investigation and awareness-raising related to cyber frauds and scams, highlights the complex and sophisticated nature of these schemes and their pervasiveness across government and other sectors. See below for a detailed outline of the Federal Trade Commission, and how it targets cyber frauds and scams, as well as a second case study, which highlights the need for agencies to cooperate in order to prosecute alleged offenders.

Private policing bodies

Private policing bodies have assumed a significant role in the policing of fraud, including that of cyber frauds and scams against individual victims. The private

Case study 7.3 A hybrid policing body, the Federal Trade Commission in the USA

A very important and significant hybrid policing body in the USA is the Federal Trade Commission. It has a wide range of responsibilities, but some of which include enforcing:

> federal consumer protection laws that prevent fraud, deception and unfair business practices. The Commission also enforces federal antitrust laws that prohibit anticompetitive mergers and other business practices that could lead to higher prices, fewer choices, or less innovation.

Whether combatting telemarketing fraud, internet scams or price-fixing schemes, the FTC's mission is to protect consumers and promote competition.

The FTC administers a wide variety of laws and regulations, including the Federal Trade Commission Act, Telemarketing Sale Rule, Identity Theft Act, Fair Credit Reporting Act, and Clayton Act. In total, the Commission has enforcement or administrative responsibilities under more than 70 laws. (Federal Trade Comission, n.d.)

The FTC usually starts on a civil basis to shut down the fraudsters. In doing so it often secures evidence to pursue criminal action. The FTC also has a criminal liaison unit which works with relevant prosecutors in the Department of Justice, US Attorneys and federal and state law enforcement to pursue criminal cases. Common areas of fraud where actions have been taken include:

- telemarketing scams;
- mortgage and other debt relief rip-offs;
- bogus health products; and
- sweepstakes scams.

The FTC also provides a variety of packages to help prevent such frauds and support and training for law enforcement in this area.

In the 2015 statistics for consumer protection, the FTC noted it had received 3,083,379 complaints. It had pursued 37 administrative actions, 52 federal actions, 18 civil penalties. It had also secured 41 administrative orders; 118 redress, disgorgement, and permanent injunctions; 12 civil penalties and 7 civil contempt. (Federal Trade Commission, 2015)

Case study 7.4 Prosecuting cyber fraud

On 13 July, 2015, the US Department of Justice issued a release which advised that six Nigerian nationals had been extradited from South Africa to Mississippi, USA, to face charges relating to fraud. A total of 20 individuals were charged in the case which comprised of romance scams, re-shipping scams, fraudulent check scams, work from home scams, in addition to bank, financial and credit care takeovers (US DOJ, 2015). Members of this group faced charges relating to identity theft, fraud and money laundering. In seeking to investigate and extradite those allegedly part of this group, the media release acknowledges the assistance of the following agencies:

> This case is being investigated by Homeland Security Investigations (HSI) and the U.S. Postal Inspection Service. Significant assistance was also provided by the Criminal Division's Office of International Affairs, the HSI Cyber Crimes Center, HSI Attachés in Pretoria and Dakar, U.S. Marshals Service's International Investigations Branch and the Southern District of Mississippi, the South African Police Service (SAPS) Directorate of Priority Crimes Investigation (DPCI) Electronic Crimes Unit, the SAPS Interpol Extradition Unit, the South African National Prosecution Authority, and the South African Department of Justice and Constitutional Development.
>
> *(US DOJ, 2015)*

This alone demonstrates the need for collaboration and mutual assistance both at a domestic level (within the USA) and internationally (with South Africa) and the logistical complexity experienced in these cases.

policing bodies can be divided between those offering commercial policing services for a fee, such as private investigators and consultancy practices, and the in-house security/investigative departments of many organisations that deal with fraud. Those offering commercial services tend to do so for other organisations, but as there are some examples of individuals using such services, they will be briefly examined. An organisation's in-house security/investigative capacity is usually targeted at protecting the organisation. However, there are a large number of organisations who use this capacity to not only protect themselves, but also their customers. Therefore this group will also be considered.

Commercial policing services

There many and varied private investigators in operation, from large corporate practices to lone operators who, for a fee, will investigate frauds as well as many other acts (Gill and Hart, 1997). Competing with the firms of private investigators are lots of large consultancy practices (such as KPMG, Ernst and Young, and BDO) and some firms of solicitors who also offer fraud investigation-related services (such as Keoghs and Hill Dickinson). The larger bodies offering these services do not come cheap and their main focus is to sell their services to other organisations who have the resources to pay for them. However, some individuals who can afford it will turn to such bodies. For instance, in August 2016 it was revealed that the movie star Eddy Murphy's ex-wife had experienced a US$7 million investment fraud and had used private investigators to investigate the case and help bring the culprit to justice (Parry, 2016). In another case with a less high-profile victim, a Canadian disabled man who had been the victim of a CAN$850,000 romance scam hired private investigators to find out what had happened and to trace the fraudsters who were based in Jamaica. This was successful with the alleged ringleader charged in August 2016 (Duffy, 2016).

The high costs of investigating frauds restrict this as an option for only the more wealthy victims of fraud. There are, however, firms of private investigators offering other services to potential fraud victims, which are more accessible to a greater number of victims. For example, the problem of romance fraud has led one firm to offer a service to check out and vet potential partners who have been met online (UK Private Investigators, n.d.). The firm notes about the service:

> What if you could actually find out who the person REALLY is? You would definitely feel safer and more confident in meeting them face-to-face and less vulnerable to a potential online scam.
>
> Our investigators are able to provide you with an extremely detailed profile on your new friend or find answers to specific questions which you may have.
>
> Our checking and vetting service is completed with absolute discretion and professionalism ensuring that the individual/s in question will never be aware of the investigation, at ANY stage.
>
> *(UK Private Investigators, n.d.)*

Another firm of investigators offering a similar service, notes:

> UK Background Checks (http://www.ukbackgroundchecks.com/) is a professional, discreet private investigation service operating across the UK. One of our largest areas of expertise is in undertaking relationship enquiries to prevent associated frauds and dating scams. We pursue enquiries on a global basis, finding dating scams originating from Africa, the Ukraine, the USA, Pakistan and India, among other nations. In most cases, we can differentiate fraudsters, scammers and liars from genuine people at an early stage to prevent our clients falling victim to a scam.
>
> *(UK Background Checks, n.d.)*

Similar services are available in Australia, with one firm, Online Investigations, advertising expertise in fraud and scam investigations which include: Online Dating Background Checks; Scam Analysis; Identity Verification; Pre-marital Checks; Romance Scam Investigations; and Verification of International Relationships (Online Investigations, n.d.).

There are clearly many firms offering a range of services in this area for potential and actual victims of fraud. It is difficult, however, to determine the extent of use.

Organisational security/investigative capacity

For many victims the start (and often the end) of an investigation into a fraud will be the counter-fraud department of the organisation they are first reporting to. For instance a person who realises they have fraudulent transactions on their credit card statement will usually first call the credit card provider. The bank or financial institution will then investigate the case and if the transactions are fraudulent and the victim was not negligent, the victim can usually have their account rectified. For many victims the return of monies or removal of illegitimate transactions is all that is required. Some victims, however, will also want justice (see Button et al., 2009a; Cross et al., 2016). Behind the scenes, the credit card company's investigators may well be investigating the case in greater depth, in some instances this may also be in partnership with the police. In a small number of cases, these investigations may even result in a successful conviction. However, the reality is that while many cases will be initially subject to an investigation simply to determine if they are fraud, if there is no evidence or leads to take the case further they will simply be filed away by the bank or financial institution. Credit cards are one of the more obvious areas where 'in-house' investigators are the frontline in investigating fraud cases for individuals. The investigative teams of these providers are also often more proactive, not just focusing upon reactive investigations based upon clients complaints. Many of these companies use sophisticated data-matching and mining tools, which are able to identify suspect transactions. Indeed one of the author's colleagues was saved from a fraud when he was contacted by his credit card provider to ask if he had just tried to purchase an airline ticket. As he hadn't, it was revealed to be an attempted fraudulent transaction, which was stopped as a result of this proactive approach. This is not an isolated incident.

Another significant area is retail, particularly online, telephone and mail order companies. Persons may find they do not receive goods or have unaccounted-for items added to their account, leading them to complain to their provider which prompts its investigative teams to examine the alleged incident. The many social networking sites and online dating websites' investigative teams may also be the frontline investigators for complaints of clients' about attempted or actual frauds. There is such an incredible diversity in areas where consumers of services who have, or have suspected they have, been targeted with a fraud may contact the service provider first in addition to those listed, such as credit reference agencies, internet service providers, email providers, IT hardware and software providers, that it is impossible to list them all here. This in-house fraud investigative sector accounts for a very substantial number of personnel, but unfortunately there is little accurate information to gauge this sector. Indeed, the potential size was illustrated by the Fraud Review Team (2006: 53), which noted there were 2,500 investigators alone in the six major banks in the UK, which substantially dwarfs the total dedicated police resources for the whole of the UK.

These investigators, when conducting reactive investigations, will usually seek to determine what has occurred. Often there will be too few leads to go on and because of the more dominant influence concerning the cost of investigations, many of these cases will be filed away without an outcome. There will be some that can be resolved and in some cases investigators will often work with the police. Unfortunately, the sheer volume of cases means that a significant number will be filed away by the organisation and at best reported to law enforcement for intelligence-building purposes with little expectation of any successful prosecution.

Voluntary policing

The rise in the problem of frauds and scams and the limited capacity/interest of official bodies has created a huge gap. Traditionally, gaps in the state response to crime have led to vigilante action stepping in to plug the gap (Johnston, 1996). The world of scams and particularly cyber frauds has also spawned a variety of what could be called organised online vigilante action. Some of these are linked to countries, others are more globally based. One prominent website http://www.419eater.com/ seeks to engage in 'scambaiting', which is defined as:

> put simply, you enter into a dialogue with scammers, simply to waste their time and resources. Whilst you are doing this, you will be helping to keep the scammers away from real potential victims and screwing around with the minds of deserving thieves.
>
> *(419eater, n.d.)*

The 419eater website is focused upon 419 scams (predominantly advanced fee fraud schemes) but encourages action against other types too. The site provides news on scams and tips on how to waste the scammers' time. There are a variety of other websites which can be found that fit this genre such as http://baita.mugu.co.uk/, http://www.ebolamonkeyman.com/ and http://www.romancescambaiter.com/. Another, such as http://www.scamorama.com/, focuses more on showcasing the variety and comedy value of some attempted scams, rather than baiting them. YouTube also provides a powerful resource for scambaiters too, where many examples of scammers are placed on this website by some of those already noted, as well as individuals. Some 'scambaiters' have not only wasted the time of the scammers and exposed them, but effectively implemented punishments on offenders that are intended to shame them and provide amusement value to those who witness. One article examining the practice noted how one group had convinced a scammer they were a member of the 'Church of the Painted Beast' and tricked the scammer into joining via their initiation rights, which included painting over their chests. In other cases scammers were persuaded to draw elaborate maps of British towns by hand, tattoo themselves, and rewrite Harry Potter books by hand (Ezer, 2011). These types of vigilante action tend to be facilitated online and open to the global (English-speaking) community, although there may be a bias to particular countries. There are a small number of studies and scholars who are seeking to examine the racial tones of these scambaiting activities, particularly the concept of '"trophy" photographs of African men and women, posed holding signs, either naked or in outrageous and bizarre outfits and positions' (Nakamura, 2014: 261). Such photos are collected and shared across a variety of social media and internet platforms and seek to evoke feelings of amusement from the viewers rather than acknowledge the discomfort and racism that is inherent in the scenes presented. This is based upon the belief that those pictured are criminal and therefore deserve the humiliation and degradation experienced. Byrne (2013: 71) brands this practice as 'digilantism'.

> Based mostly in the United States and the United Kingdom, digilantes mete out extrajudicial punishment to cybercriminals such as scammers, hackers, and pedophiles. Unlike traditional vigilantes whose notions of frontier justice required brute force to flog, tar and feather, or lynch their outlaws, for digilantes, punishing cybercriminals rests largely in the art of persuasion.
>
> *(Byrne, 2013: 71)*

The requests for photos from scambaiters usually have sexual and racial undertones, and are shared across platforms such as 419eater.com and are rated by users in this forum. Byrne (2013) asserts that there is real prestige in being able to upload a trophy image from an African offender and that those which receive the highest ratings by other users, are usually those that depict the scammer as 'nude, seminude, or holding a sign that refers to deviant sexual behaviour' (Byrne, 2013: 77). Given the small amount of research that has been conducted upon these practices and the extent to which they exist, a deeper analysis of their contribution and racial symbolicism is in need of further research. Overall, it is important to acknowledge that such vigilante action is rarely officially supported by the state police and is often viewed negatively.

The problem of fraud, however, has spawned more official initiatives encouraged by the state and law enforcement to draw in volunteer action to support the state. For example in January 2016, Hampshire Constabulary in England launched an initiative to recruit Cyber Special Constables and Cyber Volunteers.

Volunteers were expected to contribute 16 hours per month and to advise on and support digital investigations (Hampshire Constabulary, 2016). Their role would bring them into more contact with the police on a variety of investigations where digital support was required as well as some pure fraud-related investigations. Other police forces in England and Wales have also initiated such schemes and the National Crime Agency has also established a volunteer program. However, there is little information in the public domain to gauge the size of the voluntary contribution and the effectiveness of such schemes. There are a variety of not-for-profit bodies that also provide prevention advice, such as Victim Support, pensioner charities such as Age UK, and specialist charities such as Think Jessica. These will be detailed further in the next chapter.

International policing

The international nature of many frauds has been noted many times in this book. Many fraudsters cross borders multiple times in the process of developing, conducting and reaping the rewards of their scams. This was evident in the above case study, where alleged Nigerian offenders were extradited from South Africa to the USA. Many of the state and non-state policing infrastructures cooperate to conduct their various activities. There are, however, a number of transnational and international bodies that exist to support and facilitate the fight against cross-border fraud.

Europol is an EU body established in 1999 for the purpose of the coordination of collation, analysis and distribution of information and intelligence amongst the EU law enforcement community (for example, police, customs). The main areas of responsibility are terrorism, drug trafficking, illegal immigration, organised crime and money laundering. Europol has developed a number of areas, which are important in the fight against cross-border fraud. First, it hosts the European Cybercrime Centre (EC3) which investigates a variety of offences, and recognises payment card fraud and high tech crimes as two of its priority areas. Second, the broader activities of Europol do include a focus on fraud, some of which fall within the scope of this book (others include tax fraud and counterfeiting, for example). For instance in the 2014 annual review, Europol noted three coordinated actions it had been involved in to tackle airline ticket fraud as outlined in the introduction to this chapter (Europol, 2015).

Europol's 'sister' organisation Eurojust has also shown interest in cross-border fraud. Eurojust was established in 2001 to facilitate the coordination of investigations and prosecutions of the most serious crimes. Like Europol it deals with a wide range of serious crimes, but fraud and cyber crimes have been a significant area of action. Similar to Europol, many of these areas relate to frauds beyond the scope of this book. In 2015, it dealt with 647 fraud cases, which was the biggest by far of its caseload, with the next biggest category of drug trafficking at 274 (Eurojust, 2016: 28). The annual review notes its role in dealing with one set of fraudsters based in Nigeria/Cameroon targeting multiple EU countries who had netted €6 million. The review notes the important coordination role undertaken by Eurojust, which culminated in an action day, which:

> took place in June 2015, led by Italian, Spanish and Polish judicial and police authorities. Facilitated by the coordination centre at Eurojust, the action day yielded excellent operational results. A total of 49 suspects were arrested and 58 searches carried out. Through close judicial cooperation and coordination between the involved States, cybercriminals can be brought to justice in any jurisdiction.
>
> *(Eurojust, 2016: 32–33)*

Another important international body is Interpol, with 190 member countries working in a number of crime areas to facilitate cooperation between countries to more effectively tackle international crime. It covers a wide range of crimes, including a small part focused on cyber crime and fraud. Interpol offers a number of specialist databases, training courses and investigative support across a number of areas. The Stolen and Lost Travel Documents Database (SLTDD) and Counterfeit Payment Cards Database (CPCD) are hosted by Interpol and are very important tools in the fight against identity and payment card-related fraud.

There are a number of international groups which come together to support the fight against fraud. There are also some international, national government initiatives and private strategies worth noting. EConsumer.gov is a website operated by the International Consumer Protection Enforcement Network (ICPEN) which provides a portal to report complaints with foreign companies for consumers. It also enables the law enforcement community via the Consumer Sentinel Network to share intelligence (Button, 2012). Another example is the International Mass-Marketing Fraud Working Group, which was established in 2007 and comprises of several law enforcement agencies from Canada, the Netherlands, Nigeria, the UK, and the USA, as well as contributions from other countries such as Belgium, Sweden, Spain, France, Australia and New Zealand. The IMMFWG aims to share intelligence and coordinate operational matters, including enforcement and disruption activities. In 2010, it published an international threat assessment, which outlined the specific details and challenges associated with the global nature of mass marketing fraud (IMMFWG, 2010). The IMMFWG is also involved in the coordination and promotion of education and prevention messages and activities across its member countries (see RCMP, 2010).

The challenges of plural provision

This chapter has noted the multiple agencies engaged in policing fraud drawn from the public, private and voluntary sectors. This fragmented or plural patchwork of bodies creates a number of challenges which are important to note.

Responsibility

The first and one of the most important challenges is determining who has responsibility for policing. There are a large number of frauds that could and are investigated by multiple bodies. At the very base this creates challenges for the victim in ascertaining who they approach to report their case. Button et al. (2009a) noted what they called the victims 'merry-go-round' with victims sent to multiple bodies in an attempt to try and report their fraud. Part of the response in the UK to deal with this problem was the creation of Action Fraud, a central reporting agency for all frauds. Similar central reporting agencies also exist in the USA, Canada and Australia. While these are positive in terms of creating a single mechanism for reporting, their existence does not in and of itself overcome the large number of relevant bodies still involved in the fraud space. Despite the establishment of a central agency, there are still multiple bodies, creating a bewildering number of possibilities for fraud victims to navigate. The second aspect to the responsibility challenge is that, when there are multiple bodies that have a potential stake in a particular fraud, it can lead to tensions over who takes the lead. It can also have the opposite effect whereby the fraud falls between them all, because each agency thinks it's another's responsibility. Responsibility leads naturally to the next substantive challenge of coordination and cooperation.

Coordination and cooperation

The natural consequence of the challenge of responsibility is that when multiple bodies take an interest in a particular fraud they need to work together. Bringing different agencies to work together to cooperate and be coordinated in an effective way is a significant challenge. The upcoming case study of Project Sunbird will illustrate how this can be done effectively.

Inequity

Another consequence of the plural provision drawn from multiple sectors is the inequity that occurs in response to different frauds. There are some frauds where there is an overwhelming response, such as payment card fraud. This is partly because major financial institutions have a profit motive to deal with this type of crime and thus dedicate resources through their own departments and support for law enforcement to deal with it. It could also perhaps be because many of the criminals that become involved in this type of fraud are the traditional criminals the police deal with. There are other types of fraud where, because there is a strong regulatory body with responsibility in this area, there is additional interest. Thus, in the UK investment frauds attract the interest of the Financial Conduct Authority. The police have also taken interest in these types of fraud with initiatives such as Operation Broadway, possibly because of the FCA, but perhaps also for reasons that many of the victims are more influential, middle-class men.

Finally, there are also frauds that secure very little interest from any police or regulatory body. Thus, victims, depending upon the type of fraud, will face a very different prognosis in terms of action to deal with their fraud. This combines with the problem of attrition, which will be examined shortly.

Case study 7.5 Successful partnership

Three men were jailed in York after an investigation by the North Yorkshire Multi-Agency Safeguarding Team into a disabled 80-year-old woman who paid for over-priced and poor quality gardening and roof work. The team is drawn from trading standards officers, North Yorkshire Police and the safeguarding manager from adult services in the County. (MinsterFM, 2016)

Case study 7.6 Project Sunbird

Project Sunbird is a partnership approach between the West Australian Police and the West Australian Department of Commerce that targets online fraud victims through the use of financial intelligence to five West African countries: Nigeria, Ghana, Benin, Togo and Sierra Leone. Based on this intelligence, potential online fraud victims are contacted by mail, to warn them of their potential involvement in fraud and a request to cease transferring funds. Contact details are provided with both police and consumer protection agencies, in order to facilitate an open dialogue between victims and authorities. For those who continue to send money after the first letter, a second letter is sent, with the same message and the inclusion of a fact sheet specifically designed for victims of fraud. Initial evaluations from Project Sunbird indicate that 72% of letter recipients stop sending money after the first letter, and a further 50% of letter recipients stop sending money after the second letter. While there are limitations with this data and much needed work to further examine this approach, the use of financial intelligence and the partnership approach taken by both agencies, overcome two main barriers to the reporting of fraud. The first being that victims do not recognise that they are involved in fraudulent activity, and the second being the social stigma in reporting to authorities. This strategy uses police resources to target potential victims in an attempt to reduce the harm and financial losses incurred through online fraud, which acknowledges police do not generally have jurisdiction to investigate overseas offenders, but do have jurisdiction to intervene with potential victims (see Cross, 2016a; 2016b; Cross and Blackshaw, 2015). Further details of Project Sunbird and the use of financial intelligence to target online fraud will be explored in the following chapter on prevention.

Punishment of fraudsters

If there is a successful investigation into a fraud, then there is a consequential expectation that there is some form of punishment for the offender. Traditional texts on criminal justice note the following purposes for punishment:

- Retribution: seeking vengeance against the perpetrator.
- Incapacitation: preventing the perpetrator from offending again.
- Rehabilitation: changing the behaviour of the offender.
- Deterrence: deterring the actual offender (specific) and others contemplating offending (general).
- Denunciation: making clear to society the act undertaken is wrong.
- Reparation: compensation for the victim.

(Davies et al., 1995)

Much of the literature surrounding volume crimes and punishment focuses upon the sanctions from the criminal justice system. This chapter, however, has already noted the significant involvement of hybrid and private bodies, who bring with them a greater diversity in sanction options beyond the criminal justice system. Indeed, the criminal justice system itself has been used in a number of countries in more innovative ways to deal with fraudsters. Before some of these are examined, however, it is important to note the very important problem of attrition, which is relevant across many crime categories, fraud included.

Attrition

Attrition is the process by which the total number of crimes reduce as they proceed through the criminal justice system, such that sentencing the total number of crimes dealt with is significantly smaller than the total number of crimes which occurred. Attrition is a very common problem for all volume crimes. For instance Barclay and Tavares (1999) in one of the first and most significant studies noted that only 3 per cent of offences resulted in a conviction and only 0.3 per cent led to custodial sentences. Research using 'crude' methods by Button et al. (2012) on fraud offences in general, using the National Fraud Authority (2012) annual fraud indicator as a basis, estimated there were 10,133,259 (100%) frauds, of which 157,847 (1.5%) were reported and 40,709 (0.4%) resulted in sanctions. The real attrition rate for the types of fraud considered in this book is impossible to determine, but what is clear is that very significant numbers of frauds are not reported, and those which are reported are likely never investigated. Consequently only a very small percentage of frauds will ever result in a sanction. This is important because, as McGuire (2002) has noted, for deterrence to be most effective in seeking to dissuade or prevent offending actions in the first place, the possibility of sanctions must be:

- Inevitable and unavoidable,
- Administered immediately or speedily, and of
- High to maximum severity.

It is very clear that for most frauds – at least in terms of criminal sanctions – getting caught is near to impossible and can therefore not be understood as an effective deterrence mechanism, either for the individual criminal or for society as a whole. There is also evidence to suggest that the penalties are lighter in comparison to other volume crimes in many jurisdictions. Before some of the punishments are considered it would be useful to return to the very start and examine what victims want in terms of punishment.

What do victims want regarding punishment?

There have been only a few studies that have investigated what fraud victims want. Button et al. (2009b) undertook a telephone survey with closed questions, including one asking how important it was to the victims that there be 'tougher sentences for fraudsters' on a scale of 1 to 7, where 1 is not very important and 7 is very important. Of the 675 victims that responded to this question 78.7 per cent rated this 7 or very important. This was further reflected in some of their face-to-face interviews. However, there was also a realisation that many fraudsters do not reach the end-game of sentencing after a criminal trial. Victims therefore have other needs and considerations on sentencing, which warranted further analysis.

In a more focused study by Button et al. (2015b) on the views of online fraud victims on a variety of criminal penalties some of the following issues were noted.

- *Custodial sentences*: victims saw these as appropriate for frauds with most aggravating factors, but recognised that it was unlikely to reduce re-offending of the individual offender.
- *Community orders*: were not seen by some victims as providing a tough enough penalty, while others felt it was potentially a more economical punishment for lower-level fraudsters.
- *Financial penalties*: victims felt these were appropriate if the offender had sufficient resources to enable them to be 'hurt' by them.
- *Restitution orders*: victims felt these were appropriate if fraudsters had the resources such that some should be passed back to the victims.
- *Seizure of assets and various orders*: victims felt this was appropriate, particularly if the fraudsters had equipment such as computers, which could be used to perpetrate further crimes.

However, the research by Button et al. (2015b) also noted the significant opportunity for restorative justice for many fraudsters. Given that a significant group of perpetrators operate at a distance and have no or limited contact with the victims it was felt that if they had to face their victims and realise the damage and hurt they had caused them this would be an appropriate punishment.

Sanctions for fraudulent acts

Unlike other volume crimes, criminal prosecution is one part of the picture, with significant numbers of frauds dealt with by regulatory and civil action too, as illustrated in Figure 7.1 below. Some frauds encompass more than one area, such as criminal and regulatory areas. Thus, when a fraudulent act is identified by a victim, they report it to whom they believe to be the relevant body, and if that body (or bodies in some cases) takes an interest (which is a significant hurdle, as already noted) depending upon the evidence, the act and the orientation of the body, regulatory, civil or criminal actions will be pursued alone or in parallel. It is also possible that either no action will be taken or disruption activities are pursued to make it difficult for the fraudsters to continue defrauding the identified victim as well as other potential victims. Depending upon the action pursued, there is a wide range of potential sanctions that can be applied if the offender is convicted.

Criminal penalties

In many countries, when fraudsters are caught and punished by the criminal courts they often face lighter sentences in comparison to other volume crimes. Unfortunately much of the research that illustrates this is built upon fraud offences in general and does not distinguish between the different types of fraud. Nevertheless, if we consider there is not a significant difference, Levi's (2006) study found in 2004 the average length of a custodial sentence for fraud cases tried in a Magistrates' courts was three months, against four months for commercial burglary and three months for theft and handling stolen goods. For

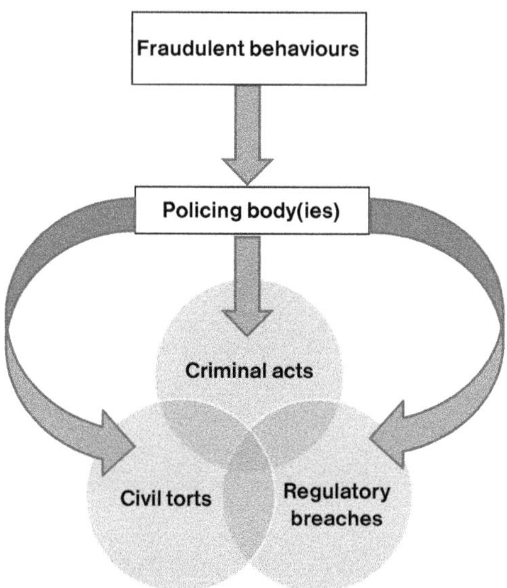

FIGURE 7.1 The sanction options for fraudulent acts.

more serious cases of fraud tried in the Crown Courts, the average sentence was 15.4 months, against 24.6 months for burglary and 41.1 months for robbery. For cases involving conspiracy to defraud, the length was 25.6 months (such cases usually involve larger amounts of money). For frauds involving in excess of £1m, and investigated by the SFO, between 2000–2005 the average sentences were 31.7 months, with the most severe sentences being 4–5 years (Levi, 2006).

There are also clear differences between countries in the sentences they apply for comparable offences. Take, for instance, Britain's 'Bernie Madoff', Kautilya Pruthi who defrauded celebrities and others out of £115 million. His sentence was 14 years, which compared to 150 years for Madoff, in the USA (Greenwood, 2012). These differences are further illustrated by a comparison of cross-border fraud offences across a range of jurisdictions (Button, 2009).

Case study 7.7 Selected penalties for cross border frauds

Boiler Room / telemarketing frauds

UK, £2.4 million fraud of 500 investors. 4 convictions and sentences (5½ years, 3 years 9 months, 2 years 9 months, 21 months). April 2009.

USA (California), $6 million fraud of 103 investors. 2 convictions and sentence (12 years – other to be sentenced later and $5.8 million restitution to victims). February 2005.

USA (New York), $6.5 million fraud of 200 investors. 11 convictions. (ringleader 7 years + £1.2 million restitution and $1.2 million to the Government). May 2008.

Canada (Toronto), $158 million over 10 years. 1 conviction (2 years and 3 years probation). July 2009.

Nigerian / advanced fee frauds

UK, 'thousands of pounds' from 11 victims. 1 conviction (20 months). April 2004.

Hong Kong, 'thousands of dollars', 1 conviction (4 years). March 2005.

USA, $1.2 million. 3 convictions. (87 months, 57 months and 57 months). April 2009.

Canada (Toronto), millions of dollars. 2 convictions. (5 years and 4 years). February 2007.

Nigeria, $2 million. 1 conviction. (376 years and $1.6 million restitution). February 2006.

The above discussion has focused upon the traditional and most severe penalties. However, the section on victims' needs also illustrated that there are other criminal sanctions that can be used. In England and Wales there have been experiments with restorative justice for fraud offences, but only with insurance fraudsters. One tool (which can also be used without conviction too) is the anti-social behaviour order (ASBO). This attaches conditions on behaviour and breach of them is a criminal offence. Trading standards officers in England have been innovative in using this in a number of cases.

In February 2012, a rogue electrician received an indefinite ASBO banning him practising as an electrician. He had been advertising himself as an electrician and, when called out to a client, was charging them a callout fee. Thus, if he is found in future to be holding himself out as an electrician in any way, he will be in breach of his ASBO (Semke, 2012). There was another example, in Lewisham in London, of a builder acting in a fraudulent way receiving an ASBO preventing him from working as a builder ever again (London Borough of Lewisham, 2007). Both these cases involved ASBOs post-conviction, but ASBOs can also be pursued before, as a civil remedy (although there is no evidence of such use for a fraud-related case yet). The section will now consider some of the alternative punishments used against fraudsters. It is, however, important to note that some fraudsters face parallel sanctions. They might face a criminal prosecution, which is successful and also followed by civil and regulatory action. Sometimes regulatory and civil action might follow a failed criminal action, based on the differential burden of proof (beyond reasonable doubt versus on the balance of probabilities) required to successfully prosecute a civil matter.

Alternative punishments

This chapter has already alluded to the wide range of alternative measures that can be, and are currently being, used against fraudsters. First of all there are civil justice measures. Civil trials centre on proving a loss due to the person committing a civil wrong and seeking damages to cover the loss. In England and Wales (and many other countries) there are a variety of civil torts whereby, if a person breaches them, that person can be sued for damages by those who have suffered losses as a result of the tort. Thus, if someone scratches a car while parking and they refuse to pay for the damage, they could be sued. This same principle applies to a person who suffers losses as a result of some form of fraudulent behaviour. Central to the pursuit of a civil case is a perpetrator with assets, because if they didn't have assets the costs of pursuing such a case would not be worth it as there would be no potential reward at the end. The advantage of a civil case, as noted, is that the burden of proof is usually lower, however the fundamental challenge for the victim is that they need the resources to pay their lawyers to pursue the case. If the perpetrator loses the case they also do not face jail, only financial penalties. There are often orders which can be sought alongside a civil action such as restrictions on the activities and travel of the defendant. In many cases civil cases are settled before trial. The victim pursues an action, the defendant comes to the table and makes an offer, a negotiation begins and an offer is agreed. As such, many civil cases never become public and therefore statistics on the number of cases are impossible to determine. The defendant is not always the fraudster, sometimes it is a body that has been negligent in some way to enable the fraud to occur, such as a bank. It is difficult to determine the extent of such actions based on the lack of public accountability with these cases.

Case study 7.8 Successful civil action

In 2016, an Australian woman won AUS$546,000 in damages after a fraudster had sold her property while she was living overseas. The woman had sued the Australian Capital Territory Government, rather than the fraudster, who could not be traced, because of their negligence in enabling the fraud to occur. (Hitch, 2016)

Regulatory action is also a very common strategy used to deal with many fraudsters. This chapter previously noted a variety of regulatory bodies that often deal with the types of fraud considered in this book. These bodies have a wide range of potential sanctions that they can often use, such as:

- Financial penalties
- Licence revocation or equivalent
- Restrictions on operation, and
- Public admonishment.

Not all regulatory bodies possess the full 'toolbox' identified above. At the top of the list are financial penalties, as some regulatory bodies have the powers to fine the individuals and organisations they regulate.

Case study 7.9 Regulator fines company for misleading it and its customers

In 2008, a British water company was fined over £20 million by the regulator OFWAT for overcharging its customers and misleading the regulator. The company had misled the regulator on its performance which had enabled it to increase its charges at a higher rate than if the real performance figures had been supplied. Customers therefore had faced higher prices than what they should have been charged. (Milner, 2008)

In many areas of commerce and professional practice a licence or authorisation is often required to operate. Many regulatory bodies have the power to take this away or to place restrictions on those operating in a particular area. In financial services in the UK, the FCA regularly bans persons from operating in financial services for life, or a lesser period, for engaging in fraudulent-type acts. Perhaps one of the most significant areas where this type of action occurs is the Insolvency Service Companies Investigation Branch in the UK, which investigates misconduct by company directors and regularly disqualifies persons from being directors. Indeed the 2015–16 report notes 1208 directors being disqualified and 434 restriction orders and 483 referrals for criminal prosecution, with a further 25 to other regulators (Insolvency Service, 2016). Finally some regulatory bodies simply publicly admonish individuals for poor behaviour, as the case study from the ASA below illustrates. Clearly most regulatory action is only effective for those perpetrators who were regulated in the first place. The 'slippery slope'-type fraudsters that Levi (1981) notes, who started off as legitimate and then fell on hard times, leading them to commit fraud or those who simply decided from the start to use a 'regulated' position to commit fraud, are the sorts of fraudsters this type of action is suited to. The grey area of fraud also means that many acts, which victims might believe to be fraud, are often re-labelled as regulatory breaches or some other type of deviant act. These acts – by their very nature – are also suited to regulatory action (Button and Tunley, 2015).

Case study 7.10 Directors disqualified for misleading investors

In 2015 in the UK, four men were banned from being company directors for a total of 14 years for running a land and carbon credit scam. They had sold very cheap land and carbon credits for grossly inflated prices on the basis it would substantially increase in value, but this was highly unlikely. The disqualification followed an investigation by the Companies Investigation Branch. (Walmsley, 2015)

Case study 7.11 ASA and the basic sanction of admonishment

The ASA had dealt with a claim related to 'misrepresentation', which revolved around Bid TV selling 'Christian Lars' watches. In this case the presenter claimed the watch was £300 to those watching, but on the screen the price came up as £69.99. This was then claimed to be an 'error', but the lower price would be honoured, which was also subsequently lowered to £59.99. The complaint was upheld, with the ASA ruling:

We considered the price claims in the ad would be understood by viewers to mean the watch was normally sold for between £300 and £400. We also did not consider it would be clear to viewers that the presenter's statements about the price error were fictional. Because Bid TV has not provided evidence that the product was usually sold for between £300 and £400 we concluded the ad was misleading.

The ad breached BCAP Code rules 3.1 (Misleading advertising), 3.9 (Substantiation) and 3.18 (Prices).

Action (Sanction)

The ad must not appear again in its current form. We told Bid TV to not make price claims without holding documentary evidence to support them. (Advertising Standards Authority, 2012)

Disruption

Many policing bodies also use disruption as part of their tools when sanctions are not possible. As this is more oriented towards prevention, some of the activities that fit this category will be considered in the next chapter in more depth, including the work of Project Sunbird as previously cited.

Conclusion

This chapter has considered the complex web of policing bodies who deal with fraud. It has illustrated that law enforcement bodies at a state level are but one of many hybrid, private, voluntary and international policing bodies, all of which have a role to play in the policing of cyber frauds and scams. This also creates distinct challenges that include designating responsibility as well as enabling effective partnerships amongst a variety of organisations. The complex mix of policing bodies is also combined with a diverse range of potential sanctions, which stretch beyond the traditional criminal sanctions to include additional civil and regulatory tools. The chapter also noted the significant problem of attrition and alluded to the use of disruption activities by some bodies. The challenges these frauds pose mean that prevention is incredibly important and disruption, along with numerous other initiatives, provides many opportunities to have an impact upon fraud. This will be the focus of the next chapter.

References

419eater (n.d.) *Scamtracker*. Available at: http://www.419eater.com/ (accessed 25 October 2016).

Advertising Standards Authority (2012) *ASA Ruling On Sit-Up Ltd*. Available at: https://www.asa.org.uk/Rulings/Adjudications/2012/12/sit_up-Ltd/SHP_ADJ_207418.aspx#.VzMQWYQguUk (accessed 25 October 2016).

Australian Competition and Consumer Commission (n.d.) *About the ACCC*. Available at: https://www.accc.gov.au/about-us/australian-competition-consumer-commission/about-the-accc (accessed 25 October 2016).
Australian Federal Police (n.d.) *Cybercrime*. Available at: https://www.afp.gov.au/what-we-do/crime-types/cybercrime (accessed 25 October 2016).
Barclay, G. and Tavares, C. (1999). *Digest 4: Information on the Criminal Justice System in England and Wales*. London: Home Office. Available at: http://webarchive.nationalarchives.gov.uk/20110220105210/rds.homeoffice.gov.uk/rds/digest4/digest4.pdf (accessed 25 October 2016).
BBC News (2007) *Woman Sentenced Over Fake Viagra*. Available at: http://news.bbc.co.uk/1/hi/england/london/7079926.stm (accessed 25 October 2016).
BIS Enforcement Team (2016) *BIS criminal prosecutions*. Available at: https://www.gov.uk/government/case-studies/bis-criminal-prosecutions (accessed 25 October 2016).
Button, M. (2002) *Private Policing*, Cullompton: Willan Publishing.
Button, M. (2009) *Countering Cross-Border Fraud: Lessons from Abroad*. Unpublished report for the National Fraud Authority.
Button, M. (2011) Fraud investigation and the 'flawed architecture' of counter fraud entities in the United Kingdom. *International Journal of Law Crime and Justice* 39(4): 249–265. Doi: 10.1016/j.ijlcj.2011.06.001.
Button, M. (2012) Cross-border fraud and the case for an 'interfraud'. *Policing: An International Journal of Police Strategies & Management* 35(2): 285–303. Doi: 10.1108/13639511211230057.
Button, M. and Tunley, M. (2015) Explaining fraud deviancy attenuation in the United Kingdom. *Crime, Law and Social Change* 63(1): 49–64. Doi: 10.1007/s10611-015-9551-0.
Button, M., Blackbourn, D. and Tunley, M. (2015) 'The not so thin blue line after all?' Investigative resources dedicated to fighting fraud/economic crime in the United Kingdom. *Policing: A Journal of Policy and Practice* 9(2): 129–142. Doi: 10.1093/police/pau037.
Button, M., Lewis, C. and Tapley, J. (2009a) *A Better Deal for Victims*, London: National Fraud Authority.
Button, M., Lewis, C. and Tapley, J. (2009b) *Fraud Typologies and the Victims of Fraud Literature Review*, London: National Fraud Authority.
Button, M., Wakefield, A., Brooks, G., Lewis, C. (2015) Confronting the 'fraud bottleneck': Private sanctions for fraud and their implications for justice. *Journal of Criminological Research, Policy and Practice* 1(3): 159–174. Doi: 10.1108/JCRPP-04-2015-0006.
Button, M., Lewis, C., Shepherd, D., Brooks, G. and Wakefield, A. (2012) *Fraud and Punishment: Enhancing Deterrence Through More Effective Sanctions*, Portsmouth: Centre for Counter Fraud Studies. Available at: http://www.port.ac.uk/media/contacts-and-departments/icjs/ccfs/fraud-and-punishment.pdf (accessed 21 October 2016).
Byrne, D. (2013) 419 Digilantes and the frontier of radical justice online. *Radical History Review* 117: 70–82. Doi: 10.1215/01636545-2210464.
Conlan, T. (2008) *ITV Fined Record £5.675m Over Phone-Ins*. Available at: https://www.theguardian.com/media/2008/may/08/itv (accessed 25 October 2016).
Crawford, A. (2003) The pattern of policing in the UK: Policing beyond the police. In: Newburn, T. (ed.) *Handbook of Policing*, Cullompton: Willan.
Crawford, A., Lister, S. and Blackburn, S. (2005) *Plural Policing: The Mixed Economy of Visible Patrols in England and Wales*, Bristol: Policy Press.
Cross, C. (2016a) Policing online fraud in Australia: The emergence of a victim-oriented approach. In: Berents, H. and Scott, J. (eds) *Crime, Justice and Social Democracy: Proceedings*

of the 3rd International Conference 2015, Crime and Justice Research Centre, Queensland University of Technology, Brisbane, QLD, pp. 1–8. Available at: https://eprints.qut.edu.au/93198/ (accessed 25 October 2016).

Cross, C. (2016b) Using financial intelligence to target online fraud victimisation: Applying a tertiary prevention perspective. *Criminal Justice Studies* 29(2): 125–142. Doi: 10.1080/1478601X.2016.1170278.

Cross, C. and Blackshaw, D. (2015) Improving the police response to online fraud. *Policing: A Journal of Policy and Practice* 9(2): 119–128. Doi: 10.1093/police/pau044.

Cross, C., Richards, K. and Smith, R. (2016) *Improving the Response to Online Fraud Victims: An Examination of Reporting and Support*, Criminology Research Grant Final Report. Available at: http://www.crg.aic.gov.au/reports/1617/29-1314-FinalReport.pdf (accessed 21 October 2016).

Cunningham, W. C., Strauchs, J. J. and van Meter, C. W. (1990) *Private security trends 1970–2000, Hallcrest Report II*, Stoneham, MA: Butterworth-Heinemann.

Davies, M., Croall, H. and Tyrer, J. (1995) *Criminal Justice*, London: Longman.

Duffy, A. (2016) *Alleged Mastermind of Love Scheme that Defrauded Disabled Man of $850k Arrested.* Available at: http://ottawacitizen.com/news/local-news/alleged-mastermind-of-love-scheme-that-defrauded-disabled-man-of-850k-arrested (accessed 25 October 2016).

Elams, B. (2016) *Money Launderer Convicted After Trading Standards Swoop.* Available at: http://www.crewechronicle.co.uk/news/crewe-south-cheshire-news/money-launderer-convicted-after-trading-11313957 (accessed 25 October 2016).

Eurojust (2016) *Annual Report 2015*, The Hague: Eurojust. Available at: http://www.eurojust.europa.eu/doclibrary/corporate/eurojust%20Annual%20Reports/Annual%20Report%202015/Annual-Report-2015-EN.pdf (accessed 25 October 2016).

Europol (2014) *118 arrested in global action on online fraudsters in the airline sector.* https://www.europol.europa.eu/content/118-arrested-global-action-against-online-fraudsters-airline-sector (accessed 25 October 2016).

Europol (2015) *General Report on Europol Activities 2014*, The Hague: Europol. Available at: https://www.europol.europa.eu/content/europol-review-2014 (accessed 25 October 2016).

Ezer, J. (2011) *Nigerian Email Fraudsters, Humbled by Vigilante Justice.* Available at: http://www.huffingtonpost.com/jonathan-ezer/nigerian-email-fraudsters_b_544362.html (accessed 25 October 2016).

Federal Trade Commission (2015) *Stats and Data 2015.* Available at: https://www.ftc.gov/node/943403 (accessed 25 October 2016).

Federal Trade Commission (n.d.) *Enforcement.* Available at: https://www.ftc.gov/enforcement (accessed 25 October 2016).

Fraud Review Team (2006) *Final Report.* London: The Legal Secretariat to the Law Offices.

Gill, M. and Hart, J. (1997) Policing as a business: The organisation and structure of private investigation. *Policing and Society* 7(2): 117–141. Doi: 10.1080/10439463.1997.9964768.

Greenwood, C. (2012) *Britain's Bernie Madoff Jailed for 14 Years for £115m Swindle: Sports Stars, Actors and A Pop Singer Among his Victims.* Available at: http://www.dailymail.co.uk/news/article-2111820/Kautilya-Pruthi-Britains-Bernie-Madoff-guilty-115m-swindle.html (accessed 25 October 2016).

Hampshire Constabulary (2016) *Project Recruits Specialist Volunteers to Support Fight Against Cyber Crime.* Available at: http://www.hampshire.police.uk/internet/news-and-appeals/2016/january/200115-cyber-volunteers (accessed 25 October 2016).

Hitch, G. (2016) *Canberra woman wins $546,000 in damages after scammers sold house from under her.* Available at: http://www.abc.net.au/news/2016-08-22/canberra-woman-wins-damages-after-scammers-sold-house/7773434 (accessed 25 October 2016).

Insolvency Service (2016) *Annual Report 2015–16*. London: Insolvency Service. Available at: https://www.gov.uk/government/publications/insolvency-service-annual-report-and-accounts-2015-to-2016 (accessed 25 October 2016).

International Mass-Marketing Fraud Working Group (2010) *Mass Marketing Fraud: A Threat Assessment*. Available at: https://www.ice.gov/doclib/cornerstone/pdf/immfta.pdf (accessed 25 October 2016).

Johnston, L. (1996) What is Vigilantism? *British Journal of Criminology* 36(2): 220–236.

Johnston, L. and Shearing, C. D. (2003) *Governing Security*, London: Routledge.

Jones, R. (2013) *Britain's Got a Talent for Scam Phone Lines*. Available at: https://www.theguardian.com/money/2013/dec/12/britains-got-talent-scam-phone-lines-im-a-celebrity (accessed 25 October 2016).

Jones, T. and Newburn, T. (1998) *Private Security and Public Policing*, Oxford: Clarendon Press.

Levi, M. (1987) *Regulating Fraud*, London: Tavistock Publications.

Levi, M. (2006) Sentencing Frauds: A Review. Paper commissioned by the Attorney General's Fraud Review. Available at: http://docplayer.net/19102643-Sentencing-frauds-a-review.html (accessed 25 October 2016).

Loader, I. (2000) Plural policing and democratic governance. *Social and Legal Studies* 9(3): 323–345. Doi: 10.1177/096466390000900301.

London Borough of Lewisham (2007) *Bogus Builder Gets 4 ½ Year Prison Sentence and ASBO for Life*. Available at: http://www.ihsti.com/lacors/ContentDetails.aspx?id=16174 (accessed 25 October 2016).

Loveday, B. (2016) Still plodding along? The police response to the changing profile of crime in England and Wales. A Paper prepared for the Nordic Police Research Seminar 8–9th September. Available at: https://www.researchgate.net/publication/308078867_Still_Plodding_Along_The_police_response_to_the_changing_profile_of_crime_in_England_and_Wales_A_Paper_prepared_for_the_Nordic_Police_Research_Seminar_8–9th_September (accessed 3 November 2016).

Mawby, R. (2003) Models of policing. In: Newburn, T. (ed.) *Handbook of Policing*, Cullompton: Willan.

McGuire, J. (2002) Criminal sanctions versus psychologically-based interventions with offenders: A Comparative empirical analysis. *Psychology, Crime and Law* 8(2): 183–208. Doi: 10.1080/10683160208415005.

Milner, M. (2008) *OFWAT Fines Southern Water £20.3 million*. Available at: https://www.theguardian.com/business/2007/nov/15/southernwater (accessed 25 October 2016).

MinsterFM (2016) *Scam roofers jailed for preying on vulnerable Easingwold family*. Available at: http://www.minsterfm.com/news/local/2088612/scam-roofers-jailed-for-preying-on-vulnerable-easingwold-family/ (accessed 25 October 2016).

Nakamura, L. (2014) 'I WILL DO EVERYthing that am asked': Scambaiting, digital show-space, and the racial violence of social media. *Journal of Visual Culture* 13(3): 257–174. Doi: 10.1177/1470412914546845.

National Fraud Authority (2012) *Annual Fraud Indicator*, London: National Fraud Authority.

Noaks, L. (2000) Private cops on the block: A review of the role of private security in residential communities. *Policing and Society* 10(2): 143–161. Doi: 10.1080/10439463.2000.9964837.

Ofcom (2015) *Ofcom Fines Unicom for Misleading Customers*. Available at: http://media.ofcom.org.uk/news/2015/unicom-misleading-customers/ (accessed 25 October 2016).

Online Investigations (n.d.) *About Us*. Available at: http://www.onlineinvestigations.com.au/ (accessed 25 October 2016).

Parry, R. (2016) *EXCLUSIVE: Eddie Murphy's Ex-Wife Nicole Murphy Tells of 'Nightmare' $7million Fraud by High-Living Conman Who is Finally Going to Trial – Five Years After his Arrest*. Available at: http://www.dailymail.co.uk/news/article-3753039/Eddie-Murphy-s-ex-Nicole-Murphy-tells-nightmare-7-million-fraud-high-living-conman-Troy-Stratos-finally-going-trial.html (accessed 25 October 2016).

Queensland Organised Crime Commission of Inquiry (2015) *Report*. Available at: http://organisedcrimeinquiry.qld.gov.au/__data/assets/pdf_file/0017/935/QOCCI15287-ORGANISED-CRIME-INQUIRY_Final_Report.pdf (accessed 25 October 2016).

Rigakos, G. S. (2002) *The New Parapolice*, Toronto: University of Toronto Press.

Ring, T. (2014) *London Police Boosts Cyber-Crime Fighting and CNI Threat Tackled*. Available at: http://www.scmagazineuk.com/london-police-boosts-cyber-crime-fighting-and-cni-threat-tackled/article/375224/ (accessed 25 October 2016).

Royal Canadian Mounted Police (2010) *International Day of Action Against Mass Marketing Fraud*. Available at: http://www.rcmp-grc.gc.ca/scams-fraudes/day-jour-eng.htm (accessed 25 October 2016).

Sarre, R. and Prenzler, T. (2011) *Private Security and Public Interest: Exploring Private Security Trends and Directions for Reform in the New Era of Plural Policing*. Sydney: ARC Report. Available at: https://www.asial.com.au/documents/item/12 (accessed 25 October 2016).

Semke, C. (2012) *Rogue Purbrook electrician who conned Hampshire residents is given an ASBO*. Available at: http://www.portsmouth.co.uk/news/law-and-order/rogue_purbrook_electrician_who_conned_hampshire_residents_is_given_an_asbo_1_3492643 (accessed 25 October 2016).

Shearing, C. D. and Stenning, P. C. (1982) *Private Security and Private Justice*, Montreal: The Institute on Public Policy.

UK Background Checks (n.d.) *Dating Scams can be Prevented with UK Background Checks*. Available at: http://www.ukbackgroundchecks.com/dating-scams.html (accessed 25 October 2016).

UK Private Investigators (n.d.) *Dating Site Scams and Investigations*. Available at: https://www.ukprivateinvestigators.com/dating-site-scams (accessed 25 October 2016).

United States Department of Justice (2015) *Six Nigerian nationals extradited from South Africa to Mississippi to face fraud charges*. Available at: https://www.justice.gov/usao-sdms/pr/six-nigerian-nationals-extradited-sout-africa-mississippi-face-fraud-charges (accessed 25 October 2016).

US Postal Inspection Service (n.d.) *Mission Statement*. Available at: https://postalinspectors.uspis.gov/aboutus/mission.aspx (accessed 25 October 2016).

Walmsley, C. (2015) *Directors Banned Over £5.5m Land and Carbon Credit Scam*. Available at: http://citywire.co.uk/new-model-adviser/news/directors-banned-over-5-5m-land-and-carbon-credit-scam/a822334 (accessed 25 October 2016).

8

PREVENTING CYBER FRAUDS AND SCAMS

Introduction[1]

The sheer scale of fraud and cyber fraud victimisation, with millions of people falling victim globally and even more being targeted each year, poses significant challenges for the law enforcement community. As was shown in the previous chapter they do not have enough resources to investigate the vast majority of these frauds. Prevention, therefore, becomes very important. Indeed, there is also the duty that befalls individuals, organisations and official bodies to develop effective strategies to prevent fraud and attempt to substantially reduce the level of victimisation. Mainstream property crime has been targeted with many preventative techniques rooted in criminological theory, and there is a corresponding body of research to justify and evaluate such initiatives. However, fraud prevention as an academic subject is much less advanced, although it is important to note that there are many fraud prevention tools used by individuals and organisations. This chapter will seek to build upon the body of knowledge on crime prevention in general, particularly the 25 techniques of situational crime prevention advocated by Clarke (2005) to identify a variety of fraud prevention tools which are regularly used. Unfortunately, because of the lack of research in this area, there is not a great deal of literature to assess how effective some of these tools are. However, this chapter will attempt to provide one of the first broad attempts to identify a wide variety of tools under the five main sub-headings used by Clarke (2005): *increasing the effort*, *increasing the risks*, *reducing the rewards*, *reducing provocations* and *removing excuses*. While the chapter focuses heavily on situational crime prevention techniques as they can apply to cyber frauds and scams, it will also offer a discussion on the perceived differences/similarities between crime that occurs across both offline and online environments to determine the suitability of existing prevention theory in this new sphere. Before we embark upon this, however, the chapter will first examine crime prevention in general.

Crime prevention in general

There has been a huge body of research that has fuelled policies and tools to prevent crime. Rooted in the importance of opportunity, rational choice theory and routine activity theory, situational crime prevention has become one of the most dominant. During the 1970s in the UK Home Office, a whole series of research studies pointed towards the importance of opportunity inspired from data on suicide and related research. This had found that when toxic town gas was replaced by natural gas, the preferred method of suicide (of switching on the gas with the head in the oven) disappeared. However, rather than use another method many chose not to take their life and the total number of suicides actually declined. As Clarke and Mayhew (1989: 36) note:

> It seems reasonable, therefore, to conclude that the overall decline of the national rate of suicide for England and Wales in the 1960s and 1970s was due to the elimination of domestic gas poisoning as a method, and, further, that this observation constitutes powerful evidence of the role of opportunity in suicide.

A similar effect was also found in the USA with the introduction of catalytic conversion on cars. It was therefore argued that if, as fundamental a decision as to take one's life was based upon opportunity, then a much lesser decision of committing a crime may also be affected (Clarke and Mayhew, 1989). This, combined with other research, led some researchers to highlight the importance of opportunity in offender motivations. The small amount of research on fraud offenders has also highlighted the importance of opportunity, although these studies have been largely pre-occupied with occupational fraudsters (Cressey, 1953; Schuchter and Levi, 2015).

Linked to the importance of opportunity and underpinning situational crime prevention is the importance of rational choice theory. Cornish and Clarke (1986) noted the idea of crimes occurring as a result of a 'rational actor' who undertakes a series of choices rooted in different influences leading to the criminal event. The criminal assesses these influences and if there is potential benefit, commits the act, although not necessarily with sound objective judgement. Clearly the ability of individuals to assess the opportunities and risks varies by criminal and type of crime.

Alongside these ideas of rational choice theory, routine activity theory emerged. This argued that three elements are required for a crime to occur: a motivated offender, a suitable victim and the absence of a capable guardian (Cohen and Felson, 1979). Gill (2005) has also highlighted that the motivated offender requires the appropriate resources and there also needs to be a law to break. Central to this theory is that crimes are associated with increased opportunities. Many activities that individuals engage in provide opportunities for crimes and with the other two aspects, this provides for the greater likelihood of a crime occurring. The theory sought to partly explain the rise in post-war crime in many Western countries, despite increasing wealth, which went against many of the social-determinist explanations for crime.

Building upon these theories, it was argued that if the environment could be enhanced to reduce the opportunities this would lead to a reduction in the level of crime. If offenders could be made less motivated to commit a crime, victims less suitable and the guardian more effective, these would all have an impact on crime. Situational crime prevention has come to encompass all of these strategies of which there are many and we will shortly note. Clarke (1997: 1) describes situational crime prevention in the following way:

> Proceeding from an analysis of the circumstances giving rise to specific kinds of crime, it introduces discrete managerial and environmental change to reduce the opportunity for those crimes to occur. Thus it is focused on the settings for crime, rather than upon those committing criminal acts. It seeks to forestall the occurrence of crime, rather than to detect and sanction offenders. It seeks not to eliminate criminal or delinquent tendencies through improvement of society or its institutions, but merely to make criminal action less attractive to offenders. Central to this enterprise is not the criminal justice system, but a host of public and private organisations and agencies – schools, hospitals, transit systems, shops and malls, manufacturing businesses and phone companies, local parks and entertainment facilities, pubs and parking lots – whose products, services and operations spawn opportunities for a vast range of different crimes.

Clarke (2005) has refined situational crime prevention to 25 techniques. As previously noted, there are five main headings: *increasing the effort*, *increasing the risks*, *reducing the rewards*, *reducing provocations* and *removing excuses*. Before these 25 techniques are examined, however, it is important to note the other major 'school' of crime prevention, centred around 'social crime prevention'. Situational crime prevention has been criticised for a number of reasons, most notably displacement, therefore it is important to consider this fundamental weakness. Barr and Pease (1990) and Reppetto (1976) have identified a number of elements to displacement:

- *Temporal.* The crime is committed at a different time;
- *Tactical.* The crime is committed using a different method;
- *Target.* The crime is committed against a different target;
- *Territorial.* The crime is committed in a different area;
- *Functional.* A different type of crime is committed;
- *Perpetrator displacement.* Prevented crimes are committed by different offenders.

The essence of this critique argues that situational crime prevention does not change the underlying behaviour of the offender or the motivations for offending behaviour to occur. To put it crudely and simply, imagine a child who wants to raid the cupboard for sweets. The situational crime prevention means to deal with this is to lock the cupboard. However, the child will still want to try and get into the cupboard, they may try to steal the key, or force the door open. Social crime prevention, by contrast, seeks to change the behaviour of the child so they would not think about raiding it for sweets. Social crime prevention, which has been defined by Sutton (1994: 10, cited in Gilling, 1997: 5) as, 'any program that can claim to affect the pattern of behaviour, values, and self-discipline of groups seen as having the potential to offend' is also important to note in a holistic preventative scheme. Clarke's techniques of situational crime prevention have evolved over the years and some, but not all, of Clarke's 25 techniques overlap with social crime prevention, particularly some of the techniques under the headings of reducing provocations and removing excuses. There are five main areas which each unlock another five areas. Each of the areas is listed below with examples of relevant techniques.

1. Increasing the effort

These strategies are designed to force the offender have to increase their effort to commit a crime and include the following five types of strategies:

Target hardening: shutters and barriers;
Controlling access: entry phones, X-ray detection for weapons/explosives, ticket gates;
Controlling exits: ticket gates, electronic tags on products;
Deflection of offenders: street closures, crowd separation; and
Control tools and weapons: restriction on spray paint sales, weapon sales controls.

2. Increasing the risks

These strategies are designed to make it more likely the offender will get caught and thus, it is hoped, less likely to commit the crime.

Extend guardianship: going out in groups, neighbourhood watch;
Natural surveillance: improve lighting, design of buildings, encourage whistle-blowers;
Reduce anonymity: require name badges, school uniforms;
Utilise place managers: caretakers, conductors; and
Formal surveillance: CCTC, security guards.

3. Reducing the rewards

These are strategies that, if the offender is successful, make the outcome of the criminal event less attractive, again with the aim of discouraging offenders.

Conceal targets: off-street parking, unmarked bullion trucks;
Remove targets: DVDs removed from display packages, pre-payment cards instead of cash;
Identify property: marking of bikes with codes, tagging of items;

Disrupt markets: monitor pawn shops, controls on classified advertisements; and
Deny benefits: blocking mobile phones, graffiti cleaning.

4. Reducing provocations

The fourth set of five strategies focus upon reducing the provocations that might influence some people to commit crimes.

Reduce frustrations and stress: remove queues, emit soothing music;
Avoid disputes: reduce crowding, fixed fares for cabs;
Reduce emotional arousal: controls on violent pornography;
Neutralise peer pressure: campaigns to say no; and
Discourage imitation: rapid repair of vandalism, block publication of modus operandi.

5. Removing excuses

The final set of five strategies seek to remove excuses as often offenders will justify their actions by claiming they did not know it was wrong.

Set rules: clear rules on expectations of behaviour;
Post instructions: 'no parking signs', 'no skate boarding signs';
Alert conscience: roadside speed displays, signature declarations;
Assist compliance: public lavatories, litter bins; and
Control drugs and alcohol: alcohol free zones, breathalysers in pubs.

The above provides a sample of some of the strategies that fall under the 25 techniques. Research, policy documents and websites provide much more depth to the techniques which can be used for different types of crime (see http://www.popcenter.org/). Most volume property crimes have been addressed by situational crime prevention. It has also been applied to terrorism (Clarke and Newman, 2006), sex offending (Wortley and Smallbone, 2006), organised crime (Bullock et al., 2010) and e-commerce (Newman and Clarke, 2003). There has been some interest in applying it to fraud in general (Button and Gee, 2013; Smith et al., 2010), but what is interesting is that there has been virtually no interest in applying the 25 techniques to the frauds and cyber frauds considered in this book. This, however, is not to say there has been no interest in preventing this type of fraud, because there clearly has. It is just they have not been grouped together in a holistic way in the model of situational crime prevention. This is particularly interesting, given the dominance of routine activity theory approaches to research in this area, which is drawn heavily from similar concepts that underpin situational prevention measures. This chapter will therefore draw out these techniques and use examples from around the world to illustrate examples of fraud prevention techniques. However, before applying these techniques to the current problem of cyber frauds and scams, it is important to examine the literature that engages in a discussion of offline/online offending, and whether traditional criminological theories (and by extension crime prevention theories) are applicable and of relevance across both mediums.

Offline crime versus online crime: the same or different?

As previously stated, situational crime prevention measures have been a dominant approach to crime prevention for several decades, and there have been many successful evaluations that have documented effective outcomes through the modification of environment factors to reduce the opportunity and ability to commit crimes. With the evolution of technology, and the increased use and role of the internet in offending, it is therefore unsurprising that there has been a desire to apply these same situational techniques to crimes perpetrated in a cyber space. However, there is little consensus as to whether there are inherent differences in crimes perpetrated in a virtual environment, and as such, if existing crime prevention theories are transferrable to the cyber world.

Grabosky (2001) asserted that online crime is no different to its offline counterpart. Instead he argued that online crime is essentially 'old wine in new bottles' (Grabosky, 2001). This is based on assumptions that the motivations to commit crimes do not change between offences regardless of the environment that they are perpetrated in. Further to this, Grabosky (2001: 248) argues 'one of the basic tenets of criminology holds that crime can be explained by three factors: motivation, opportunity and the absence of a capable guardian … Derived initially to explain conventional "street" crime, it is equally applicable to crimes in cyberspace'. This statement draws heavily from Cohen and Felson's (1979) crime triangle and demonstrates the influence of situational approaches to this argument. In a similar vein, Holt and Bossler (2014) conducted a review of all available research examining cyber crime, under Wall's (2001) cyber crime typology, which has been well established and accepted in academic fields and consists of cyber trespass, cyber deception/theft, cyber porn and obscenity, and cyber violence. Through their examination, Holt and Bossler (2014: 33) surmise 'as a whole, these studies have generally demonstrated that traditional criminological theories and postulates apply in virtual environments'. In advocating this position, they cite studies that have mainly employed 'routine activity theory, social learning and the general theory of crime' (Holt and Bossler, 2014: 33).

In contrast to this, Yar (2005) argues that there are significant differences, which can alter the applicability of traditional crime prevention theories to the new environment created by the internet. In analysing each of the main components of routine activity theory, Yar concludes that the temporal and spatial aspects of routine activity theory are limited in a virtual environment, where there are 'distinctive spatio-temporal ontologies of virtual and non-virtual environments' (Yar, 2005: 424). In this way, Yar (2005: 424) concludes that 'routine activity theory … thus appears of limited utility in an environment that defies many of our taken-for-granted assumptions about how the socio-interactional setting of routine activities is configured'.

Most recently, Leukfeldt and Yar (2016) continued the examination of applying routine activities theory to cyber crime, in an attempt to further determine its suitability from an empirical perspective. In doing this, they identified eleven previous studies, which have specifically sought to apply at least one element of routine activities theory (value, inertia, visibility, accessibility, and/or capable guardian) across at least one type of cyber crime (such as fraud, malware, phishing, and harassment, to name a few). The 11 studies outlined in Leukfeldt and Yar (2016) delivered mixed results, with five giving mostly positive results, while the remaining six were mostly negative on the application of routine activity theory. In their own analysis of the elements of routine activity theory across three categories of cyber crime (hi-tech crimes, cyber frauds and interpersonal cyber crimes) Leukfeldt and Yar (2016: 17) argue that 'overall, the usability of RAT seems to have a number of restrictions, at least in the way RAT has been operationalised in this article'. Of interest, they note 'what is striking is that within all three categories of cyber crimes victims often simply spent more time on-line … being more extensively on-line thus provides a greater chance of becoming a victim of on-line crimes' (Leukfeldt and Yar, 2016: 17).

In combination, the studies cited in this section indicate the current nature of the debate as to whether cyber crimes and those perpetrated in an offline environment are inherently similar or different, and to what degree that impacts on the application and suitability of traditional criminological theories. At present, the evidence is inconclusive at best, though there is ongoing discussion and investigation. In this context, the following statement by Henry and Powell (2014: 92) is worth keeping in mind (in this case, specifically focused on technology-facilitated sexual violence).

> It would be imprudent to overlook the qualitative distinctions between offline and online forms of criminality. Conversely, it is important to avoid a false dichotomy between 'offline' and 'online worlds' … As such it is crucial to acknowledge two key features of TFSV: first, that technology assists or facilitates the perpetration of old or traditional behaviours …; and second, regardless of whether or not these are old or new crimes, conceptual frameworks for addressing and responding to sexual violence in the technosocial world requires substantial development.
>
> *(Henry and Powell, 2014: 92)*

It is readily apparent that the underlying concept underpinning this quote has relevance for the current discussion of cyber frauds and scams. The evolution of technology has seen a shift in fraud being committed across both offline and online platforms. This has been clearly illustrated in earlier chapters and in many examples across this book. Having a clear demarcation of the medium of communication for fraud is not necessarily constructive and does little to assist the victims who experience fraud and scams. Rather, it is imperative to think about the perpetration of fraud as a whole, including both virtual and terrestrial environments. In this way, while the application of traditional crime prevention theories may have limitations and are not necessarily readily transferable to an online environment, there is still merit in thinking through how these established crime prevention theories could be modified and further developed to better assist in the prevention of fraud, across any method of communication. It is to this discussion that the chapter now turns.

Preventing fraud and cyber fraud using situational crime prevention

While the previous section has highlighted various points of consideration in applying traditional situational crime prevention techniques (developed for offline offences) to online offences, as stated, we believe there is still merit in exploring these techniques in the context of cyber frauds and scams. While acknowledging the above arguments, the following section seeks to demonstrate that there is still a valid contribution to be made through applying Clarke's five categories of situational crime prevention techniques to the current problem of cyber frauds and scams. This does not seek to ignore the previous critiques and acknowledges the overall limitations of a situational approach, from its traditional foundations as well as its application to a virtual environment. However, it builds on this discussion and uses these critiques as a means of engagement with the situational crime prevention literature.

On this basis, the following section will consider how the five broader techniques of crime prevention can be applied to scams and cyber fraud. While not all the techniques can be used or are applicable, under the five main sub-headings there remain plenty of tools and examples that are of relevance. These main sub-headings will be used to explore the different tools. It is important to note, however, such is the diversity of fraud and variety of fraud prevention tools it will not be possible to cover them all. The chapter will, however, give a very strong indication of the breadth of tools, and leads for an interested reader to pursue more examples. It is also important to note these tools can be utilised at a number of levels. The individual member of public can take actions to prevent victimisation, organisations can pursue strategies to reduce the risk of their customers becoming victims, and the relevant police bodies can also pursue action to reduce the risk to victims. It is this last point that forms a detailed case study towards the end of this chapter.

Increasing the effort

At first glance it might seem difficult to link the use of barriers and shutters in target hardening to the prevention of fraud. However there are a variety of strategies which can be used to harden targets. First of all it is important to distinguish between the target victims and the facilitating victims. Some organisations possess information on clients that is useful to fraudsters to then target those clients. For those organisations who possess such information, it is critical that they have the suitable cyber barriers in place such as firewalls, password protection, and encryption to protect that information as well as appropriate procedures and controls to prevent staff from releasing sensitive personal information by accident or design. These same lessons also apply to individuals and persons who use online tools for various transactions, and who should take the steps to protect themselves with appropriate updated anti-virus protection, the use of suitable passwords for their accounts (which contain a combination of letters, numbers and symbols), and anti-spam software, to name a few. Individuals can take many steps to target harden their online presence. There is also the option of some additional protections that can be used by consumers, such as the protective registration of Cifas in the UK. Under this scheme a person who has been the victim of an identity fraud or perceives themselves to be high risk can register with Cifas and this means any time a financial institution receives an application for a product involving that person's name they apply greater checks in line with their registration (Cifas, n.d.). This same service is also offered by a variety of credit bureaus, where customers can register to receive notifications each time a new line of credit is applied for using their details. This is particularly relevant for victims of identity theft, or those who believe that their personal information may have been compromised in some way.

While this book has concentrated on frauds perpetrated in an online environment, it is important to realise that fraud still occurs through a combination of older technologies. For example, frauds are still perpetrated by communication mediums such as the telephone. Many fraudsters gain telephone numbers of potential victims from legitimate marketing lists. In some countries it is possible for consumers to opt out so their telephone details are not circulated and therefore cannot be contacted. Of course many fraudsters get numbers from other means, but this does provide one tool to reduce the risk and increase the effort for the fraudster. Many countries have what are generically termed 'do not call' registries. For example is the USA, consumers can register on the Do Not Call Registry (https://www.donotcall.gov/) and similar initiatives exist in Australia, New Zealand, the UK and Canada. Similar initiatives also exist for other types of communication. For instance, in the UK it is possible to register with the Mail Preference Service to restrict certain types of mass marketing mail (http://www.mpsonline.org.uk/mpsr/).

Access control prevention techniques can include a variety of commonly used tools such as passwords and PIN codes for access to websites and devices. Controlling access can also be applied to fraud and cyber fraud. Many websites which facilitate online trading can apply checks on persons before they are able to use the website and prevent those who are deemed higher risk of fraud from entering. There are means to verify a person through credit referencing agencies, fraudster databases and other tools. The growing problem of romance frauds has led to a number of the major providers of this service to undertake background checks on prospective clients before they can use the services. In the USA, it was reported a number of providers checked clients against national sex offender registers, amongst others (Newcomb, 2012). It was also noted in the previous chapter how some private investigator firms also offer background checks on prospective partners found on romance websites. The same can be applied to 'controlling exits'. For instance before a large transaction is approved by some banks they will check and verify the payee and the receiver of the payment. Indeed, some banks have advised some vulnerable customers, such as pensioners, that the payment they intend to make is fraudulent, with a view to stopping them. There is an increased use of two-factor authentication across a range of agencies, such as banks and email providers, which use two separate means of identification to verify the true identity of a person and ensure that any transactions or changes to account settings are actually those of the customer and not an offender.

Another very important preventative strategy undertaken by policing bodies and some organisations is the disruption of fraudsters. The tactics here include a wide range of initiatives. For example many fraudsters use websites and once the police have identified specific fraudulent websites, they will contact the internet service provider to seek to close them down. This means the fraudster then has to set it up again, which is often possible, but makes it more time consuming and challenging to do this. Disruption can also be applied to bank accounts, email accounts, mobile phone accounts, to name some. Organisations that are impersonated by fraudsters may also become involved in this type of action, alone or in partnership with policing bodies. In the previous chapter 'scambaiting' was illustrated, which can be seen as another form of disrupting fraudsters by overloading them with information and leads which are useless, in order to waste their time, though this is not an endorsed activity in and of itself. Some organisations also provide these services to clients to target fraudsters, such as those 'phishing', with large amounts of useless information. For instance, a major US company RSA had a division which feeds phishers with large numbers of account details which are useless (Kotadia, 2006). Disruption also features highly in the case study provided at the end of this chapter.

Case study 8.1 Disrupting fraudsters

The City of London Police reported in 2015–16 extensive activities to disrupt fraudsters. They reported having sent nearly 150,000 suspension requests to partners in the UK and abroad for bank accounts, telephone accounts and websites. Some 3,889 domains in the UK had been suspended as a result of their action. (City of London Police, 2016)

In the previous chapter the use of orders such as ASBOs and potential regulatory sanctions were illustrated. These also provide tools to help prevent further frauds from occurring and make it more difficult for the fraudster to operate. The use of orders like the ASBO to restrict the potential activities of a fraudster makes it more difficult and risky to pursue that type of action. If the fraudster uses a regulated position to conduct frauds, by banning them or restricting their activities, this also increases the effort for the fraudster.

Increasing the risks

One of the most important strategies for tackling fraud is the need to share information between bodies in the public and private sectors and between countries. This enables the dots to be joined up and offenders and their modus operandi to be exposed, which then enables preventative measures and enforcement to be pursued. There are a variety of initiatives around the world, which provide good examples of such information-gathering initiatives. These techniques centre around two major types of information sharing:

> **Datamatching**: this is the scanning of different files/databases using computer technology either within an organisation or between more than one to identify inconsistencies that can then be investigated to detect fraud. (National Audit Office, 2013)
>
> **Datamining**: this is 'the process of selecting, exploring and modelling large amounts of data to reveal previously unknown patterns, behaviours, trends or relationships which may help to identify cases of fraud. Because of the large amount of data that need to be analysed, specialist computer software is used which usually contain a range of data mining tools.'
>
> *(National Audit Office, 2013: 33)*

Organisations such as financial institutions make use of such techniques to identify higher risk transactions with the purposes of preventing fraud against their customers. Thus, it is common for banks to spot potential frauds using these techniques, which highlight unusual transactions. This is also evident in the use of suspicious transaction reports in Canada, and the use of suspicious matter reports in Australia, whereby authorities are required to flag transactions that they feel may not be legitimate on a number of grounds. The example used earlier in this book of a colleague of one of the authors being phoned to ask if they were trying to purchase an airline ticket is a good example of the type of preventative work undertaken by such bodies using these techniques. These techniques are also used by policing bodies, particularly as they often receive extensive intelligence, data and reports of frauds from a variety of sources. Thus a mobile phone number from one report can be checked against multiple other reports in databases (datamatching) and this might throw up other leads which then enable the investigators to determine who the fraudster is, thus increasing their risks of getting caught.

Case study 8.2 Datamining and datamatching to reduce romance fraud

There is a company called Scamalytics (https://scamalytics.com/) which specialises in conducting various data analytics and matching to detect potential fraudsters. Some of the tools they use include analysing the profiles, messages, images of clients. They also share known fraudsters on a 'blacklist' amongst users of their service.(Scamalytics, n.d.)

Case study 8.3 Datamatching to reduce online fraud

West Australian police were able to use financial intelligence to identify the bank account of an alleged offender, who was receiving funds from a victim. The identification of this particular account and further examination of its transaction history subsequently led police to identify additional victims from other Australian jurisdictions who were also victims and sending money to this one offender. The account was closed, the offender was arrested, and the victims were notified of their involvement in fraud to reduce ongoing victimisation. (Cross and Blackshaw, 2015)

There are also a variety of databases used in the financial services sector, which enable members to share information on fraudsters or information associated to fraudulent transactions, such as Cifas and National Hunter in the UK. These are particularly strong in the UK financial services sector and make it more difficult for fraudsters to get access to financial services.

Central to good datamatching and datamining is a central repository of reports and intelligence. In the UK, as well as many other jurisdictions, fraud is a crime that presents more difficulties to report (see Button et al., 2009). There are often multiple agencies with responsibility for fraud with varying commitment towards it. Public and corporate ignorance of who to report to alongside the multiple jurisdictions involved adds to the problem for cross-border fraud. If a victim falls for a scam emanating from Costa Rica, some might think that they would need to report in Costa Rica, when they don't in the UK. England and Wales have sought to address low reporting with the establishment of a National Fraud Reporting Centre called Action Fraud, with the National Intelligence Bureau behind it. All reports as well as intelligence from a large variety of other sources are brought together to create packages which are then distributed to the most appropriate agency for action. This information is also used to alert the general public, educate them and to inform campaigns. Some of these reporting bodies are run by law enforcement agencies, however others are supported by other government and non-government agencies.

TABLE 8.1 National fraud reporting bodies

Action Fraud http://www.actionfraud.police.uk/ (UK)
Fraud Help Desk http://www.fraudhelpdesk.org/ (Netherlands)
Internet Crime Complaint Centre http://www.ic3.gov (USA)
Canadian Anti-Fraud Centre http://www.antifraudcentre-centreantifraude.ca/ (Canada)
Australian Cybercrime Online Reporting Network http://www.acorn.gov.au (Australia)
Scamwatch http://www.scamwatch.gov.au (Australia)
The Orb http://www.theorb.org.nz/ (New Zealand)

In addition to datamining and datamatching, many financial institutions use a variety of other strategies to try and protect their customers. Some fraudsters will use phone call centres to try and impersonate the victim to transfer monies or pursue other actions to facilitate a fraud. To combat this, some financial institutions use voice recognition techniques to compare the voice to the real client. Some also use technology to identify where the caller is calling from and if this does not fit with the profile it can be used to ask questions to identify if there is a higher risk to the proposed transaction. These increase the chances of the fraudster getting caught.

Individuals can also use various software installed on their home computers and devices, which are regularly executed to detect malware, viruses, and sniffer software. By regularly conducting such 'scanning' exercises, individuals are doing the equivalent of looking out their window to look for suspicious persons and activities. Similarly, any unsolicited contact offering products and services can be checked on appropriate scam awareness websites. Consumers can also check the websites they visit to determine if they are legitimate before purchasing from them. It is in this context too that policing bodies and organisations often publicise scams and other suspect activities such as suspicious websites, to raise awareness amongst the general public and their customers and to increase the risks of fraudsters being caught.

There are other means to extend some of the initiatives under this category. For instance, the extension of guardianship can be used amongst groups who are vulnerable to victimisation. Pensioners who are often targets for fraudsters can be educated, through their community groups and networks, to recognise emerging scams and frauds and what to do to prevent them. These groups can also be used as sounding boards for potential transactions/invitations before they commit to them.

Case study 8.4 Elders helping elders

In the USA a National Telemarketing Victim Call Centre was established, staffed by members of the Retired and Senior Volunteer Programme. These volunteers called potential victims to alert them to potential scams and that they might be targeted. The names of those who are called are taken from 'mooch' lists that have been seized during boiler room and other investment fraud operations, and therefore seek to warn those who are identified targets. The centre managed to make almost 20,000 phone calls in its first year of operation, in addition to the almost 8,000 calls made in a previous operation which led to the establishment of the call centre. Further to the phone calls, the Centre pursued a strategy to secure extensive media coverage of the nature and risk of frauds, estimating that over 20 million people have been made aware of telemarketing fraud through their activities. (Aziz et al., 2000)

Another tool that has been used to make it more likely for potential victims to spot a potential fraud are 'fake scams' by consumer protection bodies. For instance, the US Postal Service sent 200,000 postcards to prior victims of scams telling them they had won a prize in a draw. On calling the telephone number the victims were told this was an example of a telemarketing scam and that they should be more careful responding to such initiatives in the future (Hines, 2001). This same technique, of official bodies perpetrating a scam to see who falls for it and then seeking to educate them, has been used by a wide range of other bodies in different countries.

Reducing the rewards

There are a wide variety of ways in which the potential rewards to the fraudsters can be reduced. Websites which offer individuals the ability to sell goods and services might have scope to seize some of the monies that flow through their site from those proved to be engaged in fraud. Internet Service Providers can also be utilised to close down suspect websites and ban proven fraudsters from using them. When those fraudsters are caught, it is important to secure as many of their illegally gained assets as possible. The previous chapter noted some of the powers that are available in some countries to seize the assets of criminals.

Reducing provocations

Many frauds are simple and relatively easy to replicate. In some cases it is therefore important not to provide too much information on how the fraud has taken place as a means to prevent copycats. Many frauds use advertising techniques that often exaggerate the potential benefits. Therefore, restricting the controls on how products and services are advertised offers some protection where fraudsters use legitimate channels to promote their scams.

Removing excuses

This book has illustrated the dynamic nature of frauds and scams and how they evolve and adapt to target different groups. One of the most important aspects of a fraud prevention strategy is to educate the public of the risks and nature of scams. Every person in society has a fraud they could potentially fall for, so it is very important to develop awareness campaigns that are targeted to the likely groups who will be targeted. All the tools of a campaign therefore need to be utilised in varying ways according to the target group:

- Advertising campaigns: television, radio, newspapers, specialist publications, online
- News releases to secure media interest
- Specialists websites
- Mailshots
- Social media
- Emails, texts, tweets
- Community and interest group activities
- Storylines in dramas.

It is also important that awareness and prevention advice is targeted at those who have already become victims, to prevent repeat victimisation. In the UK, Action Fraud, which is the national reporting centre for fraud and cyber crime, regularly reports the latest frauds and scams on its news section of the website at: http://www.actionfraud.police.uk/news. Another good example is Canadascambusters, which as its name suggests is based in Canada and provides information on new and emerging scams and advice on how to avoid them https://www.canadascambusters.com/. Similar websites are accessible in several countries, such as the Federal Trade Commission in the USA, https://www.consumer.ftc.gov/, the Scamwatch website in Australia https://www.scamwatch.gov.au and the Netsafe website in New Zealand http://www.netsafe.org.nz.

Case study 8.5 FCA and the prevention of investment fraud

Investment frauds or boiler room frauds are very common. One of the strategies the UK Financial Conduct Authority uses is providing a website with extensive guidance on how to avoid a scam. One of the most important aspects of this service is a database with a list of suspect organisations that have been identified in the course of their investigations. For example, there is a website where a prospective investor can type in information about the firm or person offering the investment to see if they are listed (http://scamsmart.fca.org.uk/warninglist/search). There is also extensive advice on a variety of other factors for prospective investors to consider and nine steps are advocated:

1. Reject cold calls
2. Don't send money

3. Check if a firm is authorised or registered
4. Search the list of unauthorised firms
5. Beware of cloned firms
6. Make additional checks
7. See warnings from abroad
8. Report an unauthorised scam
9. Beware of further scams. (Financial Conduct Authority, 2016)

The alerting of conscience and assisting compliance are regularly used by financial institutions to try and prevent their customers falling for frauds. For instance, often details of a particular risk will be displayed to a customer and they will have to tick a box acknowledging that they have read it before they can continue to the services they wish to use. Some websites when facilitating a new account where a password is required will assist the user in developing a suitably complex one by rating it, with more secure passwords receiving a higher score. Similarly, with some websites, before they can be reached the user is alerted to potential risks of visiting. There are also examples of banks approaching customers who wish to transfer large sums of money to a suspect account, particularly overseas, suggesting that they should think again before doing so.

Plural responsibility for prevention

In the previous chapter, the large number of organisations who become involved in policing fraud were identified. Some of those dedicated to preventing fraud in particular were highlighted. In this section some examples will be noted of emerging organisations from around the world that have done significant work to prevent fraud.

Victim-led groups

Victim-led groups are very important for a variety of different types of crimes. Fraud victims have been notable by the smaller number of groups that exist to support such victims. This may reflect the more recent higher profile that has been given to such crimes. One notable group in the UK, however, is 'Think Jessica'. This is a victim support group founded by the daughter of a chronic scam victim. The group has gone on to provide a voice to such victims and most importantly to promote a variety of tools and policies to reduce the problems of particularly elderly victims becoming addicted to responding to scam requests (Think Jessica, n.d.).

Another example of this is MULE (http://www.stopMULEvictims.org), which is an organisation established in 2015, which brings together a group of international experts to target those involved broadly in human trafficking. It has a dedicated focus to providing assistance and education on the prevalence

TABLE 8.2 Techniques of situational crime prevention applied to cyber fraud and scams

	Increasing the effort	*Increasing the risks*	*Reducing the rewards*	*Reducing provocations*	*Removing excuses*
Individual	Protecting accounts with complex passwords, anti-virus protection. Protective registrations. Pursue measures to make personal contact information more difficult to find for third persons.	Regular cleansing of computers of viruses, spyware. Check websites, emailers and callers.	If fraudster known and has assets, pursue civil action to secure damages or seek reparation through criminal process.		
Organisation	Suitable controls to protect the personal information of clients. Background checks: verifying that clients are who they say they are.	Information sharing: datamatching and datamining. Verifying voice and location of clients.	If fraudster known and has assets, pursue civil action to secure damages or seek reparation through criminal process.		Communicate with clients to educate them of the risks and good practice to reduce the risk.
Policing Bodies	Disrupting the activities of fraudsters. 'Scambaiting' Pursue orders and restrictions on fraudster by using the civil, regulatory or criminal law.	Information sharing: datamatching and datamining. Central reporting. Publishing information on suspected scams, suspect websites. Fake scams to alert potential victims.	If fraudster known and has assets pursue civil action to secure damages or seek reparation through criminal process. Monitoring financial transfers to high-risk third countries to identify possible victims to warn them of potential victimisation.	Restrict information on how certain scams have been conducted. Regulation of advertising and promotion activities.	Communicate with general public and at risk groups to highlight the risks and good practice. Advertising campaigns: television, radio, newspapers, specialist publications, online. News releases to secure media interest. Specialists websites. Mailshots. Social media emails, texts, tweets. Community and interest group activities. Storylines in dramas.

of romance fraud victimisation as a means to coerce victims into other serious offences and there are several examples of victims on the website who have been jailed in a foreign country for their unwitting involvement as drug mules. For example, Sharon Armstrong, a romance fraud victim from New Zealand, was jailed for four years and ten months (of which she did two and a half years) in an Argentinian prison, after she was caught with cocaine in her luggage on route to meet with her 'partner' in London. Throughout the five and a half months of her relationship, she was groomed by her offender which culminated into her travelling from New Zealand to Argentina to collect business documents for her partner. Instead she was given a suitcase which contained cocaine and inadvertently became a drug mule (Sullivan, 2016). Armstrong is now a campaigner against romance fraud and one of the founding members of MULE.

Not-for-profits

There are also a variety of organisations which can be described as 'not-for-profits' which provide services to organisations largely, but often individuals too, to reduce the risk of certain types of frauds. Cifas in the UK is one such body that holds a database of known fraudsters and other relevant information that members can use to spot high-risk transactions. As was noted earlier in this chapter they also provide a protective registration service to individuals to reduce the risk of identity fraud.

Commercial bodies

There are also a number of commercial bodies that specialise in services which aid prevention. Some of the private investigation firms, noted in the previous chapter, which offer background checking services, fit this category. There are also some commercial companies that specialise in analytics to support companies in trying to prevent their customers from being defrauded, such as the previously noted Scamalytics, particularly in the romance fraud field.

The above examination has looked at how the five categories of situational crime prevention can be applied to frauds and scams within an online context. This has highlighted that despite being conceptualised originally for crimes in a terrestrial environment, there is an ability to translate these concepts into targeting prevention efforts in the virtual world. Importantly, this previous discussion has focused on how to target offenders, and seeks to reduce offending behaviours through modifications to the physical environment. However, given the challenges of enforcement activity documented in the previous chapter, the ability to successfully target offenders is difficult. While the current chapter has explored ways in which this is being done across the world, there is also an alternative argument for focusing prevention efforts on victims (Van Dijk and de Waard, 1991: 485), who argue that a distinction can be drawn between 'situation or victim-related types of crime prevention and offender related ones' (van Dijk and de Waard, 1991: 484). It is this focus on victim-based prevention to which the chapter now turns.

Using financial intelligence to target online fraud

As noted, this chapter has thus far explored the use of situational crime prevention techniques in general. This section will now explore in depth some innovative attempts at developing fraud prevention strategies. The following section presents three Australian case studies, which use financial intelligence to target online fraud victimisation. This was briefly described in the previous chapter as a policing strategy (through Project Sunbird), however the strength of this approach is based on its prevention value, therefore it will be examined in depth in this chapter.

The barriers associated with reporting online fraud have been documented in earlier chapters. Underreporting is entrenched with these types of crimes, through a combination of factors, which include not knowing one is a victim; not knowing who to report to; an inability to lodge a report with any authority; not believing that anything will be done; the high levels of shame and stigma associated with this type of crime; and the overwhelmingly negative experiences of those who do attempt to report. These have all been well established. In addition, the challenges of policing online fraud have been examined in the previous chapter, focusing predominantly on the transnational nature of offences; the prevalence of identity crime; and the continued evolution of technology used by offenders to avoid detection and prosecution. It is in this context, that Australia has seen the emergence of an innovative approach to targeting online fraud, through the use of financial intelligence in a victim-oriented approach, across three distinct programmes.

The following section provides an overview of the three Australian programmes that use financial intelligence to target online fraud victimisation: Project Sunbird (West Australian Police and West Australian Department of Commerce); Operation Disrepair (South Australian Police); and the National Scams Disruption Project (Australian Competition and Consumer Commission). It details the main tenets of these case studies, in order to provide an understanding of how each operate (see Cross, 2016, for further details on each of these). It also sets up the foundations on how each can be located within existing crime prevention theory and provides an example of the elements detailed earlier within the chapter, albeit from a victim perspective.

Project Sunbird

The West Australian Police (WAPOL) established Operation Sunbird in 2012 to target advance fee fraud (AFF) and romance fraud victimisation in Western Australia. As noted in earlier chapters, AFF is a common fraudulent approach where a victim sends a small amount of money in the hope of receiving a large sum of money at a later date (for example inheritance, lottery, investment and employment schemes) (Ross and Smith, 2011), and romance fraud is an approach which uses the guise of a legitimate relationship to defraud an individual

(Rege, 2009). Operation Sunbird was later renamed Project Sunbird, and a formal partnership was entered into between WAPOL and the West Australian Department of Commerce (Commerce), who were also concerned about the victimisation of individuals (Department of Commerce, n.d.).

Project Sunbird targets financial transactions between Western Australia and five West African countries: Nigeria, Ghana, Togo, Sierra Leone, and Benin (Department of Commerce, 2014). These financial transactions include those submitted via financial institutions or banks as well as those processed through remittance agencies. It is a five-stage process, with the stages shared across both agencies. The first is identification, whereby WAPOL access financial intelligence. They screen this list for likely legitimate transactions and then forward the remaining details to Commerce. The second stage is intervention, whereby Commerce sends a letter to the households on the list, which acknowledges that the person is sending money to one of the five identified countries and outlines the reasons why WAPOL/Commerce believe the recipient of the letter may be a victim of fraud. The letter encourages the cessation of financial transactions and provides a point of contact to discuss the matter further. If the individual continues to send money three months after this initial letter, a second letter is sent, outlining the belief that the person could be the victim of fraud and further encourages the termination of transactions. In addition, a fact sheet developed specifically for victims of fraud is enclosed.

The third stage is interruption, whereby Commerce liaises with banks, remittance agencies, and other relevant organisations, to block accounts of identified offenders and potential victims. This also includes education campaigns and media releases to increase the overall awareness of society. The fourth stage revolves around intelligence, and takes information gathered by Commerce and WAPOL from letter recipients who make contact. This leads into the last stage of investigation, whereby WAPOL focus on local offenders if relevant or make appropriate referrals of intelligence to other national and international police agencies (see Cross and Blackshaw, 2015 for further details about Project Sunbird).

Operation Disrepair

Following on from their West Australian counterparts, the South Australian Police (SAPOL) established Operation Disrepair in 2013 (SAPOL, 2014: 27). This targets South Australians who transfer funds to Nigeria and Ghana (SAPOL, 2014: 27). In a similar approach to Project Sunbird, SAPOL identify potential victims and send a letter out which conveys their suspicion that the individual may be a victim of online fraud (Nankervis, 2014). The stages of Operation Disrepair mirror Project Sunbird, with the only difference being that SAPOL is not working in partnership with a consumer protection agency. Instead, they undertake the five stages themselves.

National Scams Disruption Project

In August 2014, the Australian Competition and Consumer Commission (ACCC) launched their National Scams Disruption Project (NSDP), which adopted the same model as both Project Sunbird and Operation Disrepair. The most notable difference is that the ACCC is a consumer protection body and not law enforcement. The NSDP initially targeted citizens across New South Wales and the Australian Capital Territory, who were sending money to either Nigeria or Ghana. In July 2015, this was expanded to include Victoria, Tasmania and the Northern Territory (ACCC, 2015: 2). Similar to Sunbird and Disrepair, the ACCC access financial intelligence to send letters to individuals considered to be likely fraud victims and encourages them to desist their money transfers (Bainbridge, 2014). While the ACCC is an enforcement body, it has different powers and legislative authority compared to police agencies, particularly as relevant to online fraud. Therefore, they work in collaboration with local law enforcement when necessary.

Locating a victim-oriented approach within a crime prevention framework

The use of financial intelligence to identify alleged victims of online fraud and notify individuals of this suspicion is a notable shift in policing, given that police generally initiate an investigation only after an alleged victim has made a complaint. It has been argued elsewhere that there are distinct benefits to this approach, namely that it provides a more accurate picture of the crime problem; it reduces the impact and losses of online fraud; it increases the legitimacy of online fraud victims; it improves the effectiveness of resource allocation for police; and it improves police operations and investigations (Cross and Blackshaw, 2015). In addition, it has been argued that this victim-oriented approach overcomes two of the largest barriers to the underreporting of online fraud: an acknowledgement from the individual that they are a victim of fraud, as well as the stigma and shame associated with this particular type of victimisation (Cross, 2016).

It is understandable that the victim-oriented approach to targeting online fraud can be considered a movement away from traditional reactive, policing methods. However, the approach is better understood within the framework of crime prevention, particularly tertiary prevention principles. Therefore the following section uses these three Australian case studies to demonstrate how this approach can be understood as an example of tertiary prevention. In particular, the discussion focuses on two aspects: the prevention of revictimisation and the timing of the intervention. Where available, data from each of these case studies has been provided to illustrate the initial results obtained through this approach. However it is important to note that it is not the intention of this section to assert a direct link between these case studies and a reduction in online fraud victimisation. Rather it is the purpose of this analysis to provide evidence of the theoretical crime prevention framework of the approach taken by Australian jurisdictions targeting online fraud victimisation. More research is needed to make further assertions on the relationship between the intervention (sending of the letter) and victim behaviour (increase/decrease in sending funds).

Preventing revictimisation

Tertiary prevention seeks to prevent the recurrence of offending. In the context of victim-oriented prevention, it attempts to intervene to prevent repeat victimisation, through a focus on those known to have experienced previous crime and/or victimisation (Crawford and Evans, 2012: 772; Sutton et al., 2014: 23). The targeting of known victims is evident across Sunbird, Disrepair and the NSDP. Sending a letter to a suspected online fraud victim is a deliberate act of intervention with the specified goal of reducing the number of victims and their overall financial losses. It cannot prevent victimisation from occurring in the first place, but it does seek to prevent the continued victimisation of individuals.

Initial results from Sunbird, Disrepair and the NSDP observe a positive outcome, through a reduction in the number of individuals who continue to send money. The following provides statistics obtained from each of the case studies.

Project Sunbird

Between March 2013 and August 2015, approximately $51.5 million was sent from Western Australia to West Africa. Of those funds, approximately $17.9 million was identified as the result of fraudulent transactions. Between March 2013 and October 2015, 3,001 first letters and 1,503 second letters were sent out. Monitoring of recipients occurs three months prior to sending a letter, excludes the month that the letter is sent, and then continues for three months after. Based on this, of those senders that received a first letter between March 2013 and July 2015, 73 per cent stopped sending money and 13 per cent reduced the amount of money sent. Of those who received a second letter during this same time period, 53 per cent stopped sending money and 27 per cent reduced the amount of money sent. A small percentage of individuals also continued to send money despite the intervention. This is illustrated in Figures 8.1 and 8.2.

These graphs indicate that a large percentage of letter recipients appear to cease financial transactions. It also indicates that there are a small percentage of individuals who continue to send money or who restart sending money after they have stopped. However, for the most part, these graphs indicate at face value a reduction in the number of likely online fraud victims.

Operation Disrepair

Between January 2013 and March 2014, 1,555 letters were sent to potential victims. There were 824 letters sent to individuals between January 2013 and June

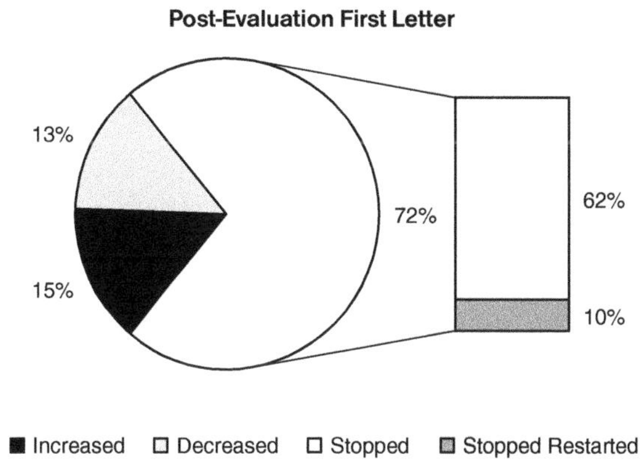

FIGURE 8.1 Sending activity of individuals after receiving a first letter (Project Sunbird, unpublished data file).

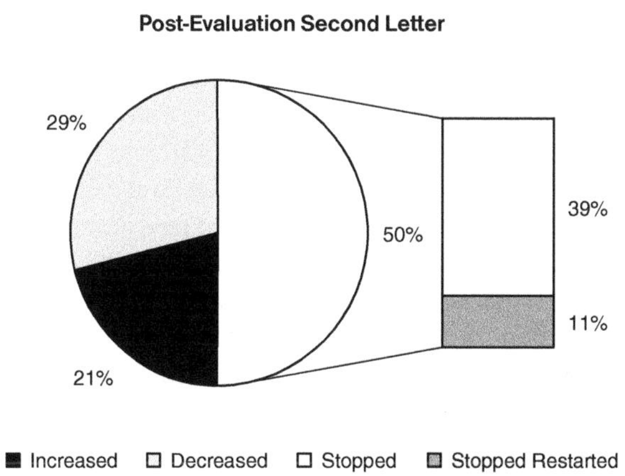

FIGURE 8.2 Sending activity of individuals after receiving a second letter (Project Sunbird, unpublished data file).

2014. In July 2014, the content of the letters was changed and up until March 2015, 477 first letters were sent and 254 second letters were sent. Monitoring of letter recipients with Disrepair is for a one-month period after receipt of the letter and records indicate only 76 individuals identified as continuing to send money during this period.

National Scams Disruption Project

Between August 2014 and September 2015, over 4,700 letters were sent, which includes 874 second letters. This represents $61 million in transactions from Australia to high-risk West African jurisdictions in a 13-month period. Approximately 5% of letter recipients contacted the ACCC in response to the letter, with

75% (178) confirmed victims of online fraud. Of those who received a first letter, 77% have not sent money to any overseas jurisdiction for a follow-up period of six weeks or more.

Summary

In combination, these statistics point towards an observed reduction in the number of individuals identified as sending money to West Africa through online fraud victimisation. Arguably, if fewer victims are sending money, then this will also see a reduction in the financial losses incurred by victims as well as the overall level of harm and non-financial losses associated with online fraud victimisation.

As alluded to previously, there are limitations to the data provided, which need to be acknowledged. Each jurisdiction monitors the transactions of letter recipients across different time periods and across different countries. At this point in time, it is also unknown as to whether the letter received by recipients is one of the reasons that individuals cease their remittance of funds, or whether there are other factors in operation. Also, the data is unable to provide a direct link between the receipt of a letter and a cessation in transactions. Rather, at this stage it is an assumption on the part of agencies, based on anecdotal evidence provided to them by victims, which requires more rigorous investigation. Despite these limitations, at face value the data provided does appear to depict the letter as a positive intervention which has the potential to reduce the levels of online fraud victimisation, and as a result, reduce the ongoing and repeat victimisation of suspected online fraud victims. These observations provide a strong foundation for further research to better understand the relationship (if any) between the victim's receipt of a letter and their subsequent financial transactions.

The timing of the intervention

There is an extensive body of literature that has examined how early intervention approaches can influence and reduce the likelihood of criminal and antisocial behaviour (National Crime Prevention, 1999; Sullivan, 2013). The purpose of early intervention is to focus involvement 'early in the pathway [however] this may or may not mean early in life' (National Crime Prevention, 1999: 9). Further to this, there is strong evidence to suggest that 'tackling problems early may prevent them from escalating and intensifying' (Lee et al., 2012: 54).

This last point is significant in applying the concept of early intervention to a victim-oriented, tertiary approach to online fraud prevention. The main purpose of Sunbird, Disrepair and the NSDP is to identify and notify potential online fraud victims through their financial transactions. It aims to reduce the harm and losses suffered as well as prevent ongoing and repeat victimisation. For many online fraud victims, their involvement will not be restricted to one scenario. It is not unusual for victims to experience several different types of approaches across a period of time, or for one approach to morph into another one (for example an initial romance fraud may develop into an investment fraud) (Cross et al., 2016). There is also the problem of recovery fraud, whereby offenders will sell or trade victim details, and these victims will then be targeted in the future with additional fraudulent scenarios (Cross et al., 2014). It may be a scenario that promises to get their money back, or it may be an entirely new scheme.

In order to facilitate early intervention, police and consumer protection agencies are using West African countries as likely indicators of online fraud victimisation, based on known intelligence. From within a tertiary perspective, the purpose of sending a letter is not to prevent victimisation from happening in the first place (given that at least one financial transaction has already taken place); rather, it is to intervene as early as possible, with the intention of reducing the length of time a victim is involved in fraud and the corresponding amount of money which is lost. There is no transaction limit or designated amount, which will attract the attention of authorities. Any amount transferred to one of the identified countries could come within the ambit of each project.

It is also important to recognise that, while West African countries are used to identify likely victims, online fraud is a global phenomenon. Fraudulent transactions are not restricted to West African nations. However, data obtained by the ACCC through the NSDP, suggests that using Nigeria and Ghana to conduct an initial assessment of individuals, can indicate extended victimisation. For example, the ACCC examined the sending histories of 94 confirmed victims from the NSDP. The following table provides a list of the countries, in addition to Nigeria and Ghana, that victims were remitting funds to, and the percentage of the overall transactions.

TABLE 8.3 List of countries that victims are remitting funds to (ACCC, unpublished data file)

Country	*Percentage of transactions*	*Country*	*Percentage of transactions*
Philippines	34.70%	Yemen republic	0.60%
Cameroon	17.50%	France	0.40%
Malaysia	9.10%	Hong Kong	0.20%
USA	7.20%	Netherlands	0.20%
South Africa	5.80%	Bhutan	0.20%
United Arab Emirates	4.90%	Tanzania	0.20%
Thailand	4.60%	Panama	0.10%
India	2.70%	Turkey	0.10%
UK	2.20%	Singapore	0.10%
Spain	1.90%	Italy	0.10%
Benin	1.50%	Greece	0.10%
Qatar	1.30%	Ukraine	0.10%
Kenya	1.20%	Uganda	0.10%
Russian federation	0.90%	Germany	0.10%
China	0.70%	Canada	0.10%
Togo	0.70%	Zambia	0.10%
Cote d'Ivoire	0.70%	Mali	0.10%

While this is a small, non-representative sample of online fraud victims, and is only able to ascertain the first destination country of the financial transaction after Australia (as it is likely that these funds may be laundered through a number of accounts in various jurisdictions), it demonstrates one very important point: the global nature of online fraud. It is not surprising that victims are sending financial transactions to multiple jurisdictions across the world. It is well established that offenders will create complex situations and narratives that compel the victim to send money across an extended period of time. It is not unusual for these scenarios to involve multiple characters across a number of countries, rather, it is sometimes essential for this to occur in an attempt to maintain the ruse. This also reiterates that online fraud is not exclusively a West African problem. While online fraud has a strong history in countries such as Nigeria (Schoenmakers et al., 2009) the above demonstrates that victims are increasingly asked to send money to a multitude of non-African nations.

Overall, it can be seen that conceptualising the transfer of funds to West African nations as an indicator for potential involvement in online fraud, can be an effective mechanism. As demonstrated by data obtained through the NSDP, sending money to Nigeria or Ghana can be indicative of extended financial losses to a range of other countries. The large number of countries is not surprising given the known characteristics of online fraud and the ways in which the scenarios unfold. However, it is not logistically possible for law enforcement or consumer protection agencies to screen all international transactions for fraudulent activity. Therefore, West African nations appear to be a viable indicator for transactions to other countries. There is a strong need to do further work to determine if the trend observed by the ACCC is consistent with other jurisdictions and if the West African nations selected are the most effective and appropriate countries to use to initially identify potential online fraud victims. However, it provides a solid basis from which to work.

There is also evidence to illustrate the potential benefits and success of financial intelligence approaches as an early intervention tool, from both Sunbird and Disrepair. As stated, Project Sunbird sends an initial letter (1st) to individuals who are identified as sending money to one of five West African nations (Nigeria, Ghana, Sierra Leone, Togo and Benin). Monitoring of these individuals continues for three months after the receipt of the letter (excluding the month that the letter was sent) and covers only the five countries targeted. In that time, individuals are recorded as doing one of three actions, increasing the amount of money sent, decreasing the amount of money sent, or ceasing financial transactions altogether. If an individual continues to send money in this period, they will then receive a follow up (2nd) letter from Sunbird. Again, monitoring of the three-month period subsequent to this letter (excluding the month that the letter was sent) to the five identified West African countries will place individuals in one of the three same categories. The following table indicates the amount of money that a Sunbird letter recipient has sent at the time they receive a letter (both first and second).

TABLE 8.4 Average amount of money sent by Project Sunbird letter recipients, 2013–2015 (Project Sunbird, unpublished data file)

Summary of average amount sent per individual (March 2013 to July 2015)		
Action after letter	1st letter	2nd letter
Ceased transactions	$2,554.35	$5,991.62
Decreased amount sent	$10,052.87	$18,439.53
Increased amount sent	$15,531.25	$22,055.79
All persons	$5,331.57	$12,787.08

This table indicates that those who cease transactions after receiving the first letter have, on average, sent only $2,554. In contrast, individuals who increased their amount of financial transactions after receiving a second letter have on average already sent $22,055. Even those who continued to send money after receiving the first letter, had previously sent higher average amounts of money ($10,052 for those who decreased and $15,531 for those who increased). This table suggests that intervention (through the sending of a letter) to a potential online fraud victim may be of more benefit and effectiveness early on in the victim/offender relationship. It is likely that the letter may have a greater impact on individuals who have not invested large amounts of money in the relationship. Those who are recorded as stopping their transactions, have much smaller average amounts compared to those who continue to send money, despite the letter's warning.

This is further reiterated through data obtained by Operation Disrepair. The following graph in Figure 8.3 illustrates the number of months alleged victims of online fraud have been sending money to either Nigeria or Ghana.

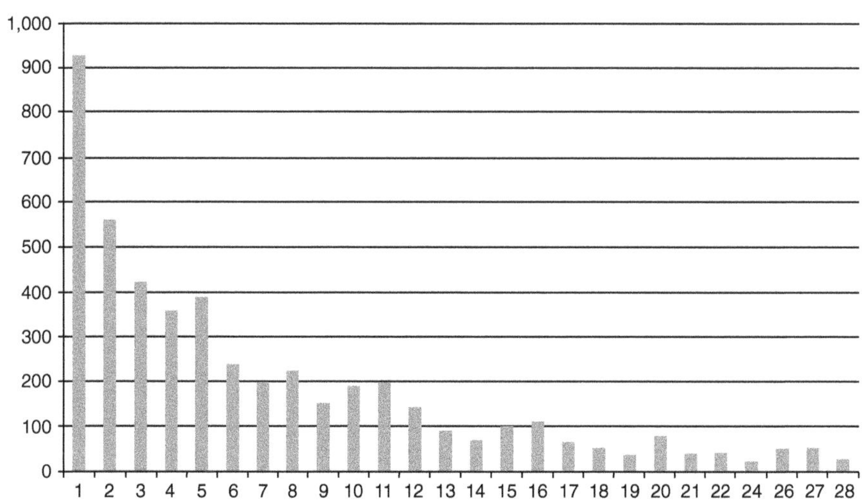

FIGURE 8.3 Number of recurring months that individuals have remitted funds (Operation Disrepair, unpublished data file).

This graph indicates the sharp decline that is evident across the number of months that individuals transfer funds overseas. There is a clear downward trend in the number of individuals who transfer money for a period greater than twelve months. Again, it highlights the prospect that the receipt of a letter towards the beginning of a victim's involvement with online fraud may have a greater influence on their decision to cease transactions, compared to those who are involved over a longer period of time. This graph also reveals a small group of chronic victims who in some circumstances have been remitting funds overseas for more than two years. These are likely to be victims who have accumulated substantial monetary losses and are heavily invested in their relationship with the offender. Once this level of involvement has been established, the receipt of a letter is unlikely to have any impact on this situation.

Summary

These statistics from Sunbird and Disrepair suggest that early intervention, both in terms of the amount sent and the time that funds have been remitted, is important to disrupting the relationship between the victim and offender. Early intervention, as witnessed by Sunbird, Disrepair and the NSDP, is premised on alerting suspected victims to reduce the number of victims and the harm they experience. It is also clear that there is a group of chronic victims. Further work needs to be done with this particular group, to determine the most appropriate method of intervention, as a letter is unlikely to have the disruptive effect required.

The use of early intervention across Sunbird, Disrepair and the NSDP targets victimisation rather than offending behaviour. However, there is limited evidence to demonstrate that a benefit of this approach may also be in the reduction of offending behaviour from victims as a result of their ongoing involvement in fraud (Cross and Blackshaw, 2015). This is exemplified through situations where the victim feels compelled to commit criminal offences (such as theft) to obtain the money needed to maintain their relationship with the offender and meet their financial demands. Early intervention in the victim pathway may also reduce the likelihood that victims remain involved to the point where they perpetrate offences themselves.

Overall, it can be seen that targeting potential victims and intervening as early as possible, can have a positive impact. While further work is needed to determine if the inferences made are consistently accurate, the evidence presented suggests a positive starting point to continue this approach, as well as the use of West African countries as an indicator of extended online fraud victimisation.

Applying the five categories to cyber fraud and scams

In light of the earlier analysis in this chapter on the five situational crime prevention techniques, the current case study exemplifies each of these techniques and how they can apply to a victim perspective of prevention. The following is an exploratory application of these five categories to a victim perspective of online fraud, and provides an important step for further research in the area.

Increasing the effort

Alerting victims to the fact that they may be involved in fraud is an attempt to strengthen the knowledge of victims and reduce the likelihood they will engage in a fraudulent scheme in the long term. By law enforcement and consumer protection agencies directly contacting potential victims, it seeks to empower the victims to take their own action and cease their relationship with the offender as well as cessation of any further funds transfers. Providing information on warning signs of fraud victimisation, and details about the various scenarios of different approaches, aims to give the victim knowledge and attempts to reduce their current victimisation as well as harden them against revictimisation at a later stage.

Increasing the risks

By alerting victims to the fact that authorities are aware of their transactions and that they might be involved in fraud, it helps to remove the secrecy that offenders seek to establish with victims in order to maintain their compliance. This attempts to break the relationship and offer the victim a way out (through support and guidance from authorities) and ultimately attempts to stop any further transactions being sent to the offender. In addition, known victims may have their accounts blocked and sending ability removed in an attempt to reduce their ongoing sending behaviour. This type of disruption work can be undertaken by both police and consumer protection agencies targeting known victims and offenders.

Reducing the rewards

The letters seek to try and break the relationship between the victim and the offender and the web of lies and deceit that the victim has experienced. While the victim may have been told by the offender that they have an inheritance or investment coming, or believe that they are involved in a genuine relationship, the direct engagement with law enforcement and consumer protection agencies seeks to provide an alternative narrative. For some, this is confirmation of a suspicion that they have previously held, but for others, it is not able to break through the high levels of trust and rapport that have been established by the offender. It seeks to empower victims with the knowledge and support they need to end their relationship with the offender and stop sending money.

Reducing provocations

The education and awareness of online fraud is a main part of each of these operations, particularly that of Project Sunbird and the National Scams Disruption

Project, through the ongoing work of Scamwatch. Agencies will use opportunities to gain media coverage on the issue, and where possible, they will support actual victims in coming forward to share their story in an effort to break down the barriers and stigma associated with victimisation. These campaigns are important in alerting current and potential victims to the types of warning signs they should look out for, in order to protect themselves from these types of schemes.

Removing excuses

The use of a letter to intervene with potential online fraud victims is an important step in opening up a legitimate conversation with potential victims involved in online fraud. Through the information contained within the letter and the contact details provided, it provides a simple mechanism for letter recipients to engage with authorities in a non-confrontational and non-judgemental manner. It also removes the need for victims to negotiate the system themselves, and ensures that their first contact is with someone who knows what is going on and can offer advice and support to the individual. In some cases, it can also alert victims to the reality of what they have been involved in. In some cases, offenders will use victims as money mules, and ask them to transfer funds for them into overseas accounts. Direct engagement by law enforcement and consumer protection, can alert victims to the gravity of their actions and potential consequences if they continue with their behaviour.

As can be demonstrated from the above, there is merit in thinking about the use of financial intelligence to target online fraud from a variety of perspectives, including the situation prevention techniques canvassed within this chapter. The above application of the five categories of situational prevention is a starting point for further consideration of how situational measures could be used across both victim and offender perspectives, into the future.

This last analysis also points to the use of awareness and education as an important tool for victims in terms of prevention. Therefore, it is worthwhile to examine the nature of these prevention messages in and of themselves, and it is to this that the final section of this chapter now turns.

The challenge of prevention

This chapter has thus far, established the need to focus on prevention as it relates to cyber fraud and scams, given the immense challenges noted previously around the ability to effectively police this particular crime type. In particular, this chapter has explored the use of situational crime prevention techniques as well as providing an Australian case study on the use of financial intelligence as a means of victim-oriented prevention activity. In doing this, the importance of education and awareness was highlighted in several places. Prevention messages related to online fraud are an important component of many agencies and their work in this area. However to date, there have been few analyses which have examined the effectiveness or otherwise of these prevention campaigns. Smith and Akman (2008) examined the effectiveness of a media awareness campaign across Australia and New Zealand, which specifically focused on consumer fraud, with the slogan 'Scams target you – Protect yourself'. The campaign ran for a month and focused on four key aspects (one per week) in relation to protecting oneself from scams: 'protect your money, protect your phone, protect your computer and protect your identity' (Smith and Akman, 2008: 1). This analysis concluded that the intense publicity campaign undertaken 'was effective in raising awareness of the risks of consumer fraud throughout the community and increasing the reporting of cases' (Smith and Akman, 2008: 6), though this analysis was highly focused on an association of website hits with corresponding media releases and the number of reports received during the campaign period. Focused on the broader notion of cyber security, a government inquiry held in Australia in 2010 noted that 'cyber security education in Australia remains fragmented, and more consistent and effective messaging is needed to achieve the cultural change necessary' (Australian Government, 2010: 221). This includes education targeted towards consumers and the public around cyber frauds and scams and is argued to not be a specific problem in Australia.

It is evident that all countries have agencies (both government and non-government) who aim to educate individuals against the risks posed by cyber frauds and scams. However, there is little evidence to suggest a consistent message on a global scale. The *Little Black Book of Scams* was first published in Australia by the Australian Competition and Consumer Commission in 2008. Since then it has been adopted by agencies in the UK and Canada, and has undergone several revisions. Therefore, it can be argued as the closest available resource which illustrates the nature of prevention messages related to fraud prevention at a global level. The following section provides a short analysis of this publication (across Australia, the UK and Canada) to demonstrate some of the issues which currently exist with current prevention messages.

'The Little Black Book of Scams': demonstrating current prevention approaches

As stated, the ACCC first released The Little Black Book of Scams (LBBS) in 2008 (ACCC, 2008). This was promoted as a guide to 'scams, swindles, rorts and rip offs' (ACCC, 2010). The booklet contained an array of information on a large number of frauds. The edition was revised in 2010, but was revamped and released as a second edition in 2012. It promoted itself as 'a pocket sized guide to spotting, avoiding and reporting consumer fraud' (ACCC, 2012). The booklet has both hard copy and electronic versions.

The LBBS is an example of a victim-oriented approach to crime prevention, which targets the general population and aims to provide them with information and awareness to reduce the collective likelihood of victimisation (Barthe, 2003; Van Dijk and de Waard, 1991). Smith and Akman (2008: 2) assert that 'in order to reach as many victims as possible, it is necessary to deliver fraud prevention information on an extensive scale' and the LBBS is a prime example of this. The premise of the LBBS is to provide potential fraud victims with the knowledge and skills to avoid future victimisation. This can be linked to routine activity theory, first advocated by Cohen and Felson in 1979 (and further developed by many scholars since), whereby for a criminal act to occur, there needs to be the presence of a motivated offender, a suitable victim and the lack of capable guardianship. Awareness campaigns targeted at crime prevention, generally base themselves on this model, through the intention to 'exert influence over one or more of the three routine activity theory elements' (Johnson and Bowers, 2003: 498). In this case, the LBBS is seeking to 'reduce the vulnerability of potential victims, and hence opportunities for crime, by protecting them from motivated offenders' (Johnson and Bowers, 2003: 498). The provision of information about the variety of frauds is the key element to this publication and its intention to prevent fraud victimisation.

The publication of the LBBS is significant for three reasons. To begin with, it is arguably the first comprehensive resource published in an Australian context, which examines the issue of consumer fraud across all mediums (online, phone, mail and door-to-door contexts), though there is a strong focus on fraud within the online environment. Second, it provides a detailed description of many types of fraud. The first edition canvassed 15 different categories, while the second edition details 'the scammers black list – the top 10 scams to avoid' (ACCC, 2012: 3). It also provides insight into how an offender may defraud a person in a section called 'the scammers toolbox' (ACCC, 2012: 27) and advice on how to avoid victimisation (ACCC, 2012: 29). Third, it has had significant influence on the global message of prevention. The LBBS has been adopted by both the UK and Canada through The Little Book of Big Scams (Metropolitan Police) and The Little Black Book of Scams: Your Guide to Protection Against Fraud (Competition Bureau Canada). Both were explicitly adopted from the original Australian version.

The LBBS is an important tool in prevention efforts. The key element to any fraudulent offence is the transfer of money or personal details. Without this, there is generally no fraud offence and no victim. The success or failure of all prevention messages and awareness campaigns culminates in the decision of a person to comply or not comply with such a request, across all circumstances. Consequently, this section asserts two things: that the current message is overly complex and information heavy; and second, that the need to classify fraud into discrete categories is redundant from an offender's perspective. Both of these are important to consider in terms of improving prevention messages for future campaigns.

Too much detail

The LBBS is a victim-oriented approach to crime prevention, which relies upon the presentation of a large amount of detail about this crime category. Examples of this are found within all jurisdictional versions of the LBBS. In combination, the three publications detail over 20 different categories of fraud, with some crossover (dating and romance scams are detailed in all three publications, as are health and medical scams). However, there is not necessarily any consistency in the publications regarding what constitutes each category of fraud. For example,

Australia uses the category 'online shopping, classified and auction scams', which is termed 'internet scams' in Canada and the United Kingdom. The same category of 'internet scams' also encompasses phishing in Canada and the United Kingdom, but is a separate category of 'banking, credit card and online account scams' in Australia. This demonstrates the inconsistency that exists with definitions of fraud and the characteristics of what each type of fraud category encompasses.

Regardless of the arbitrary nature of fraud categories and their overlap, each publication is based on providing the reader (or potential victim) with detailed information about these fraud categories, which includes common characteristics of each type of fraud (how it generally presents to potential victims and how it is perpetrated for example). All publications offer things to look out for, rules, handy hints and guidance on how to avoid becoming the victim of a fraud, as well as outlining how to report victimisation if it should occur.

It is evident that these publications provide a high level of detail on each potential fraud type. However, it can be argued that this is not an effective prevention or awareness mechanism because it overwhelms the individual and provides an excessive amount of information to process. It also directs potential victims to look for characteristics or 'plotlines' in a fraud that may not exist in an approach directed specifically at them. Cross and Kelly (2016) detail several scenarios whereby the victim is aware of one type of fraud, but is unaware of the type of fraud they fall victim to.

Case study 8.6 Lack of awareness of fraudulent schemes

Ruth was a romance fraud victim who had heard about frauds where a person was required to send money. However she did not associate that to her own experience, despite the fact she was sending money overseas in exactly the same manner as the other types of fraud. For Ruth, the approach (in this instance through her perception of a legitimate relationship) did not allow her to see that she was being defrauded in the same way as other schemes she was aware of.

RUTH: ... I had no idea about that [romance fraud]. Not romance sort of scams. I guess I had heard scams wanting to send money but there was no emotional involvement in those sorts of things so they are easy to detect. But this wasn't easy initially, and then all of a sudden ...

INTERVIEWER: You are in the middle of it?

RUTH: You are in the middle of it and there are often times in the beginning I think, oh I wish this was a scam, it would be easy just to get out of but there was no indication that there was initially. (Cross and Kelly, 2016)

While each version of the LBBS highlights the vulnerability of all individuals to fraud, this example (and others provided by Cross and Kelly, 2016) illustrates the fact that educating about specific types of fraud is not always effective. Rather, education messages need to focus on the key element of all frauds, which in all scenarios, is the transfer of money. In this example, the victim (Ruth) was aware of other types of fraud where a victim sends money overseas, but was not able to associate or apply this to the approach used against them. Despite the victim's knowledge about other fraud types, the offender was successful in subverting this knowledge and gaining substantial amounts of money.

A critical point to emerge from this analysis stems from the fact that the fraudulent approach is not a static characteristic. From an offender's perspective, the way that a victim is approached is not important so long as the attempt is successful and results in the acquisition of money or personal information. An awareness of advance fee fraud did not help Ruth in her identification of the romance fraud she was involved in. However, in this circumstance (and many others similar to this), the offender was successful in obtaining money from these victims, and the way in which it was perpetrated is of little relevance to them. It is this point to which the paper now turns.

The differentiation of fraud types is redundant to offenders

As highlighted in the previous section, one critique against fraud classifications is that it assumes the plotlines are differentiated enough from one approach to another, and that they require a separate category or classification. However, the only real differences from one approach to another are the micro-details of the initial pitch and the subsequent dollar amounts associated with each request. Though there is arguably some value in tracking the prevalence of certain fraud approaches and victimisation, this chapter argues that there is limited value in such categorisation when it comes to prevention initiatives, as indicated by the example presented above. Rather, the categorisation of fraud types can work against prevention, with victims believing that because their situation or 'plotline' is different to what they know or have heard, it is not fraudulent.

For an offender, the type of approach selected is irrelevant, so long as it successfully targets a weakness or susceptibility identified in a potential victim. On this basis, an offender will select a plotline or an approach specifically tailored to appeal to the intended victim. This is evident in the following examples (provided by Cross and Kelly, 2016).

The first example illustrates how the first plotline (through a perceived legitimate relationship) soon transitioned into an investment plotline, where Frank was invited to assist in the mining and sale of gold. To the offenders, the details of the plotline are irrelevant, so long as Frank remains involved and continues to send and invest money. This can also be seen in the emergence of recovery schemes, where victims who have been defrauded and ceased contact with their offenders, are approached by individuals purporting to be law enforcement who claim they can recover their lost funds for a fee.

Case study 8.7 Changing plotlines

Frank was originally defrauded in the context of a relationship. Frank had recently lost his wife to a particular illness, and it was through this same illness that he initially sent money to the offender/s.

> … and then her brother calls me, sends me an email under her [offenders] name and said she got hit by a car, her brains bleeding anyway, I just lost my wife with a brain haemorrhage, and they wanted $1000 for the doctor, to operate, they won't do anything unless you pay so I sent them $1000 $1200. Then it started, as you say it's all bull** it wasn't nothing about it that's what they do, and then I went over there, and then she [offender] had gold you see and this sounds good, but not knowing anything about mining or gold you know, 1500kg of gold, that her [offender's] father had left her…
>
> *(Cross and Kelly, 2016)*

Case study 8.8 Recovery schemes

Julia was originally defrauded through a romance scheme, however she realised she was involved in fraud and ceased contact with her offender. She was later targeted (unsuccessfully) in a recovery scheme.

> But I even had the EFCC ring me. We have taken over your case, we have discovered that you have been scammed, blah, blah, blah. We will get you in contact with an agent and you can talk to him about what to do. I did all that and the agent says ok, they are going to reimburse your thirty four thousand dollars. I said, oh, that's really good. But you need to send ten thousand dollars. I said, yeah likely story … They really play with your mind.
>
> *(Cross and Kelly, 2016)*

The case of Julia is a prime example of how recovery frauds can operate. The Economic and Financial Crimes Commission (EFCC) is an enforcement agency in Nigeria established to combat fraud perpetrated from Nigeria. The legitimate existence of this agency provides the guise through which offenders will try to obtain further money from victims, who may send the money thinking that they are assisting with law enforcement and they will be able to recover some of their funds. However, the reality is that they simply are revictimised and lose further amounts of money.

These two examples demonstrate how an offender will utilise a variety of plotlines and approaches in order to exploit a wide range of potential victims' needs or vulnerabilities. Offenders are not tied to one specific approach, rather the type of plotline they employ has no specific meaning or relevance beyond whether it was successful or not.

Overall, it has been argued that current fraud prevention approaches are overly complex and irrelevant from an offender's perspective. It is asserted that they are characterised by 'white noise' in that they fail to adequately articulate the critical point of any victimisation experience, being the sending of money or personal details. All prevention messages culminate in success or failure at the point where a person is confronted with the decision to send or not to send. Based on the evidence and arguments presented above, future prevention approaches need to be focused on the simplistic message of protecting money and protecting personal information. While detailed knowledge and information of different fraud types and how they are perpetrated is important, it should not be the basis for a prevention approach. As evidenced by the current content of the LBBS across Australia, the United Kingdom and Canada, the essential prevention message should be far more simplistic and universal around the protection of money and personal information, rather than divesting it into an extensive and highly detailed, fraud classification system. This is a challenge relevant to all agencies globally (including law enforcement, government, non-government and corporate organisations) who see consumer protection and fraud awareness as part of their role.

Conclusion

This chapter has highlighted the importance of prevention in attempting to reduce the harm and losses associated with cyber frauds and scams. It is clear that prevention is a critical aspect of seeking to reduce victimisation associated with cyber frauds and scams. While policing and other law enforcement activity is important, it has been argued that prevention efforts are likely to have more direct impacts across many jurisdictions, given the transnational nature of many cyber offences and the likelihood that the victim is within one's jurisdiction while the offender is located overseas.

This chapter has provided a particular focus on situational crime prevention techniques and how the five categories evident in crime prevention theory (increase the effort; increase the risks; reduce the rewards; reduce the provocations; and remove excuses) may be applied to fraud within a virtual environment. This analysis was located within a broader discussion, which acknowledged the limitations of relying solely on a situational and environmental approach (such as displacement, lack of addressing structural and other factors, and victim blaming) but still argued for the merits of these potential measures being implemented in the current context. While this analysis was distinctly focused on the offender and seeking to reduce and prevent offending, this chapter also presented the merits of adopting a victim-focused approach, exemplified through the use of financial intelligence to target online fraud victimisation in Australia. This analysis demonstrated how this approach can be understood from within existing crime prevention theory (a victim-oriented, tertiary perspective) and also provided a preliminary application of the five situational categories to this overall case study. Lastly, the chapter concluded with an examination of crime prevention messages that are currently used to target potential victims and educate them as a means to reduce their likely victimisation. This analysis pointed to the 'white noise' of current messages and the need to reduce complexity associated with messaging to a clear simplistic message focused on the sending of money or personal details.

Overall this chapter has sought to demonstrate the challenges that currently exist in seeking to effectively prevent cyber fraud and scams globally. As observed with policing in the previous chapter, the task is great. While there are many approaches to crime prevention, across a variety of sectors (not restricted solely to law enforcement), this poses both a strength and a weakness to current practices. While there are many examples of good work across the globe, there are equal numbers of areas for improvement, and the ongoing reality of victimisation to highlight the perpetual need for improved work and practice in this area. The last chapter of this book seeks to bring all of the arguments throughout together, and offer some hope and optimism for targeting cyber frauds and scams as we move into the future.

Note

1 Part of this chapter first appeared as Cross, C. (2016) Using financial intelligence to target online fraud victimisation: Applying a tertiary prevention perspective. *Criminal Justice Studies* 29(2): 125–142. Doi: 10.1080/1478601X.2016.1170278 and Cross, C. and Kelly, M. (2016) The problem of 'white noise': Examining current prevention approaches to online fraud. *Journal of Financial Crime*. 23(4): Online first. Doi: 10.1108/JFC-12-2015-0069.

References

Australian Competition and Consumer Commission (2008) *The Little Black Book of Scams*, Canberra: Commonwealth of Australia.

Australian Competition and Consumer Commission (2010) *The Little Black Book of Scams*, revised edition, Canberra: Commonwealth of Australia.

Australian Competition and Consumer Commission (2012) *The Little Black Book of Scams: A Pocket Sized Guide to Spotting, Avoiding and Reporting Consumer Fraud*, 2nd edition, Canberra: Commonwealth of Australia.

Australian Competition and Consumer Commission (2015) *Targeting Scams: Report of the ACCC on Scams Activity 2014*. Canberra: Australian Competition and Consumer Commission. Available at: http://www.accc.gov.au/publications/targeting-scams-report-on-scam-activity/targeting-scams-report-of-the-accc-on-scam-activity-2014 (accessed 21 October 2016).

Australian Government (2010) *Inquiry into Cyber crime*. Available at: http://www.aph.gov.au/Parliamentary_Business/Committees/House_of_representatives_Committees?url=coms/cybercrime/report/chapter10.htm (accessed 30 October 2016).

Aziz, S. J., Bolick, D. C., Kleinman, M. T. and Shadel, D. (2000) The National Telemarketing Victim Call Center: Combating telemarketing fraud in the United States. *Journal of Elder Abuse and Neglect* 12(2): 93–98. Doi: 10.1300/J084v12n02_10.

Bainbridge, A. (2014) *ACCC Launches Action to Stop Australians Falling Victim to Dating and Romance Scams*. Available at: http://mobile.abc.net.au/news/2014-08-11/accc-launches-actionagainst-romance-dating-scams/5661438 (accessed 30 October 2016).

Barr, R. and Pease, K. (1990) Crime placement, displacement and deflection. In: Tonry, M. and Morris, N. (eds) *Crime and Justice: A Review of Research*, Chicago: University of Chicago Press, pp. 277–318.

Barthe, E. (2003), *An Evaluation of the Effect of Offender-Oriented Publicity on Autocrimes*, PhD Thesis, Michigan: Rutgers University. Available at: http://www.popcenter.org/library/scp/pdf/15-Barthe_2003.pdf (accessed 30 October 2016).

Bullock, K., Clarke, R. V. and Tilley, N. (eds) (2010) *Situational Prevention of Organised Crimes*, Cullompton: Willan.

Button, M. and Gee, J. (2013) *Countering Fraud for Competitive Advantage*, Chichester: Wiley.

Button, M., Lewis, C. and Tapley, J. (2009) *A Better Deal for Victims*, London: National Fraud Authority.

Cifas (n.d.) *For Individuals*. Available at: https://www.cifas.org.uk/pr_for_individuals (accessed 31 October 2016).

City of London Police (2016) *National Policing Lead for Economic Crime Annual Review 2015–16*, London: City of London Police. Available at: https://www.cityoflondon.police.uk/advice-and-support/fraud-and-economic-crime/Documents/ECD-annual-review-2015-16.pdf (accessed 30 October 2016).

Clarke R. V. (1997) Introduction. In: Clarke, R. V. (ed.) *Situational Crime Prevention Successful Case Studies*, New York: Harrow and Heston, pp. 1–43.

Clarke, R. V. (2005) Seven misconceptions of situational crime prevention. In: Tilley, N. (ed.) *Handbook of Crime Prevention and Community Safety*, Cullompton: Willan, pp. 39–70.

Clarke, R. V. and Mayhew, P. (1989) Crime as opportunity: A note on domestic gas suicide in Britain and the Netherlands. *British Journal of Criminology* 29(1): 35–46.

Clarke, R. V. and Newman, G. R. (2006) *Outsmarting the Terrorists*, London: Praeger Publishers.

Cohen, L. E. and Felson, M. (1979) Social changes and crime rates: A routine activities approach. *American Sociological Review* 44(4): 588–605.

Cornish, D. and Clarke, R. V. (1986) *The Reasoning Criminal: Rational Choice Perspectives of Offending*, New York: Springer.

Crawford, A. and Evans, K. (2012) Crime prevention and community safety. In: Maguire, M. Morgan, R. and Reiner, R. (eds) *The Oxford Handbook of Criminology*, Oxford: Oxford University Press, pp. 769–805.

Cressey, D. (1953) *Other People's Money*, Belmont, CA: Wadsworth Publishing.

Cross, C. (2016) Using financial intelligence to target online fraud victimisation: Applying a tertiary prevention perspective. *Criminal Justice Studies* 29(2): 125–142. Doi: 10.1080/1478601X.2016.1170278.

Cross, C. and Blackshaw, D. (2015) Improving the police response to online fraud. *Policing: A Journal of Policy and Practice* 9(2): 119–128. Doi: 10.1093/police/pau044.

Cross, C. and Kelly, M. (2016) The problem of 'white noise': Examining current prevention approaches to online fraud. *Journal of Financial Crime* 23(4): Online first. Doi: 10.1108/JFC-12-2015-0069.

Cross, C., Richards, K. and Smith, R. (2016) *Improving the response to online fraud victims: An examination of reporting and support*, Criminology Research Grant Final Report. Available at: http://www.crg.aic.gov.au/reports/1617/29-1314-FinalReport.pdf (accessed 21 October 2016).

Cross, C., Smith, R. G. and Richards, K. (2014) Challenges of responding to online fraud victimisation in Australia. *Trends and Issues in Crime and Criminology*, no. 474. Canberra: Australian Institute of Criminology. Available at: http://aic.gov.au/publications/current%20series/tandi/461-480/tandi474.html (accessed 21 October 2016).

Department of Commerce (n.d.) *Project Sunbird*. Available at: http://www.scamnet.wa.gov.au/scamnet/Fight_Back-Project_Sunbird.htm (accessed 30 October, 2016).

Department of Commerce (2014). *Project Sunbird Flying High*. Available at: http://www.scamnet.wa.gov.au/scamnet/Types_Of_Scams-Advanced_fee_frauds-Operation Project_Sunbird.htm (accessed 18 January 2017).

Financial Conduct Authority (2016) *Avoid Scams and Unauthorised Firms*. Available at: https://www.fca.org.uk/consumers/avoid-scams-unauthorised-firms (accessed 30 October 2016).

Gill, M. (2005) *Learning from Fraudsters*, Leicester: Perpetuity Research and Consultancy International.

Gilling, D. (1997) *Crime Prevention Theory, Policy and Politics*, London: UCL Press.

Grabosky, P. (2001) Virtual criminality: Old wine in new bottles? *Social and Legal Studies* 10(2): 243–249.

Henry, N. and Powell, A. (2014) The dark side of the virtual world: Towards a digital sexual ethics. In: Henry, N. and Powell, A. (eds) *Preventing Sexual Violence: Interdisciplinary Approaches to Overcoming a Rape Culture*, Basingstoke: Palgrave Macmillan UK. pp. 84–104.

Hines, J. (2001) Telemarketing fraud upon the elderly: Minimizing its effects through legislation, law enforcement and education. *Albany Law Journal of Science and Technology* 12: 839–862.

Holt, T. and Bossler, A. (2014) An assessment of the current state of cybercrime scholarship. *Deviant Behaviour* 35(1): 20–40. Doi: 10.1080/01639625.2013.822209.

Johnson, S. and Bowers, K. (2003) Opportunity is in the eye of the beholder: The role of publicity in crime prevention. *Criminology and Public Policy* 2(3): 497–524. Doi: 10.1111/j.1745-9133.2003.tb00011.x.

Kotadia, M. (2006) *Fighting Fraud by Baiting Phishers*. Available at: http://www.cnet.com/uk/news/fighting-fraud-by-baiting-phishers/ (accessed 30 October 2016).

Lee, S., Drake, E., Pennucci, A., Bjornstad, G. and Edovald, E. (2012) Economic evaluation of the early childhood education in a policy context. *Journal of Children's Services* 7(1): 53–63. Doi: 10.1108/17466661211213670.

Leukfeldt, E. R. and Yar, M. (2016) Applying routine activity theory to cybercrime: A theoretical and empirical analysis. *Deviant Behaviour* 37(3): 1–18. Doi: 10.1080/01639625.2015.1012409.

Nankervis, D. (2014) *Operation Disrepair Find South Australian Lost More than $2 million in 4261 Transactions to Foreign Scams*. Available at: http://www.adelaidenow.com.au/news/south-australia/operation-disrepair-finds-south-australians-lost-more-than-2-million-in-4261-transactions-to-foreign-scams/story-fni6uo1m-1226842491763 (accessed 30 October 2016).

National Audit Office (2013) *Good Practice Guide: Tackling External Fraud*. London: NAO. Available at: https://www.nao.org.uk/wp-content/uploads/2013/02/Tackling_External_Fraud.pdf (accessed 30 October 2016).

National Crime Prevention (1999) *Pathways to prevention: Developmental and early intervention approaches to crime prevention in Australia*. Canberra: Developmental Crime Prevention Consortium. Available at: https://eprints.qut.edu.au/4482/ (accessed 30 October 2016).

Newcomb, T. (2012) *Major Online Dating Sites to Start Background Checks on Users*. Available at: http://newsfeed.time.com/2012/03/21/major-online-dating-sites-to-start-background-checks-on-users/ (accessed 30 October 2016).

Newman, G. R. and Clarke, R. V. (2003) *Superhighway Robbery*, Cullompton: Willan.

Rege, A. (2009) What's love got to do with it? Exploring online dating scams and identity. *International Journal of Cyber Criminology* 3(2): 494–512.

Reppetto, T. (1976) Crime prevention and the displacement phenomenon. *Crime and Delinquency* 22(2): 166–177. Doi: 10.1177/001112877602200204.

Ross, S. and Smith, R. G. (2011). Risk factors for advance fee fraud victimisation. *Trends and Issues in Crime and Criminal Justice*, no. 420, Canberra: Australian Institute of Criminology. Available at: http://aic.gov.au/publications/current%20series/tandi/401-420/tandi420.html (accessed 21 October 2016).

Scamalytics (n.d.) *What is Scamaltyics?* Available at: https://scamalytics.com/ (accessed 30 October 2016).

Schoenmakers, Y., de Vries, R. and van Wijk, A. (2009) *Mountains of Gold: An Exploratory Research in Nigerian 419 Fraud*, Netherlands: SWP.

Schuchter, A. and Levi, M. (2015) Beyond the fraud triangle: Swiss and Austrian elite fraudsters. *Accounting Forum* 39(3): 176–187. Doi: 10.1016/j.accfor.2014.12.001.

Smith, G., Button, M., Johnston, L. and Frimpong, F. (2010) *Studying Fraud as White Collar Crime*, Basingstoke: Palgrave.

Smith, R. and Akman, T. (2008) Raising public awareness of consumer fraud in Australia. *Trends and Issues in Crime and Criminal Justice*, no. 349, Canberra: Australian Institute of Criminology. Available at: http://www.aic.gov.au/publications/current%20series/tandi/341-360/tandi349.html (accessed 30 October 2016).

South Australia Police (SAPOL) (2014) *Annual Report 2013–2014*. Available at: https://www.police.sa.gov.au/__data/assets/pdf_file/0008/58616/Annual-report-2013-2014_INTERNET.pdf (accessed 30 October 2016).

Sullivan, C. (2013) Enhancing translational knowledge on developmental crime prevention. *Criminology and Public Policy* 12(2): 343–351. Doi: 10.1111/1745-9133.12037.

Sullivan, R. (2016) *Sharon Armstrong Spent Two Years in an Argentinian Jail After Being Caught in an Online Dating Scam*. Available at: http://www.news.com.au/lifestyle/sharon-armstrong-spent-two-years-in-an-argentinian-jail-after-being-caught-in-an-online-dating-scam/news-story/200a2a7e68566f203fc76fbf10174a96 (accessed 30 October 2016).

Sutton, A., Cherney, A. and White, R. (2014) *Crime Prevention: Principles, Perspectives and Practices*, 2nd edition, Cambridge: Cambridge University Press.

Think Jessica (n.d.) *Welcome to Think Jessica*. Available at: http://www.thinkjessica.com/ (accessed 30 October 2016).

Van Dijk, J. and de Waard, J. (1991) A two dimensional typology of crime prevention projects: With a bibliography. *Criminal Justice Abstracts*: 483–503.

Wall, D. (2001) *Crime and the Internet*, London: Routledge.

Wortley, R. and Smallbone, S. (eds) (2006) *Situational Prevention of Child Sexual Abuse*, Monsey, NY: Criminal Justice Press.

Yar, M. (2005) The novelty of 'cybercrime': An assessment in light of routine activity theory. *European Journal of Criminology* 2(4): 407–427. Doi: 10.1177/147737080556056.

9

CONCLUSION

The future of cyber frauds and scams

This book has provided an in-depth examination of the many facets of cyber frauds and scams which exist on a global level. As stated in the introduction, the purpose of this book was to argue for a greater need to understand and respond to cyber fraud and scams in a more effective and victim-centred manner. While the chapters in this book have highlighted the challenges, negative experiences, barriers and current inadequacies that exist within current systems, it is not our intention to dwell on the negative. Rather, we wish to argue that this book has brought together a body of evidence that clearly agitates for the need to improve current practices, across the prevention, policing and victim support aspects of these crimes. There are several best practice examples listed throughout the chapters and numerous case studies which illustrate the positive work and outcomes which can be achieved in this area. Rather than be the exception, we would argue that these should become the normalised standard, and something which is routine practice, rather than a welcome outlier.

Cyber fraud and scams have the ability to devastate their victims, as well as their friends, family, colleagues and society as a whole. The extent of this problem requires a coordinated, partnership approach amongst a large number of organisations. That in and of itself poses challenges, but also provides the sharing of the burden and allows the strengths of different organisations to be better utilised to respond where needed.

It is clear that cyber fraud victimisation poses challenges to law enforcement and other agencies by its very characteristics. There is merit in further research that acknowledges the similarities and differences exhibited by these incidents and how current theories and approaches can be adapted, modified or reinvented to respond to cyber fraud more effectively. The continuing evolution of technology will be critical to this. As demonstrated, fraud is not new, and it is far too simplistic to argue that improvements in technology are directly responsible for the current trends in cyber fraud and scams. However, what is readily apparent, is the influence that technology (particularly the internet) has had on the ability of offenders to modify their approaches to potential victims, their ability to communicate with potential victims, and the ways in which they perpetrate their offences. The combination of traditional offline methods with those enabled through technology and the internet has reshaped the fraud landscape. Offenders are nimble and flexible in their ability to modify their activities to better target their victims and avoid law enforcement. Unfortunately, law enforcement and other agencies, and society itself, has not been as readily able to change as needed and respond through prevention, policing and victim support practices. Rather, as demonstrated throughout this book, there are large inadequacies and areas that require immediate and radical improvement.

It is unlikely that cyber fraud and scams will dissipate into the near future. Instead, it is foreseeable that these approaches will continue to successfully target victims worldwide and continue to wreak havoc and devastation on the lives of many. As we argued in the opening chapter of this book, the consistent decline in property crime rates across recent years is more likely to reflect a displacement of traditional crimes into the virtual environment rather than a reduction in crime per se. We anticipate that this will continue to be the case into the near future, and we are witnessing evidence of this in places such as the UK, where the inclusion of fraud and cyber offences has seen a dramatic increase in the overall numbers of crime recorded.

Without adequate recognition and acknowledgement of cyber fraud offences, it is unlikely that any real positive change can be achieved. It is imperative that society as a whole shifts beyond the view that cyber frauds and scams are victimless incidents that are the responsibility of those who fall for them. That is too simplistic and ignores the role of the offender in the equation, and their ability to deceive, manipulate and coerce victims into complying with their demands. Despite the low reporting rates of cyber frauds and scams, victims are still more visible and identifiable than those who offend against them. The cultural change needed in understanding the reality of cyber fraud and scams is a challenge by itself that will require significant resources and buy-in from many sectors across society.

Despite the challenges ahead, we are optimistic for the future. There have been significant shifts and improvements made with other crime types across the world, and we believe that cyber frauds and scams are gaining position on the list. It is our hope that coming years will see many positive changes to practices in this area, which ultimately seek to reduce the likelihood of victimisation in the first place, but also better support those who have been victimised to recover and move forward. It is for this reason that we also advocate a strong prevention agenda, as we continue to believe that a reactive approach left primarily to law enforcement and other authorities is not the most appropriate way forward. While not undervaluing the role of police action in seeking to identify, arrest and prosecute offenders who perpetrate these crimes, a focus on reducing harm and victimisation in the first place is a more optimal solution and one that avoids the trauma associated with victimisation.

It is our hope that this book can provide a starting point for future conversations that initiate discernible action in this area. There are many opportunities for further research to inform improved practices across all aspects of cyber fraud and scams. Acknowledging that there is a problem to address in the first place is the first step, and we believe that this book contributes to that much-needed body of evidence to start the required dialogue.

INDEX

For Product Safety Concerns and Information please contact our EU
representative GPSR@taylorandfrancis.com
Taylor & Francis Verlag GmbH, Kaufingerstraße 24, 80331 München, Germany

www.ingramcontent.com/pod-product-compliance
Ingram Content Group UK Ltd.
Pitfield, Milton Keynes, MK11 3LW, UK
UKHW021506240926
475702UK00035B/503
* 9 7 8 1 1 3 8 9 3 1 1 9 0 *